Dedication. Vision. Heart.

The CalPERS *Story*

First Edition
ISBN 1-882771-19-2
Library of Congress Control Number 2007927566

A full list of image credits appears on pp. 258-259.

Published by The History Factory
14140 Parke Long Court
Chantilly, VA 20151
www.historyfactory.com

Contents

Preface

What follows on these pages is the first published account of the history of the California Public Employees' Retirement System, from its Progressive Era beginnings as a cherished cause among a group of California reformers to its present-day stature as the nation's largest public pension system. A host of past and present CalPERS Board Members, Executive Officers, and employees played vital roles in bringing this book to fruition, as did numerous other individuals interested in chronicling the rich history of CalPERS as a protector of public retirement funds, provider of health care benefits, and pioneer in the corporate governance movement.

In particular, credit for this book is due to Professor Christopher J. Castaneda, Chair of the Department of History at California State University, Sacramento, and author of the original manuscript for this book. In 1998, CalPERS approached Dr. Castaneda, an expert in public and business history, about a possible collaboration. Dr. Castaneda conducted in-depth research into CalPERS history, interviewing 27 key officials and examining myriad historical documents from the organization's archive, as well as public repositories. From this extensive study, he authored an approximately 200-page manuscript covering the start of the System through 1999, which forms the basis for this book. Historical information for the period of 2000 and beyond was added by CalPERS to complete the story.

This book is based on a historical compilation by Professor Christopher J. Castaneda, Chair of the Department of History, California State University, Sacramento.

CalPERS wanted to find the ideal opportunity to publish the full history. That opportunity presented itself as official planning began for the CalPERS 75th anniversary. Dr. Castaneda's work was augmented with images from the CalPERS archive and other State libraries and agencies. Short vignettes were also developed to highlight other moments in CalPERS history.

Of course, none of these stories would exist without the members, employers, and stakeholders of CalPERS—the hundreds of public agencies and millions of people who have contributed to and championed the System from its inception. This book— and CalPERS itself—is a testament to them.

Introduction

CalPERS today is among the world's most influential public pension systems—a leader in the corporate governance movement, one of the largest purchasers of health benefits in the United States, and a provider of benefits to more than 1.5 million people and their families worldwide. But the organization started very small in Sacramento, California, in 1932.

In 1921, a few State employees talked about setting up a retirement fund. Their goal was simple: to make sure that the people who serve the public would be able to pay the rent or mortgage, buy groceries, and get proper health care and retirement in exchange for a life of loyal dedication and service to the State.

Rob Feckner, President of the CalPERS Board of Administration, 2007.

Governor C. C. Young endorsed a study of the idea soon after he came into office in 1926. Two years later, he called for a popular vote, and California citizens approved a Constitutional amendment to create the pension fund with only 1 percent of the vote to spare. In January 1932, the doors of the State Employees' Retirement System opened.

It took 64 years to break the $100 billion mark in investment assets. Just nine years later, it broke $200 billion. The first public employer joined the health program in 1967, and today CalPERS provides health benefits to more than 1.2 million public employees and their families. It began with a staff of six full-time employees and 14,000 members. The staff is now 2,000 strong and membership has topped 1.5 million. CalPERS got this far by starting small and thinking big in investments, retirement, and health benefits.

Throughout the pages of this book, you will read about the legendary people who built CalPERS. You will read about Earl Chapman, the first CEO, who once said, "When I become old enough, I will be assured of an income in my old age, and will not be dependent upon charity …" You will learn about Rene Rothschild, the first investment adviser for the CalPERS Board, who in the early years continually challenged the System to broaden its thinking in relation to investment opportunities. You will be introduced to Jesse Unruh, the legendary former California Assembly Speaker whose leadership and foresight helped develop the corporate governance program in the 1980s. And, you will become familiar with many of the Board Members who collectively have laid strong tracks in the right direction for CalPERS for more than seven decades.

This book describes CalPERS evolution and achievements throughout those years, and the people who made CalPERS what it is today. It is about people doing the people's business for a greater good—with dedication, vision, and heart.

Rob Feckner
President
CalPERS Board of Administration

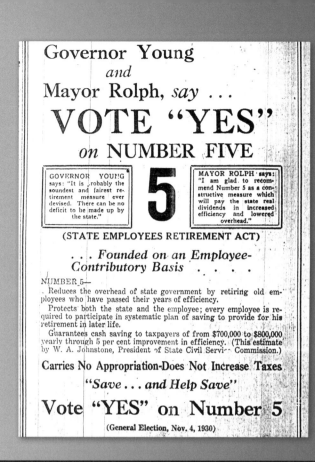

1: A Progressive Proposition

In the 1920s, inspired by a climate of sweeping national reforms, a small but dedicated group of California workers rallied for a cause of their own— a retirement system for State employees. They hoped to provide retirees with financial security and the State a more efficient workforce.

The workers fought against both political opposition and public apathy, but they waged a vigorous campaign when the matter went before voters in 1930—and they triumphed. With victory at the polls came their next challenge—working out the necessary details so that the California State Employees' Retirement System could open for business.

The origins of California's State Employees' Retirement System date to the Progressive Era, a time when numerous social, political, and economic reforms became law in both California and the nation. Women's suffrage; business regulation; civil service reform; direct primaries; and the initiative, referendum, and recall were among the reforms addressed and enacted during the era, which spanned the last years of the 19th century and the first two decades of the 20th. Progressive reforms at the state level included those that sought to make government more efficient, often by devising new workplace methods and technologies that improved worker performance and productivity. Henry Ford's assembly line, for example, speeded up the automobile production process and Frederick Taylor's "scientific management" brought labor efficiency to factories and offices. Civil service reform also sought to protect the interests of workers. In 1913, the California Legislature passed the State's first civil service act. This legislation created the State Civil Service Commission, which administered the act and set

A group of women exhibiting their award-winning canning method at a West Virginia 4-H Fair, 1921. Throughout the United States, people endeavored to find more efficient ways of doing work during the Progressive Era.

Dedication. Vision. Heart. The CalPERS Story

procedures to ensure that all State workers were selected on the basis of "merit, efficiency, and fitness."[1]

Creating a Civil Service Commission and establishing a retirement system were distinct yet closely related measures. Retirement system advocates, however, had a more difficult time promoting their cause than did civil service reform advocates. Critics of retirement systems contended they were nothing more than providers of "hand-outs" and welfare for the indolent. Retirement system supporters argued that aged State employees afforded with a reasonable retirement salary could leave the active payroll yet maintain a decent lifestyle.

The California Legislature passed a law in 1883 that provided funds for the institutional care of elderly indigents. Lawmakers later modified the law to include some support for people living at home. In 1895, however, the Legislature repealed this measure and charged individual counties with the responsibility for local retirement, annuity associations, and indigent care. In 1907, the State Legislature considered a bill that would make retired employees eligible for 50 percent of their average monthly salary as calculated during the last 12 months of service. Both the Assembly and Senate failed to pass the measure.[2]

Despite these setbacks, support continued to grow in California for the creation of a State welfare system that included a retirement plan for State employees. Most indigent elderly people at the time were forced to live in squalid, county-funded "poorhouses." The State attempted to bring some centralized control over these institutions in 1903, when it created the State Board of Charities and Corrections. Implicit in its name was the idea that the organization was concerned with *charity* rather than human *welfare*, and the board initially limited investigative and supervisory powers over poorhouses. But it gained authority over time and changed its name to the Department of Public Welfare in 1925 and then to the Department of Social Welfare two years later.[3]

California's teachers fared better than the elderly during these years when it came to retirement benefits. In 1913, the Legislature passed an act creating a Statewide retirement plan for public school teachers. This legislation included the establishment of the Public School Teachers' Retirement Salary Fund, later known as the California

Men on the porch of the Sacramento County Hospital, 1900. Before pensions and retirement plans were widespread, poverty among the elderly was rampant throughout the United States.

"The Old Tends to be Thrown Out"
California Poorhouses

The founders of CalPERS lived in a time when the outlook for Californians too old to work was often very bleak. With little in the way of public assistance, elderly people in need of shelter frequently turned to poorhouses.

It was this concern that led to the campaign to provide public employees with a financially secure retirement—a way to protect the welfare of those who had spent many years in service to the State of California.

Widely referred to as "human dumping grounds," poorhouses generally contained conditions that were not only physically deplorable, but oppressively bleak as well. Hopelessness permeated the atmosphere of poorhouses. In an 1895 study of a women's almshouse in San Francisco, social sciences professor Mary Roberts Smith described the state of the institution as "piteous, vulgar, tedious, perhaps, but real and inevitable." The misery of the inhabitants affected them nearly as much as the filth, Smith suggested in her findings. "It is a curious fact," she wrote, "that women in an almshouse appear on the average ten years older than women of the same age outside."

The fact that so many poorhouse occupants were elderly had an unfortunate effect on society's perception of both poverty and old age. "When we consider how many of the poor are old, we cannot escape the conclusion that poverty is essentially a trouble of old age," scholar Charles Booth wrote in *Pauperism: A Picture*. Many people became complacent to the existence of the poorhouses, and even adapted systems of

political corruption around them. Smith reported that during elections, competing parties often sent "lines of carriages to the gates of the grounds, and to induce the inmates to go to the polls by offers of money and whiskey."

Booth, who studied conditions of poverty extensively in the late 1800s, reflected in his work on why the elderly were ending up in poorhouses in increasing numbers during this period. "Life runs more intensely than it did," he wrote, "and the old tends to be thrown out."

Elderly men sleeping in a Sacramento Men's Shelter, 1930. Poorhouses were unfortunately common institutions in California in the late 1800s and early 1900s, when CalPERS founders were planning the Retirement System.

State Teachers' Retirement System. The plan required members to contribute $12 per year. Employers did not contribute to the system, but the State contributed 5 percent of each fiscal year's inheritance tax revenue.[4]

Renewed interest in retirement plans and old-age pensions surfaced in the early 1920s. Various groups of state employees around the country and members of state and national organizations, such as the Fraternal Order of Eagles, Abraham Epstein's American Association for Old-Age Security, and the American Association for Labor Legislation, advocated state-sponsored support for old-age pensions. The Eagles were the most active of these organizations in California, where the group had more than 4,000 members in the 1920s. The organization promoted old-age pensions by distributing voluminous amounts of literature describing the great many aged persons living in poverty throughout the country. In cooperation with the American Association for Labor Legislation, the Eagles drafted a single old-age pension bill, which it introduced to 22 state legislatures in 1923; three of these Legislatures passed the bill.[5] This old-age pension plan, however, allowed individual counties to decide whether or not they would participate in their state's pension program. Most counties decided not to participate; scholars estimate that by 1928, fewer than 1,000 people in the six states with pension plans actually received a pension.[6]

Fraternal Order of Eagles National Convention in Milwaukee, Wisconsin, 1906. The Fraternal Order of the Eagles came into national prominence as social reformers in the early 1900s, and played a key role in old-age reform in California.

The Eagles also promoted an old-age pension bill in California during 1923. State Senator D. C. Murphy, a member of the brotherhood, introduced the bill to the Senate, while Assemblyman Otto Emme introduced a similar bill in the Assembly. The Legislature amended the bill into a proposal for studying the feasibility of a retirement system, but Governor Friend W. Richardson vetoed this measure.

The Eagles continued to push for an old-age pension system in California. In 1925, Murphy and Assemblyman William Byrne, also a member of the Eagles, introduced another old-age pension bill. While this one passed the progressive-minded Legislature, Governor Richardson again vetoed it. He stated that such a measure "would tend to encourage wastefulness and extravagance and would be an injustice to those who practice thrift and economy."[7] Richardson also noted that current law already provided for the care of aged persons. The Eagles did not give up. They

Governor Friend W. Richardson, 1920s. Governor Richardson was not receptive to pension reform efforts, vetoing a measure backed by the Eagles to study old-age pensions in 1923, and reportedly throwing State workers out of his office when they approached him about a retirement system for State employees years later.

Governor C. C. Young, 1930. Elected in 1926, Governor Young was interested in pension reform, and helped advance the cause of State workers seeking to establish a retirement system.

achieved success in 1929 when the California Legislature passed what became known as the Eagles Old Age Pension Act, which Richardson's successor, Governor Clement "C. C." Young, signed into law. In adopting this measure, California enacted the United States' first mandatory old-age pension system.[8]

Although it is unclear whether State workers were directly involved with the Eagles' initial effort to create an old-age pension plan, it is known that during 1923 workers began planning a State employees' retirement system. About 15 employees personally financed the effort that year, meeting regularly at the District Court of Appeals in Sacramento.[9] They contacted Governor Richardson with a proposal to create a retirement system for State workers, but he was not supportive, tossing them out of his office when they approached him, according to one of the group's members.[10]

The California Civil Service Commission, however, supported the formation of a State retirement system, making strong statements in its Biennial Reports of 1922, 1924, and 1926 advocating such a plan. "Civil Service and the merit system have become a permanent function of the State government," the Commission stated in its 1926 report. "To insure their greatest effectiveness and to bring about greater efficiency in service there must be adopted … a pension and retirement plan which will be adequate and comprehensive so far as employees are concerned and politically sound from a financial and actuarial standpoint."[11] The Commission's support for a State retirement system was important. The Commission was an agency that lawmakers could not ignore.

Prospects for a State retirement program improved even more when C. C. Young defeated Richardson in the 1926 governor's race. The progressive-minded Young was openly concerned about the aged in California, and he was interested in supporting legislation that promoted humanitarian goals as well as increased efficiency in government.

Commission on Pensions of State Employees

With mounting support for a retirement system, a small cohort of State workers approached Governor Young in 1927 and requested that he back an effort to examine the practicality of a State retirement system. Young assented. On May 10, 1927, he signed Assembly Bill No. 38, creating the Commission on Pensions of

Lofty Goals:
The Eagles' Progressive-Era Activism

The Fraternal Order of Eagles was one of the most effective advocates of old-age pensions and other social reforms during the Progressive Era. At first glance, it was also one of the unlikeliest.

The Eagles began in 1898 as a social club for the theater community in Seattle, Washington. Its inaugural meeting consisted of a half-dozen theater owners sitting on a pile of lumber at a local shipyard to discuss their concerns over a musicians' strike. Soon, the men were gathering on empty stages with actors, stagehands, and others in the local theater community—rolling out kegs of beer once they finished their business.

These early members traveled a great deal to perform, and as a result the Eagles quickly grew into a national club. As the organization expanded, so did its sense of purpose. The Eagles' concept of brotherhood had always included the notion that members would help each other financially in times of distress. The club also provided members with insurance coverage, another reason for its rapid growth. Soon, the brotherhood was actively looking out for the well-being of workers and families outside the organization.

In 1908, the Eagles sponsored the first mother's pension law in the United States. Three years later, the club pushed through the nation's first workman's compensation law.

Club members then turned their attention to old-age pensions. The Eagles worked with labor groups to draft an old-age pension law that passed the Montana, Nevada, and Pennsylvania legislatures in 1923. These laws were also the first of their kind.

Four other states passed similar legislation over the next four years. But because counties could choose whether to participate under these laws, they had little practical effect.

It was in California that the Eagles successfully changed this. With members and sympathizers in the State Legislature, the club was able to get the first mandatory old-age pension passed. The measure provided for State supervision of and contributions to the System. By early 1931, California had already approved more than 5,000 pension applications.

Reformers hailed the Eagles' success in California as a turning point for old-age pension law. The organization continued to advocate for social reform, including the federal Social Security Act. Its work on the landmark legislation was so significant that the Eagles received a signing pen from President Franklin Roosevelt, who was himself an Eagle.

Mother's Day Observance

by

SACRAMENTO AERIE NO. 9

FRATERNAL ORDER OF EAGLES

Opening Remarks -	Eugene Welch, Worthy President
Invocation - - -	Rt. Rev. Bishop Robert Armstrong
Song "Mother" - - - - - - -	Mary Lucich
Piano Accompaniment - - - -	Mr. Howard Scott
Song "Little Irish Mother of Mine" -	Phillis Duval
Oration - - - - - - - -	Mr. Peter Mitchell
Song "Mother Macree" - - - -	Phillis Duval
Violin Selections	
"Songs My Mother Taught Me"	
"Dream" - - - - - - - -	Trudy Husing
Song "For My Mother" - - - -	Mary Lucich
Benediction - - - - - -	Rev. Clarence A. Kircher

. . . COMMITTEE . . .

James J. Burke   Stephen Marietta   Jack Ryan
William A. Carroll   Henry A. Senf
Joseph M. Lannon, Chairman

Pamphlet for a Mother's Day observance sponsored by a group of Sacramento Eagles, date unknown. In addition to sponsoring the nation's first mother's pension law in 1908, the Eagles called for the establishment of a national Mother's Day as early as 1904—which many believe led to the founding of the holiday in the United States.

State Employees (Pension Commission).[12] The Pension Commission's stated purpose was to inquire into "the subject of retirement pensions, allowances and annuities for state officers and employees, especially with reference to the method of establishing and maintaining the fund from which such pensions, allowances and annuities shall be paid."[13] The Assembly bill provided the Commission with $6,000 to complete this task. This marked the beginning of a significant movement to create a retirement system.

During November 1927, Governor Young appointed the Pension Commission's five members, none of whom received a salary for their work, although they were eligible for expenses including travel. The chairman of the State Civil Service Commission, W. A. Johnstone, also became chairman of the Pension Commission. The members held their first meeting on November 21, 1927, and met several times over the next year in Sacramento. They also held public meetings in Sacramento, San Francisco, and Los Angeles.[14]

One of the Commission's first actions was calling for an actuarial study to provide the statistical and financial information needed to make an informed recommendation. State employment statistics as of December 31, 1927, provided the basic data. As of that date, California employed 7,553 workers deemed eligible for retirement benefits with a combined annual salary of $13,284,459.[15]

California State Employees, 1927

Occupation	Gender	Number	Annual Salary
Clerical, administrative, and skilled labor	Male	3,462	$7,671,890
Clerical and administrative	Female	1,631	2,320,957
Institutional	Male	1,789	2,439,582
Institutional	Female	671	852,030
TOTAL		7,553	$13,284,459

Source: Report of the Commission on Pensions
of State Employees, December 31, 1928, p. 45.

The Commission hired Barrett N. Coates of Coates and Herfurth, a San Francisco actuarial consulting firm, to be its consulting actuary, and University of California insurance professor H. H. Mowbray as the advisory actuary. The Pension Commission had attempted to secure the full-time services of Professor Mowbray, but his university duties allowed only for a part-time affiliation with the study. Coates received a fee of $35 per day and Mowbray received $50 per day.[16]

To direct its own work over the next two years, the Commission drafted a general outline of issues that required consideration. These included the general nature of the proposed system, employee eligibility, service retirement benefits, disability retirement benefits, death benefits, and withdrawal of benefits.[17] These topics were the focus of both the Commission's private and public meetings, the latter of which were well attended by representatives of State employee groups and other organizations, as well as interested individuals.

The Commission did not conduct its inquiry in a vacuum. Many other public and private retirement systems were operating at that time, which the commission studied carefully. Commissioners looked at the state retirement systems of New York, Massachusetts, and New Jersey, as well as public systems in New York City, Baltimore, Chicago, and San Francisco, observing how these systems and other private ones operated in terms of eligibility, benefit structure, and operating budgets.[18]

Members of Chicago's Pension Commission Board, 1925. In compiling its recommendations, California's Pension Commission studied a number of established pension systems nationwide, including Chicago's.

The Pension Commission's enabling legislation required it to report recommendations to the Governor before July 1, 1928. With an extraordinary amount of work to complete and numerous complicated issues to consider, Commission members did not quite make their deadline, submitting a preliminary report on this date and the final report on December 31, 1928. In it, the Commission stated that a well-structured retirement system provided obvious advantages to both employee and employer. A retirement system increased workplace efficiency and provided a sense of security to workers, who could depend on income during old age or disability. Therefore, a sound retirement system attracted qualified workers to State employment. This was a growing concern; the Commissioners noted that the "increasing complexity of state governmental and regulatory functions makes it of the utmost importance to secure and hold the best possible type of employees." While the Commissioners realized that the promise of future retirement benefits would not prevent some employees from leaving, retirement benefits, they wrote, would at least prevent what otherwise might be a very large loss of "efficient employees [who] leave the service because of superior opportunities elsewhere."[19]

The Commission's report described how a retirement system would allow the State to better deal with elderly employees who no longer performed their work efficiently. "In the absence of a retirement system, the aged or disabled employee is left in active service as long as he can 'go through the motions,'" the report stated. Some workers were already "really retired on the job," the Commissioners wrote. "To a very considerable extent," they keenly observed, "the state pays for a retirement system even though none is established."[20]

The Commissioners argued that "the discharge of a superannuated employee without adequate provision for his future needs is repugnant to every instinct of humanity." Nevertheless, they wrote, a retirement system should not be confused with "charity, doled out to the aged employee." Rather, a sound retirement system "is an orderly method of providing for his retirement at the end of his normal service-life, using a capital fund which has been built up during his active service with this very eventuality in prospect." And in language that in retrospect sounds ahead of its time, the Commissioners wrote that a retirement system "prevents the stagnation which besets a department when the avenues of advancement are closed to the younger employee

because of the continued employment of men and women far beyond their best days, but whose long service has won them the highest places within the department's command."[21]

The Commissioners did warn against creating a retirement system founded on poor financial planning, which they believed would be worse than having no retirement system at all. They urged that a retirement system for California's State employees be created on "a sound financial basis," with liabilities "provided for as they are *incurred*, rather than when they mature." The Commissioners cautioned against establishing a system that "proposes to provide funds only as they are needed to meet disbursements …" This would "invite disaster," they wrote. "Unseen liabilities [would] continue to mount, and the time will come when they will begin to mature in such volume as to cause serious embarrassment to the state, forcing it either to make staggering appropriations, or to default in its obligations to members of the system."[22]

The Commissioners made several other recommendations as well. They proposed that membership in the retirement system be compulsory for all State workers whether or not they had civil service status. However, part-time employees, elected officers, officers appointed for fixed terms, teachers, employees of public schools, and the University of California were not to be included. After a six-month probationary period, all eligible employees joined the system.[23]

The determining factors for eligibility, apart from being a full-time employee whose salary was fully paid by the State, were age and service. The Pension Commission recommended that the minimum voluntary retirement age should be 60, with 20 years of service. The Commissioners also recommended a maximum retirement age of 70, except for current State employees. These employees would not face compulsory retirement until a minimum of five years after the retirement system was established.[24]

Envisioning a retirement system that benefited both the State and employees, the Commission expected both State and employee to contribute equally to the retirement fund. The employee's contribution to what "for all practical purposes [is] a savings account" would be "matched" by the State for salaries up to $5,000 per year. Technically, each employee would purchase an "annuity" that accumulated interest until the retirement date while the State matched the annuity with a "pension." The combined annuity and pension would equal the employees' retirement allowance.

Headline in the *Los Angeles Times*, January 6, 1929. The Pension Commission's study, which recommended that the minimum age for retirement be 60 and the maximum 70, was of interest to many Californians.

STATE PENSION PLAN OFFERED

Commission Recommends Adoption of Bill

Four Major Points Contained in Program

Retirement Ages Range from 60 to 70 Years

One particularly difficult issue concerned the current employees' State service prior to the adoption of a retirement system. The commissioners stated that the "question of 'prior service' is inevitably the storm center of the discussion of any proposed retirement system."[25] Whether the State should be liable for a worker's contribution for "prior service" was problematic both financially and politically. Ultimately, the final report recommended that in fairness to current employees a prior service allowance be granted to State workers upon retirement. This prior service formula stated that, "when any present employee retires at age 65 or older, and enters upon his service retirement benefit consisting of the 'annuity' and the 'pension' … he receive in addition thereto, a special allowance for each year of 'prior service' equal to one-seventieth of his average salary for the three years previous to the adoption of the system." In no case would a present State employee receive less than $40 per year in retirement benefits.[26]

Under the Commission's plan, employees would be eligible for four types of benefits: service retirement, disability retirement, death benefits, and withdrawal benefits.[27] According to the Pension Commission's original plan, employees could retire at age 65 and receive one-seventieth of their final compensation for each year of service. Employees retiring earlier or later than age 65 (with 20 years of service) would receive less, or more, than 1/70th of their final year's salary, accordingly. Employees who became severely disabled would be eligible for a disability retirement allowance after 10 years of service. Considering that a retirement system is intended to "take care of faithful employees who become incapacitated either on account of age or of physical or mental disability," the Pension Commission decided to offer only a nominal death benefit. The final report called for the accumulated contributions of a deceased employee to be paid to the employee's beneficiary. If these accumulated contributions were less than $500, the retirement system would contribute additional funds so that the total payment was $500.[28]

The Pension Commission also tackled the thorny issue of contribution rates. After considering the establishment of a contribution system based on an employee's specific occupation, the commission requested that the actuaries keep to a minimum any contribution-level distinctions. Consequently, the actuaries created only two contribution rates: one for men and one for women. The Commission reported that the reason for the gender-based rates was the difference in the average life spans of men and

Elderly woman in the yard of a Sacramento women's home, 1900s. The Pension Commission suggested that actuaries set different contribution rates for men and women based on the longer life expectancy of women.

women. "It is a well-established fact," the report stated, "that women who have the advantage of an annuity, or pension, live materially longer than men in the same situation." Since women lived longer than men, the report continued, "it is therefore necessary that the contributions made by the women be slightly higher." Overall, the average employee contribution was expected to be approximately 4.09 percent of salary, and the report proposed a retirement system funded equally, and on an annual basis, by the employee and State.[29]

The retirement system's startup required funding. The actuaries proposed that the State contribute $1,368,200 in order to fund the first 18 months of the retirement system's operation. The State would then provide annual funding based upon employee contributions.[30]

Campaigning for the State Employees' Retirement System

Since the new retirement system would become a permanent item in California's State Budget, Governor Young and a majority of California's Legislators in 1929 agreed that the retirement system had to be submitted to California's voters for approval. The California State Assembly and Senate passed a resolution during the Legislature's 48th Regular Session in 1929, proposing Assembly Constitutional Amendment Number 37. This resolution, filed with the Secretary of State's Office on May 15, 1929, required that Californians vote on a constitutional amendment paving the way for a State retirement system. Significantly, the proposed amendment did not in itself create a retirement system, but rather granted the Legislature the power to create one. This amendment became known as Proposition 5.[31]

Almost immediately, a collection of State employees who supported establishing a retirement system began to coalesce into an organization. Even before the Legislature passed the resolution, several loosely connected groups of State employees had initiated an effort to unite California's employees to improve relations between workers and management and to maintain and protect the State's civil service system.[32]

The State Assembly Chamber in Sacramento, date unknown. In 1929, the State Assembly passed a significant resolution giving Californians the power to vote on a Constitutional amendment allowing for the creation of a State retirement system.

There were apparently three loosely connected and informally organized groups, or chapters, of State employees in California prior to 1929. The largest of these groups was in Sacramento. Two other chapters were located in San Francisco, one at the State Building and another located at the San Francisco harbor. In 1929, a fourth group formed in Los Angeles. According to the Los Angeles group's 1930 president, George Shaw, these four chapters, though not actually part of a Statewide organization, represented the first organized effort among California's State workers to promote the establishment of a retirement system.[33]

A panoramic view of the San Francisco harbor, 1920s. With the possibility of a retirement system becoming more substantial, State employees gathered in groups to strategize on how to bring the idea to fruition. The San Francisco harbor served as the meeting place for one group of State employees.

Members of these chapters and other interested State employees then established a formal committee, the State Employees' Retirement Campaign Committee (SERCC), to actively push for the retirement plan. The Committee consisted of 12 people—four each from Sacramento, San Francisco, and Los Angeles. Headquartered in Sacramento, the Committee was the only Statewide organization that represented State employees, although its specific goal was promoting Proposition 5. Thomas E. Stanton served as the Committee's first chairman. The Committee also hired a young Clem Whitaker to manage the campaign and direct publicity for Proposition 5. Whitaker would later found Campaigns, Inc., the first professional campaign management firm in the United States.[34]

On October 29, 1929, about five months after the California Legislature adjourned, the Wall Street stock market crashed. The crash marked the beginning of the Great Depression, the worst economic collapse in the history of the modern industrial world. Thousands of banks closed their doors and as much as 25 percent of the U.S. workforce became unemployed. The financial hardship of this era affected all segments of society, from individual citizens and businesses to local and state governments. The onset of difficult economic times for the nation, as well as for California and its Budget, created some pessimism among even those people who most strongly supported the proposed retirement system. The system's advocates knew that they had to encourage California's citizens to vote in favor of the plan, even though it would cost the State money during an economic decline. At the same time, the nation's economic crisis must have emphasized to many Californians the value of having a retirement system to protect the welfare of citizens who had spent many years of their lives in service to the State. The Campaign Committee sent State employees a solemn, carefully crafted letter in the summer of 1930 emphasizing that retirement plans were not novel or radical. The July 25 letter noted that President William Taft, "a conservative statesman," had spoken out in favor of a retirement plan in 1911. In an attempt to counter criticism that the idea of a State retirement plan was "socialistic" and that such a system would be a mere provider of "charity," the letter stressed that this was a "retirement salary system." By using the term "salary," the SERCC emphasized that retirement funds were monies that had been earned, not received as an unearned dole.

The letter stated:

The retirement salary system plan is not an innovation. It has long since passed the experimental stage and has proven itself. As a governmental policy it has been approved and adopted by the Congress of the United States, by the Legislatures of several States, including New York, New Jersey, and Massachusetts, by the Territory of Hawaii, by San Francisco, Los Angeles, New York City, Chicago, Baltimore, and many other municipalities, and by foreign countries. As a sound investment from a business viewpoint it has been put into operation by many of the largest business concerns in the Nation, some of which are the New York Stock Exchange, Metropolitan Life Insurance Company, Pacific Gas and Electric Company, Southern Pacific Railroad Company, Standard Oil Company, Union Oil Company, Southern California Edison Company, United States Steel Corporation and General Motors Corporation.[35]

The State Employees' Retirement Campaign Committee decided to execute its major push for Proposition 5 after the August 1930 primaries, even though this gave Committee members only about two months to wage their campaign. Clem Whitaker set the basic framework for the effort. The Campaign Committee developed a strategy, consisting of five parts: organization of the employees, a letter-writing campaign, personal work undertaken by employees and friends, gaining endorsements, and public appeals and advertising.[36] One of the most important elements of the campaign was the personal appeal made to State employees. Campaign workers visited State offices and agencies located in cities and towns throughout California. Whitaker urged the formation of local campaign committees that could gain local support more easily than one centralized organization, while also emphasizing the need for these local committees to "KEEP IN TOUCH WITH THE STATE COMMITTEE HEADQUARTERS AT SACRAMENTO."[37]

After providing State employees with good reasons for supporting this effort, the SERCC instituted a formal fund raising campaign. It mailed pledge cards to State employees and requested contributions. In early September, the SERCC requested that each State employee contribute $1 per month for three months. "Don't be a shirker!" Committee members implored in a letter. "Do your bit, financially, whatever it may be, and then get out and work for the act among your friends and associates."[38]

Proposition 2 billboard, 1949. Clem Whitaker, with his wife and business partner, Leone Baxter, continued to work in support of sound pension systems after leading the CalPERS campaign. The pair successfully campaigned for Proposition 2, a 1949 State ballot measure that enacted several pension reforms, including the restoration of an old-age assistance plan for the blind.

Early Steps of a Campaign Trailblazer

The members of the State Employees' Retirement Campaign Committee were breaking new ground in more ways than one when they set out to found a retirement system for California State workers.

Clem Whitaker with his business partner and wife, Leone Baxter, in their office, 1957. Half of the groundbreaking public relations team of Baxter and Whitaker, Clem Whitaker launched one of his early campaigns in 1930 in support of Proposition 5, which allowed for the establishment of a retirement system for State employees.

In choosing a manager for the Proposition 5 campaign, the Committee was among the first groups to enlist the campaign services of a young Clem Whitaker—co-founder of the first political consulting firm and architect of the modern American political campaign.

Whitaker, who began his career as a Sacramento reporter, had not yet established his seminal campaign firm when Proposition 5 landed on the ballot in 1930. He had only recently started working in lobbying and public relations when the Campaign Committee decided to hire him.

It was a wise decision. Proposition 5 passed, and Whitaker's career soon blossomed. In 1933, he joined with a woman named Leone Baxter, then head of a local Chamber of Commerce, to support a water project on the ballot. The pair prevailed, and went on to found Campaigns, Inc. (later renamed Whitaker and Baxter). In doing so, they essentially created a new professional field—political campaign consulting.

Whitaker and Baxter enjoyed extraordinary success over more than two decades in the business, winning all but a handful of the 85 political campaigns they handled. Their business partnership also led to a romantic one: five years after opening their firm, Whitaker and Baxter married.

Staunch Republicans, the couple successfully campaigned against author Upton Sinclair's run for California Governor in 1934, and led the successful gubernatorial campaigns of Earl Warren and Goodwin Knight. Many of their standard campaign maneuvers—issuing extensive mass mailings, blanketing city streets with campaign collateral, and otherwise bombarding citizens with pithy messages and reminders to vote—were ones Whitaker had used during the Proposition 5 campaign.

While Whitaker and Baxter worked tirelessly at keeping the spotlight turned on their campaigns, the media found their personal story hard to resist. Newspapers and magazines often remarked on Baxter's good looks and the couple's unusual relationship. "They alternate at being president and vice president, switching jobs every year," a *Time* reporter wrote in a 1955 profile. "Usually, they answer telephone calls together on two extensions, divide profits equally [and] plot their campaigns together (often in the seclusion of an oceanside resort)."

A number of those campaigns over the years involved pension issues. Whitaker and Baxter fought against several fiscally dubious pension proposals, including an infamous plan known as "Thirty Dollars Every Thursday" and other "zany schemes that have characterized California politics of the past generation," in the words of the *Time* profile.

Whitaker and Baxter emphasized that they worked only for campaigns they actually supported. Their record suggests that it was not mere opportunism that motivated Whitaker to work for the campaign to create CalPERS at the dawn of his remarkable career. The fiscally sound pension plan was a concept he fought for time and again.

Altogether the Campaign collected approximately $41,000 through voluntary contributions, primarily from State employees. Late in the summer, the Committee instituted a massive letter-writing campaign. Before it ended, the Committee had mailed more than 1 million letters. The SERCC mailed approximately 400,000 "Dear Friend" letters along with thousands of targeted letters to State employees, teachers, doctors, druggists, chiropractors, engineers, and veterinarians, urging their support for Proposition 5.

The Committee distributed a wide variety of other campaign material to State employees and supporters. In early October, State workers received campaign cards, auto stickers, and form letters to distribute to friends and acquaintances.[39] One campaign card provided "5 Reasons for Voting 'Yes' on Number 5." The reasons included reducing State government overhead costs by "retiring old employees who

State Employees' Retirement Campaign Committee: Expenditures for Proposition No. 5 Campaign

Item	Amount
Salaries—Campaign Managers	$1,900.00
Salaries—Office	3,819.00
Printing	7,333.54
Postage	9,225.91
Postal Cards	4,000.00
Advertising—Newspapers	6,645.10
Advertising—Radio	590.00
Travel	545.13
Telephone & Telegraph	392.79
Office Expenses	441.65
Express	55.12
Miscellaneous	313.77
TOTAL	$35,262.91

Source: Report on Campaign for Proposition
Number 5, December 1930.

have passed their years of efficiency," providing old-age financial security, saving taxpayers' money through improved State efficiency, placing State business on the same footing as the private businesses that had pension plans, and providing for retired workers without requiring new appropriations or taxes.

A few days prior to the election, Clem Whitaker personally signed letters to members of the Fraternal Order of Eagles. Noting that the Eagles had led the fight for old-age pensions nationally and in California, he urged their support for Proposition 5. "Number 5," Whitaker wrote, "has the unqualified endorsement of Governor C. C. Young, who, a few years ago, signed the Eagles Old Age Pension Act, and also has the enthusiastic support of [San Francisco] Mayor James Rolph, Jr., the Republican Nominee for Governor."[40]

Indeed, Whitaker used supportive statements from both Rolph and Young in other campaign material. Advertisements appeared in newspapers declaring Young's and Rolph's support for Proposition 5. As Mayor of San Francisco, Rolph had approved a retirement plan for city employees. Now, as the Republican nominee for Governor, Rolph offered strong support for a Statewide plan, declaring that, "I am glad to recommend Number 5 as a constructive measure which will pay the state real dividends in increased efficiency and lowered overhead."[41] As election day approached, Proposition 5 supporters were enthusiastic. The measure had drawn much support. But Committee members contended with indifference and opposition as well. The SERCC reported that several newspapers had taken a position against the measure, while others took no position at all. The *Los Angeles Times* was one major newspaper that didn't offer a recommendation, while newspapers in the McClatchy chain, including the *Sacramento Bee*, recommended voting against the measure.[42]

Nevertheless, on November 4, 1930, California's voters narrowly approved Proposition 5. With more than 1 million ballots cast, the measure passed with barely 51 percent of the vote.[43] Proposition 5 became Section 22A, Article IV, of California's Constitution. The SERCC disbanded, but not before calling for the creation of a permanent Statewide employee organization to continue representing and advocating State employees' rights.

Republican gubernatorial candidate and San Francisco Mayor, James Rolph, ca. 1929. Rolph believed strongly in pension reform, and as Mayor had been instrumental in the founding of a retirement plan for San Francisco municipal workers in the early 1920s.

Flying Signs & Ferry Lines:
The Campaign for Number Five

The State Employees' Retirement Campaign Committee worked feverishly in the last days of the Proposition 5 campaign to win every vote possible. In a report released after the election, committee members described in vivid detail some of their final campaign maneuvers:

Vote appeals for Number Five were flashed on the screens of sixty theatres in San Francisco and the bay district; in both San Francisco and Los Angeles our campaign cards were scattered over the cities during the final days from airplanes; several toll bridge and ferry companies generously distributed our campaign cards to all patrons; speakers were sent before scores of women's clubs and other organizations; members of the Legislature spoke in our behalf throughout the State in their respective communities; flying squadrons of workers were sent into doubtful territory to distribute our cards in office buildings, factories, etc; another worker made a canvass of mercantile establishments in some fourteen of the larger cities, securing the cooperation of the management in placing cards in the hands of all employees of the stores; the Ferry Building in San Francisco was decorated with Number Five banners during the last days of the

campaign so that every commuter was forced to see the message morning and night; a 'Number Five airplane' was entered in a big air meet, with campaign banners flying from both sides; and above all— every employee was busy working, each with his own style of campaigning and each determined to put it over.

Passengers exiting a boat at the Ferry Building in San Francisco, 1933. Campaigners for Proposition 5 bombarded ferry-boat crowds in California cities with promotional material for the measure.

The intense campaign in favor of the State retirement plan had brought Committee members together and given them a new sense of unity. In February 1931, the State workers who had supported the retirement system plan created a new Statewide organization, the California State Employees Association (CSEA).

With the passage of the Proposition, it was up to the California Legislature to pass the legislation needed to establish a retirement system. In early 1931, Senator B. S. Crittenden

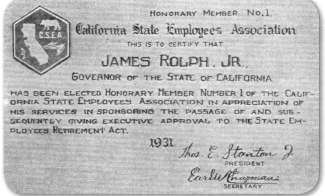

Above
Governor James Rolph's honorary CSEA membership card, 1931. Grateful for Rolph's support, the newly formed CSEA presented him with a certificate declaring him the association's first honorary member on June 10, 1931.

Left
Inaugural parade for newly elected Governor James Rolph, 1931. Many of Rolph's supporters were presumably also backers of Proposition 5, which he publicly endorsed while running for Governor.

Intertwining Roots: CSEA & SERS

It would be impossible to tell the story of the creation of CalPERS without detailing that of the California State Employees Association.

The origins of the two organizations are inextricably linked: founding members of CSEA initially formed the association to push for the establishment of the Retirement System; CalPERS would not have started without the State workers who formed CSEA.

Those workers got together to campaign for Proposition 5—the measure allowing for the creation of the Retirement System—when California's lawmakers placed it on the 1930 ballot. Some of these employees had worked together in the past on issues of concern for State workers, but during the intense weeks of the Proposition 5 campaign, they developed into the tight-knit working group. They called their organization the State Employees' Retirement Campaign Committee (SERCC).

After the proposition passed, SERCC members met in Sacramento to discuss parlaying their organization into a comprehensive Statewide group. They named their new group the California State Employees Association (CSEA).

The proposed constitution they drafted during their meeting described the group's mission as "promoting a sense of civic responsibility among State employees; disseminating a knowledge of departmental activities to the end that cooperation, efficiency and harmony may prevail; and promoting the welfare of State employees in any and all ways which are compatible with the best interests of the State."

Organizers agreed to meet again in February 1931 and to form new chapters. Forty-eight representatives from 10 chapters attended this second meeting—the first CSEA General Council. These 10 became the CSEA charter chapters.

Since CSEA was a direct outgrowth of SERCC, it was natural for CSEA members to draw their leaders from the former SERCC

CSEA Charter Members February 1931

Chapter	Members
San Francisco	400
Sacramento	1,856
San Francisco Civic Center	475
Los Angeles	451
District IV Highways (San Francisco)	375
Patton	359
San Bernardino	312
Redwood Empire	200
Norwalk	222
San Luis Obispo	182
TOTAL	4,832

organization. CSEA members elected former SERCC Chairman Thomas E. Stanton to be the first CSEA President. Former SERCC Vice Chairman E .J. Callan became CSEA Vice President and former SERCC Treasurer James Byrne, Jr. assumed the same position for CSEA. The fourth elected CSEA officer was Earl W. Chapman, who had also served on the SERCC executive committee.

It was also natural for the new CSEA leadership to feel a particularly strong connection to the Retirement System that they had worked so hard to build. In fact, Callan and Stanton began serving on the System's first Board of Administration in 1931, and Chapman became its first Executive Officer. Though they would represent State workers on a wide variety of issues, CSEA would continue to play a role in the Retirement System's history.

CSEA has worked closely with the Retirement System on numerous key benefits changes over the years, including the addition of death benefits, lowering of the mandatory retirement age, and establishment of survivors' benefits.

The association has also fought vigorously—both through the legal system and in the court of public opinion—against any attempts by State officials to use the Fund for anything other than its mandated purpose. CSEA filed a lawsuit in 1982 to prevent the Legislature from using pension funds to reduce the State's budget deficit.

The California Supreme Court ordered the State a year later to repay $187 million in employer contributions that it had withheld.

In 1991, when Governor Pete Wilson tried to take $1.9 billion from the CalPERS Fund to balance the State budget, CSEA again came to the System's defense. CSEA was a major promoter for Proposition 162 in 1992, a ballot measure that would protect the Fund from such encroachments in the future.

Along with other groups, CSEA campaigned tirelessly for the proposition, which voters narrowly approved. The landmark measure gave the CalPERS Board fiduciary authority over the Fund and administration of the System, ensuring that the Fund would be used solely for the benefit of members.

In recent years, CSEA has continued defending the Retirement System against attempts to do away with the defined benefits plans CalPERS has offered from its inception. In the mid-2000s, Governor Arnold Schwarzenegger and other State officials began to push for a switch to 401(k)-type defined contribution plans. CSEA was among the most outspoken opponents of such a change.

Providing public employees with a sound retirement system was the reason CSEA founders started their organization more than 75 years ago. Protecting the System they helped create remains a focus of CSEA today.

CSEA members gather signatures at a rally for Proposition 162, 1992. Proposition 162, which gave CalPERS control over the administration of its Fund, is among the most important voter-approved measures in CalPERS history.

of Stockton introduced Senate Bill 683 to create the State Employees' Retirement System (SERS). The Legislature began considering the bill later that year.[44] The retirement system provided for in the bill was very similar to the program recommended by the Pension Commission. All the benefits included in the Commission's report were retained in the plan under consideration. The proposed system also included State college teachers and employees appointed by the Governor among those eligible for benefits, and a larger death benefit than the program detailed in the Commission report.[45]

The proposed legislation had strong support. The newly created State employees' association supported it, as did State Director of Finance Rolland A. Vandegrift. And James Rolph, Jr., who had endorsed Proposition 5 as Mayor of San Francisco, continued to support the proposed retirement system after winning the Governor's election in 1930. The Legislature recognized the desire and need for a State retirement system. After receiving a recommendation from the Senate Finance Committee, the Senate passed S.B. 683 by a vote of 29 to 5.[46] The Assembly subsequently approved the bill by a vote of 56 to 2. Governor Rolph signed it into law on June 9, 1931.[47] In addition to creating the initial compendium of State employees' retirement law, the bill also articulated SERS first statement of purpose, stating the System existed to "effect economy and efficiency in the public service by providing a means whereby employees who become superannuated or otherwise incapacitated may, without hardship or prejudice, be replaced by more capable employees, and to that end providing a retirement system consisting of retirement compensation and death benefits."[48]

Organizing the State Employees' Retirement System

Once Governor Rolph signed the bill, the process of creating the SERS organizational structure began immediately. This was no simple task. SERS required an organizational structure, a staff to carry out the System's tasks, and policy guidelines and a process to implement them. Organizing a Board of Administration was among the first steps required to create the SERS administrative organizational structure. The law required that the new Board be composed of seven positions: the State Director of Finance, the president of the State Civil Service Commission, a life insurance company

Pivotal Propositions:
Voting on CalPERS Destiny

The California ballot proposition is a sometimes celebrated, sometimes maligned, but ever-present fact of voting life in the Golden State.

Men waiting in line to vote in a Los Angeles city primary, 1945. California's initiative process stretches back to 1911, when the Legislature enacted the initiative, referendum, and recall.

California voters decide on more Statewide ballot propositions in a given election year than many voters face in a lifetime. Through the decades, California voters have cast ballots on propositions involving hundreds of topics, from stem cell research to greyhound racing to working on Sundays to the ability to vote for "none of the above" in general elections.

They have also voted on several propositions vital to CalPERS history, beginning with the ballot measure that provided for the System's creation—Proposition 5 in 1930 (a ballot that also included propositions on Daylight Savings Time, San Francisco harbor improvements, and livestock slaughter in times of disease).

Other voter-approved propositions central to CalPERS history include:

Proposition 1, 1966: This measure allowed the System's Board of Administration to invest Fund assets in common stocks. Previously, the Board could only invest in bonds and mortgages, limiting investment returns for the Fund. Increased returns translated to both the ability to expand benefits and reduction in the cost of benefits to taxpayers. The passage of this measure, which many in the State felt was long overdue, brought substantial growth to the Fund.

Proposition 21, 1984: Proposition 21 broadened the investment authority the Board gained under Proposition 1. Before the 1984 measure, the Board was only able to invest up to 25 percent of the Fund's portfolio in stock. Proposition 21 eliminated that requirement, enabling the Board to greatly expand and diversify the portfolio. In a 2005 *Pensions & Investments* article, Board Vice President Bob Carlson credited Proposition 21 with adding $40 billion to CalPERS assets.

Proposition 140, 1990: This measure required Legislators (Senators and Members of the Assembly) first elected after November 7, 1990, to participate in no other retirement system besides the federal Social Security program. It also introduced legislative term limits. Due to the effects of Proposition 140, the Legislators' Retirement System is in transition. Since the number of Legislators eligible for membership is declining as incumbents leave office and are replaced by representatives not eligible to participate, eventually the only active members of the program will be approximately 16 Constitutional Officers and approximately four Legislative Statutory Officers.

Proposition 162, 1992: The passage of this proposition was a true watershed for all California public pension systems. For CalPERS, this landmark measure granted the Board exclusive authority and fiduciary responsibility for the administration of the System and investment of funds. It also granted a level of protection against future attempts by other State officials to use trust monies for purposes other than paying the benefits of members.

official, a bank official, and three representatives elected under Board supervision from the SERS membership. For the first Board, the Governor appointed the first three employee members from a list of nominees presented by State employees. In subsequent years, State employee members would elect representatives for these three positions.

The three employee members of the Board, as representatives of the workers that the new System served, were particularly significant appointments, both symbolically and politically. John R. Cornwell, at the time of his appointment, was manager of the Los Angeles office of the State Compensation Insurance Fund, and had also served as the President of the Los Angeles Chapter of the employees' association. He later became the fourth President of CSEA, and continued to serve on the Board until he retired from State service in the mid-1950s.[49] Edward J. Callan was Vice President of CSEA and President of Harbor Chapter No. 1 in San Francisco when appointed to the Board. He had worked for the State for 20 years and had served as an Assemblyman from his San Francisco district. In 1931, he held the position of revenue officer of the Board of Harbor Commissioners. He served on the SERS Board until his death in 1941.[50] Thomas Stanton was a materials and research engineer for the Division of Highways when he joined the Board. He had worked for the State for 19 years and had been Chairman of the SERCC. Stanton also became the first President of the California State Employees Association.[51]

Thomas Stanton, 1950. The first President of CSEA, Stanton also served on the Retirement System's Board for nearly 10 years.

The first Board of Administration met twice before SERS became operational. Board Members held their first meeting on October 23, 1931, at the office of State Director of Finance Rolland A. Vandegrift. Civil Service Commission President Hugh K. McKevitt attended, as did the chosen banking representative, Joseph H. Stephens, President of the Merchants' National Bank of Sacramento, and the three Governor-appointed employee members, Stanton, Cornwell, and Callan. The men met at Vandegrift's office again on November 4, this time choosing Vandegrift to serve as the Board's President.

State Employees' Retirement System Board of Administration, January 31, 1932		
Name	**Employment**	**Board Position**
Rolland A. Vandegrift	Director of Finance	President
Hugh K. McKevitt	Civil Service Commission President	Member
Joseph H. Stephens	Bank Officer	Member
Edward J. Callan	State Employee	Member
John R. Cornwell	State Employee	Member
Thomas Stanton	State Employee	Member

One of the Board's first moves was hiring Earl W. Chapman to serve as principal accountant for the Retirement System, at a salary of $325 per month. Chapman had been working as the principal accountant in the Department of Finance, and Rolland Vandegrift assigned him "to assist in the formative stages of the System and to organize its office." Chapman had also managed funds and helped raise money for the State Employees' Retirement Campaign Committee's Proposition 5 campaign. The Board also appointed Ralph R. Nelson, a well-known actuary in the retirement field, as the SERS consulting actuary. Nelson received a $500-per-month salary for four months, with an option for renewal.[52]

As Nelson reported at the Board's November 4 meeting, a few issues needed to be addressed before January 1, 1932, SERS official start date. Officials planning for the new Retirement System needed to determine the status of teachers in teachers' colleges and University of California clerical staff under the new retirement law. They also needed to secure the prior service records of the State workers the System would cover, and to devise rules about the value of board and lodging provided to some employees in addition to their cash compensation.[53]

Earl Chapman, date unknown. CalPERS first Executive Officer, Chapman was also one of the System's first hires. The Board brought him on as Principal Accountant in 1931.

Nevertheless, by the end of 1931, California's State Employees' Retirement System was essentially ready to begin operations. After about five years of intense lobbying and careful planning, organizers had realized their goal. California's State workers would enjoy a carefully structured Retirement System that would provide them an important new benefit. With a retirement allowance, aged employees who were no longer performing their jobs satisfactorily could leave State service and not worry about being able to support themselves financially. As the Pension Commission noted, this gave thousands of California workers the ability "to retire in dignity and comfort."[54]

Opposite page

Clerk of the Court for the Third Appellate District John T. Stafford (*right*), ca. 1930. As one of the original promoters of a retirement system for State employees, Stafford played an important role in getting Proposition 5 on the ballot.

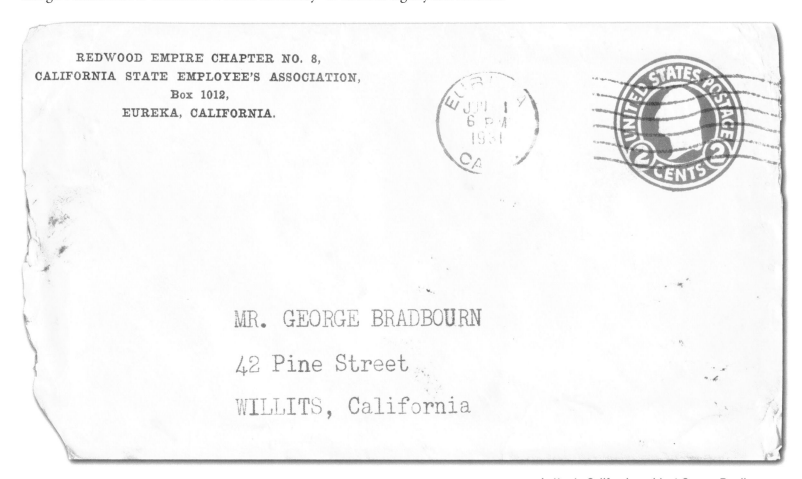

REDWOOD EMPIRE CHAPTER NO. 8,
CALIFORNIA STATE EMPLOYEE'S ASSOCIATION,
Box 1012,
EUREKA, CALIFORNIA.

MR. GEORGE BRADBOURN

42 Pine Street

WILLITS, California

Letter to California resident George Bradbourn from CSEA, 1931. On July 6, 1931, CSEA sent letters to members and supporters triumphantly announcing the creation of the State Employees' Retirement System.

Sacramento County California
WAR LOAN DRIVE

3rd DRIVE
County Quota $18,788,800
Total Sales $19,207,231
Coca Cola Employees SOLD 4.8%

4th DRIVE
County Quota $16,422,852
Total Sales $18,719,575
Coca Cola Employees SOLD 6.2%

5th DRIVE
County Quota $19,556,744
Total Sales $20,532,917
Coca Cola Employees SOLD 4.8%

6th DRIVE
County Quota $16,620,000
Total Sales $19,676,179
Coca Cola Employees SOLD 4.7%

CalPERS first Executive Officer, Earl Chapman, with (*from left*) employees Lillian McCoy, Everell Luke, and Nora Jane Krell, 1946. The System had only six full-time employees and 14,000 members when it began. By 1946, CalPERS membership had more than tripled, though its workforce remained relatively small.

Opposite page
Woman holding a Sacramento County War Loan Drive poster, 1940s. Even in its early years, the Retirement System was secure enough to take on several important new responsibilities, including issuing war bonds for the State during World War II.

Left
Cover of a Retirement System handbook, date unknown. The guidelines and policies CalPERS established in its first years in operation provided a solid foundation that would guide the System for years to come.

2: The Defining Years

The United States was in the throes of its worst economic crisis when California's new public Retirement System opened for business. SERS leadership steered the System adeptly through the havoc of the Great Depression, methodically putting in place initial benefits plans, contribution rates, and investment policies. SERS even grew sturdy enough in this time to support a significant addition, allowing local public agencies to join as contract members in 1939. The System continued to expand both in membership and Fund assets through World War II, while also navigating new administrative duties and policy issues that came with the war.

Pension Plan Expert Hired for State Job

SACRAMENTO. Nov. 10. (AP)— Ralph R. Nelson, secretary-manager of the San Francisco employees' retirement system, has been retained by the State to put into effect its employees' retirement plan.

Rolland Vandegrift, Director of Finance, announced today Nelson has been hired by the State at $500 a month to work four months putting the system into effect.

Article on Ralph Nelson in the *Los Angeles Times*, November 10, 1931. As CalPERS first actuary, Nelson implemented numerous measures that helped establish the Fund.

The State Employees' Retirement System officially began operating on January 1, 1932. The new Board of Administration did not waste any time in tackling its duties. On January 4, Board Members met to begin the process of certifying contribution rates for individual employees.[1] They had already mailed Prior Service Statement Forms to every State government office and department to deal with the prior service requirement. As of their meeting on the 4th, Board Members had received about 12,500 forms.[2]

To finance the initial start-up of the Retirement System, the State Legislature appropriated funds for 18 months to ensure the System's financial viability through July 1, 1933. The Legislature granted SERS $35,000 for its operating expenses.[3] In addition, the State provided a continuing appropriation that represented the employer share of member contributions. These funds came from the State's General and Special funds. The State agreed to contribute a sum equal to 3.25 percent of the current State payroll, which amounted to a contribution of $1,368,200 for the first 18 months. Although there was some concern that the State's contribution level might eventually need to be increased to 5 percent of the State payroll, the benefits schedule provided for in the original act required a maximum State contribution of only 3.75 percent.[4]

Of perhaps more concern to the 13,652 eligible State employees as of March 1931 were the contributions required of them. State employees could now count on a retirement salary, but they would have to contribute funds out of their current salaries to fund their retirement allowance. Contributions by individual employees varied depending upon the employee's age and gender. The original member contributions for men ranged from 2.62-6.16 percent and 2.77-7.02 percent for women. Women's rates were higher than men's because of women's longer life expectancy.

SERS also was responsible for investing its member contributions in sound financial instruments. It was essential that SERS members be absolutely confident that their contributions and the contributions of their employers be safeguarded and enhanced through prudent investment. Until 1947, SERS invested only in municipal and government bonds. SERS conservative investment policy was designed to provide a 4 percent credit to individual retirement funds.[5]

SERS Investments, 1932

Date of Purchase	Date of Delivery	Kind	Maturity	Basis	Par Value	Cost
12/14/31	2/16/32 2/25/32	East Bay 5 percent Municipal	1942 to 1946	4.70 Net to 4.70 Less ¼ of 1 percent	$80,000.00	$82,888.50
11/30/31	2/10/32 3/8/32	Los Angeles 5 percent School District	1939 to 1946	4.75 Less ¼ of 1 percent	$60,000.00	$60,877.05
1/29/32	3/8/32	California 4½ percent Veterans Welfare	1947	4.35 Net	$50,000.00	$50,820.00
TOTAL					$190,000.00	$195,564.03

Ham and Eggs retirement plan cover, 1930s. California was a hotbed for questionable old-age pension schemes during the Great Depression. The Ham and Eggs plan, which called for the government to dispense $30 every Thursday to unemployed Californians age 50 and above, was among the most popular—and controversial.

Faced with the nation's crippled 1930s economy, however, the SERS Board discovered that the 4 percent credit was not realistic. In 1937, due to the decreasing interest returns on the high-grade bonds in which the System invested, the Board lowered the interest rate calculation from the 4 percent rate used since the System's formal beginning to 3½ percent, effective June 30, 1938. The Board later lowered the interest rate again to 3 percent, effective June 30, 1941, due to the continuing decline in the return on the System's bond investments.[6]

After its first full year of operation, SERS requested the State Legislature enact some technical amendments to the original act. The requested changes were considered minor and helpful to the administration of the System and the bill providing for them passed both houses with no opposition.[7] Through 1934, it was apparent that the Retirement System was working efficiently and State employees were taking advantage of its benefits. As of June 30, 1934, the System had handled 118 service retirements, 122 disability cases, and 232 lump-sum death benefits paid.[8]

New Deal Social Welfare Programs

While the California State Employees' Retirement System has unique origins, it was part of a larger social welfare movement. The same trends both in Europe and the United States that led to the creation of various forms of pension, retirement, and old-age assistance programs facilitated the political and social acceptability of the SERS plan in California and similar plans in other states.

Prior to the Great Depression, the social welfare movement was not a major issue in mainstream American politics. Although Germany had created a social insurance system much earlier in the 1880s, the American social welfare movement was limited more to ideas than actual programs. Men such as John B. Andrews, Isaac Rubinow, and John R. Commons were pioneers of the American social welfare movement and had discussed, taught, and written about social welfare policy. Nevertheless, it remained a largely obscure topic.[9]

Before the Great Depression began, the federal government had only sponsored two social programs during the first three decades of the 20th century. These included a grant program begun in 1920 to reimburse states for one-half the cost of establishing and maintaining vocational rehabilitation programs. The second program, the Sheppard-Towner Act, provided grants between 1921 and 1929 for child and maternal welfare through the U.S. Children's Bureau.[10]

When Franklin D. Roosevelt campaigned for the U.S. presidency he promised Americans a "New Deal." Herbert Hoover had been reluctant and slow to use the federal government's powers to slow the rising tide of the Great Depression. Roosevelt, however, promised to engage the federal government in the process of solving the nation's economic woes. During his first 100 days in office, Roosevelt's administration issued a slew of legislation aimed at stabilizing the American economy and restoring confidence in its citizens. His administration sponsored reforms of the banking system, the stock market, the utilities industry, and agriculture, among other industries. He also created several jobs programs early in his administration.

Cooks at a Civilian Conservation Corps (CCC) camp in Litchfield, California, 1938. The CCC was among the New Deal programs President Franklin Roosevelt started in the early 1930s to create jobs and stimulate the economy. At its peak, there were more than 150 CCC camps in California.

But Roosevelt did not act fast enough for other popular political leaders, including populist Louisiana Senator Huey P. Long. In 1934, Long established his "Share Our Wealth" movement, which called for very high tax rates on the rich and a minimum income for all Americans. He also advocated numerous government-sponsored welfare programs, including old-age pensions, unemployment insurance, and public relief.[11] His movement was tremendously influential, attracting five million members by 1935, and Long was considered a likely presidential candidate in 1936. However, he was assassinated at the Louisiana Capitol building in Baton Rouge in 1935.

Long's downfall did not mean the end of aggressive calls for a national social welfare policy. California was the birthplace of another extremely influential social movement—one specifically aimed at securing federal support for the elderly. Dr. Francis E. Townsend, once the assistant medical officer in Long Beach, California, had treated many elderly men and women without the financial means to take care of themselves. At age 66, he lost his own job due to a change in local government administrations. Pondering his own situation and those of his former patients, Townsend began formulating a plan for securing financial support from the federal government for the nation's elderly.[12]

In an apocryphal story, Townsend one morning observed three elderly women rummaging for food in garbage cans. He reportedly reacted strongly, recalling that "A torrent of invectives tore out of me, the big blast of all the bitterness that had been building in me for years. I swore and I ranted, and I let my voice bellow with wild hatred I had for things as they were." Although some scholars question the veracity of this account, Townsend did go on to propose a sweeping national plan to provide welfare assistance to the nation's elderly.[13]

Townsend called his movement the Old Age Revolving Pension Plan. It called for federal pensions of $200 per month for every American over age 60. Recipients, however, would be required to spend that money each month. This, he reasoned, would stimulate the economy while guaranteeing the elderly a minimum monthly income.

As the nation lingered in the financial throes of the Great Depression, President Roosevelt responded to his critics while seeking ways to ameliorate the nation's crippling economic conditions. His administration created a variety of jobs programs, such as the

Senator Huey Long, 1935. Revered by the poor and reviled by the wealthy, Huey Long rose to political power as Governor and Senator of Louisiana and gained a national reputation for his social reform agenda.

Pension Plans & Dreams:
The Townsend Movement

As CalPERS was building a Retirement System in the 1930s for California's public workers, a former Long Beach public servant was busy drumming up support elsewhere in the State for his own pension scheme.

Dr. Francis E. Townsend, 1957. After losing his job with the Long Beach city health office in 1933, Townsend began devising a proposal for a national pension plan that would give $200 a month to retirees over age 60—a plan that quickly gained the support of millions of Americans.

For a brief time, the big promises of Dr. Francis E. Townsend's plan captured the attention of millions of people across the country.

Both derided as a crackpot and celebrated as a savior of America's elderly, Townsend developed one of the most popular concepts for retirement plans in the 1930s. Born to a poor Illinois farm family in 1867, Townsend settled in Long Beach, where he practiced medicine. After losing most of his savings at the outset of the Depression, he took a job as assistant director of the city health office. But he lost that job in 1933 due to city cutbacks and soon found himself in the same straits as millions of other poor, unemployed, elderly citizens.

As a result, Townsend developed the Old Age Revolving Pension Plan, or Townsend Plan for short. The straightforward plan involved the federal government paying $200 per month to everyone over the age of 60 who agreed to stop working. Previous employment was not required; the major rule was that recipients had to spend all $200 each month. These payments would be financed by a 2 percent tax on all business transactions in the country.

Townsend believed in his plan and its promise to protect the elderly and jump-start the economy through increased spending. Millions of hopeful Americans did too. In 1936, Townsend presented Congress with petitions containing 10 million signatures supporting the plan.

The economics behind it, however, proved the plan's promises unfeasible. The $200 per month was above the national average for income, so the plan would create a nation of upper-middle-class elderly people supported by younger workers. And Townsend's calculations that the 2 percent tax would cover the nearly $30 billion needed to cover the annual payments were incorrect. During Congressional hearings, Townsend himself testified that he could not validate this assertion, and the economist he brought in to testify actually proved the tax-revenue estimates were significantly off.

While Congress ultimately did not adopt the Townsend Plan, many argue that its phenomenal public support influenced President Roosevelt's decisions and rapid action in the development of the Social Security Act, whose benefits Townsend ultimately enjoyed until his death in 1960 at the age of 93.

Works Progress Administration (WPA) and the Civilian Conservation Corps (CCC), aimed at putting people to work on useful projects, but many critics continued to attack Roosevelt for not doing more to help the unemployed. Jobs programs alone, they contended, could not solve the unemployment problem.

According to Historian Gerald Nash, Roosevelt "decided to preempt and forestall his critics by supporting a comprehensive social welfare program of his own."[14] While the federal government did not offer any wide-ranging social welfare programs prior to 1935, many states did. By 1918, most states had workmen's compensation laws and noncontributory means-tested pensions for indigent elderly people at age 65 or 70. Every state but South Carolina had enacted mothers' pensions and 24 states (of 48) had pension programs for the needy blind.[15] In addition, a few states offered unemployment insurance prior to federal Social Security.

In 1935, a new agency created by Roosevelt's administration, the Committee on Economic Security, issued a report on a national social welfare policy, which outlined a federal Social Security program. Congress received the report for consideration on January 17 and on August 14, 1935, after only a seven-month legislative process, Roosevelt signed the Social Security Act into law. The legislation's prologue stated the Social Security Act would:

Provide for the General welfare by establishing a system of Federal old-age benefits, and by enabling the several States to make more adequate provision for aged persons, blind persons, dependent and crippled children, maternal and child welfare, public health, and the administration of their unemployment compensation laws; to establish a Social Security Board; to raise revenue; and for other purposes.

The 32-page act contained 11 titles providing federal involvement in nine social welfare programs, although some of these programs previously existed on the state level. The act also created one new program, the Old-Age Insurance (OAI) program.[16]

The OAI program, Title II of the Act, created a system of contributory old-age pensions covering nearly all employees in commerce and industry. The program's qualifying retirement age was 65 and pension payments were scheduled to begin in 1942. The maximum benefit was $85 per month.[17]

Mass meeting of WPA workers protesting a cut in relief appropriations in San Francisco, 1939. Although the WPA and other New Deal programs helped employ many people, critics often complained that they did not do enough to solve the problem.

Poster from the Social Security Administration, 1935. The national Social Security Program would be an important factor in CalPERS policies in decades to come.

A Daughter's Work Is Never Done

The challenges CalPERS dealt with in the 1930s were mostly the usual glitches encountered by startups—procedural issues requiring adjustment, financial projections needing refinement, lack of familiarity among customers.

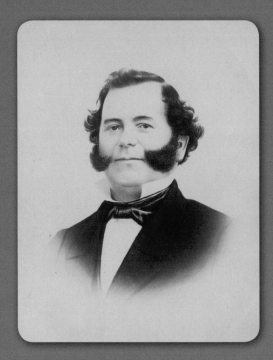

General Mariano G. Vallejo, date unknown. Born in 1808, Vallejo played a key role in California's Statehood efforts. His daughter worked as caretaker for his home after it became a State Historical Monument, which posed an early challenge for CalPERS because she was well past retirement age.

Opposite page
Lachryma Montis, 1933. After losing much of his fortune and his ranch near Petaluma, Vallejo and his wife moved to Lachryma Montis, or Mountain Tear, a gothic cottage he built in the 1850s and lived in until his death in 1890.

But in 1939, Executive Officer Earl Chapman faced a predicament from a very unusual suspect—the octogenarian daughter of one of the most revered figures in California's early State history.

General Mariano G. Vallejo was California's first Military Governor and a member of the first Constitution of California convention. He played a key role in guiding California through the process of statehood, providing strong leadership during a seminal time.

In 1933, more than four decades after his death in 1890, General Vallejo's home in Sonoma, Lachryma Montis, became a State Historical Monument. As part of the agreement made during the family's transfer of the home to the State, the California Division of Parks allowed Vallejo's daughter, Luisa Emparan, to live in the home and employed her as custodian and caretaker of the property at a salary of $100 a month.

Emparan applied for membership with the Retirement System in 1939. She was 84 at the time—well over the mandatory retirement age of 70 stipulated in the State Employees' Retirement Act. Earl Chapman responded to her request by denying her application and asking the Department of Natural Resources to find a replacement for her position as the Lachryma Montis custodian.

Chapman confidently believed that he had correctly interpreted the law, but he soon found himself at the center of a political controversy. His decision met with a quick response from California Senator Herbert W. Slater, who asked Chapman "to withhold the retirement for the present."

At present her being there to receive people is one of the greatest assets which in fact overshadows the colorful history and glamour of by-gone years when her illustrious father, the late General M. G. Vallejo, was military governor of northern California, and still later on when he was a member of the first Constitution of California convention; the man who did more than anyone else to transfer California into the United States of America and who was also my illustrious predecessor in office as Sonoma County's first member of the state Senate.

Other high-ranking government officials, including State Attorney General Earl Warren, eventually jumped into the fray as well.

Finally, in the spring of 1940, State officials decided on a compromise. Emparan continued to serve as the home's custodian, but she did not become a member of the Retirement System. This exempted her from the System's membership rules, including the mandatory retirement age. Though she suffered a heart attack in January 1940, she continued to serve as custodian to her family's historic home. She passed away in 1943.

U.S. Congressman Daniel Reed, 1954. Reed, a conservative Republican from New York, was a vocal critic of the Old-Age Insurance program created under the Social Security Act, believing that it overstepped the federal government's boundaries.

A California Highway Patrolman, 1933. In 1935, Patrol Officers became the first CalPERS members to receive a separate retirement benefit formula, which recognized the hazards of their jobs.

The OAI program faced some prominent opposition. Senator Daniel O. Hastings (DE) and Congressman Daniel Reed (NY) both spoke publicly against it. Hastings stated that OAI might "end the progress of a great country and bring its people to the level of the average European" and Reed worried that the "lash of the dictator will be felt and 25 million American citizens will for the first time submit themselves to a fingerprint test." Roosevelt would not budge, however, and OAI remained part of the Social Security Act.[18]

SERS & the Public in the 1930s

As the federal government instituted national retirement and social welfare programs, the California State Employees' Retirement System educated the public about its own operations. SERS outreach and education efforts proved quite challenging, largely because during each legislative session, lawmakers enacted new changes to the State employees' retirement law.

During the 1930s, Earl Chapman spent a great deal of time explaining to Californians how SERS operated. Chapman wrote one article titled "Retirement Act: Amendments Improve Administration of Law, Assure Continuance of System …" for the *Midstate Review*, a publication of the Stockton chapter of the CSEA.[19] In another *Midstate Review* article Chapman explained to readers the value of membership in the State Retirement System by listing six reasons why he personally appreciated it:

- *Because it provides an automatic 'painless' method of saving*
- *Because the Retirement System provides a death benefit without cost to me*
- *Because I have disability protection*
- *Because when I become old enough I can retire from service*
- *Because when I am 70 and compulsory retirement applies, I will be assured of an income in my old age and will not be dependent upon charity*
- *Because I know that the Retirement System is carefully managed by a Board of Administration of which three members are employees who I help elect.*[20]

In the mid-1930s, SERS restructured its membership categories. The Legislature in 1935 passed the California Highway Patrol Retirement Act, which created a separate system of benefits for officers in the Highway Patrol. As a result of this act, SERS membership split into two general categories, which would later be defined as miscellaneous members, or general State employees, and patrol members, or members who performed potentially dangerous duties as part of their employment.[21]

Dangerous Duty

California's highways had a reputation in the 1930s as particularly treacherous places to drive. East Coast newspapers wrote of reckless drivers and "speed mania" in the State.

A California Highway Patrol official saluting a Patrol Academy memorial dedicated to fallen officers, West Sacramento, ca. 1979. For more than 70 years, CalPERS has offered a retirement benefit formula created specifically for Patrol Officers.

State Fish and Game Patrol, 1938. Fish and Game officers became a special member category in 1945, with benefits similar to those of Patrol members.

Time magazine ran a story in 1936 about the Ridge Route, a scenic stretch of highway connecting Los Angeles and Bakersfield, where 51 motorists were killed over 15 months.

The officers patrolling these highways were not immune to their hazards. CalPERS recognized the dangers these officers faced on the job and restructured the System's benefits to reflect this. With the passage of the California Highway Patrol Retirement Act in 1935, the Retirement System instituted for the first time a class of benefits based on profession.

Highway Patrol Officers received a larger service allowance at a younger retirement age than CalPERS members in other professions. They also gained an industrial disability retirement benefit and an industrial death benefit for a beneficiary through the 1935

legislation. Of course, in a contributory system like CalPERS, these benefits did come with an extra cost.

Nevertheless, the Patrol benefits plan was well-received. Once the Retirement System began allowing public agencies to join as contractors in 1939, these agencies could secure a similar benefits structure for their police officers, firefighters, peace officers, and other public safety officials.

Over the years, the System also extended various levels of benefits to other groups of State and local employees who face on-the-job hazards, including prison workers, firefighters, fish and game wardens, and harbor police. Today, CalPERS continues to provide benefits reflecting the potential dangers many of its members brave every day in protecting California's citizens.

Patrol members, in recognition of the hazards of their occupation, received a service retirement allowance of approximately half their salary at age 60 or above, provided the member also had a minimum of 20 years' service credit. As of January 1, 1937, the compulsory retirement age for patrol members decreased from 75, as stipulated in the original act, to 65. (The mandatory retirement age for miscellaneous members was also reduced—from 75 to 70 years.) Additionally, patrol officers were eligible for an industrial disability retirement allowance and an industrial death allowance for a beneficiary. Enhanced benefits for patrol officers did not come without cost, however. SERS had been founded on the policy that benefits would be based on sound financial planning. Thus, the enhanced patrol member benefits required a higher level of contributions from both patrol officers and the State.[22]

Further significant revisions to the State employees' retirement law came out of the 1937 legislative session. Perhaps the most important amendment was a provision that enhanced the Board of Administration's powers. The Board gained broad authority over the management of the SERS Fund through the new legislation. For example, while the original act set employee and employer contribution rates, the 1937 provision gave the Board the authority to adjust these rates to ensure the Fund's adequacy and stability in changing economic times. The first few years of SERS operations had made it clear that the Board needed such authority. As of July 1, 1938, SERS increased contribution rates for males from a range of 2.68-6.16 percent to 3.15-6.38 percent; for females, the rate ranges increased from 2.88-7.02 percent to 3.41-7.31 percent.[23] The 1937 legislation also increased the State's contribution level, from 3.25 to 3.75 percent for miscellaneous members. The State's contribution for Highway Patrol officers increased to 9.2 percent.[24]

In a related issue, the State Legislature agreed to give the Board authority to adjust the rate of interest SERS paid on its accumulated member contributions. The original act required SERS to pay 4 percent interest on member contributions, but this rate was too high for SERS to maintain during the difficult economic times of the Great Depression. The SERS Board noted that its investment in bonds yielded an average return of 3.75 percent, but excess interest earned on investments was offset by the late receipt of members' contributions. The State's contribution was sometimes delayed as well, because officials had to make sure that they had received all monthly wage and

University of California, Davis employees testing milk, 1910. In 1937, the California Legislature voted to allow nonacademic employees of the University of California into CalPERS.

salary information before calculating the contribution. This situation resulted in less revenue for the SERS Fund. Following the passage of the 1937 legislation, the Board used its new authority to lower the interest rate on all member and employer contributions from 4 percent to 3½ percent effective July 1, 1938.[25]

In 1937, the Legislature also addressed the issue of nonacademic employees of the University of California. The original SERS act did not specifically include the nonacademic employees of the University of California, and the UC retirement system did not cover this group of about 2,000, either. A bill introduced to the Legislature in 1937 was designed to include the non-academic UC employees in the University's retirement system. However, the Legislature enacted certain technical amendments to public employee retirement law that the State Attorney General interpreted as providing for the inclusion of these workers into the SERS. As a result, nonacademic UC employees became SERS members on August 27, 1937. The Legislature granted them credit for prior service the next year.[26] The addition of this new group of members also prompted the creation of an eighth position on the SERS Board, for a member chosen by the University of California Regents.[27]

Cafeteria workers for the Hayward Elementary School District, 1953. In 1940, the school district became the first organization to contract for classified employee benefits with CalPERS.

The most dramatic change in SERS membership came in 1939, when the Legislature passed a bill that allowed cities, counties, school districts, and special districts in California to participate in SERS on a contractual basis. This legislation brought an immediate and major expansion in SERS membership. In 1940, membership reached 32,000; five years earlier, it had been half that. Contract agency members did not account for the entire increase, of course, but they did represent a significant portion of it.

The new law became effective on September 19, 1939. Public agency members were relatively slow to join initially. The first contracting school organization, the Hayward Elementary School District, became part of SERS on December 1, 1940. The San Mateo Union High School District was the System's second contracting agency, joining on January 1, 1941. Only employees other than teachers in such school districts were covered under SERS; certified school teachers had retirement benefits through the California State Teachers' Retirement System.

Redwood City, looking north on El Camino, 1946. In 1942, Redwood City became one of the first seven cities to join CalPERS. The city's slogan, "Climate Best by Government Test," is based on an obscure climatological survey conducted by the U.S. and German governments prior to World War I. The city tied for the world's best climate with the Canary Islands and North Africa's Mediterranean coast.

Although school districts joined the System in greater numbers at first than other public agencies, the benefit of having employees in the State System soon attracted a wide variety of agencies. By December 1942, 16 school districts and seven cities had joined SERS. The seven cities were:

- Beverly Hills
- Hillsborough
- Redwood City
- Burlingame
- Palo Alto
- San Mateo
- Berkeley (exclusive of firemen and policeman)

By June 30, 1946, there were 113 agencies under contract, including eight counties, 38 cities, 56 school districts, and 11 other districts. These agencies accounted for 13,658 individual SERS members.

CalPERS & Beverly Hills:
A Mutual Investment

View looking west on Wilshire Boulevard, 1947.

CalPERS began allowing local public agencies to contract for retirement benefits in 1939. Among the earliest municipalities to sign up was the City of Beverly Hills.

Since 1942, the city and its employees have been members of the Retirement System. In those 65 years, they have forged a strong relationship that illustrates the profound impact CalPERS has on the lives and communities of its members.

"From a personal standpoint, I see CalPERS strengthening Beverly Hills in that with the great benefits that it offers in terms of retirement, you see so little turnover. Turnover in the police department is virtually nil."
—Micaela Garland, Lieutenant, Police Department

"CalPERS provides a lot of safety and security to the employees and I think it takes the stress out of knowing that their health care is taken care of, that their pension is taken care of. And I think it's important for employees to have that kind of security to do a good job."
— Linda J. Briskman, Councilmember

"You have a comfort in knowing that CalPERS is there. I don't worry about my finances for my future retirement. I just know they're there. I don't worry about the kind of quality of health care in my medical plans that I'm going to pick because CalPERS has done all of the work behind the scenes … What is the connection between Beverly Hills and CalPERS? Well I think it's called mutual investment."
— Raymond Navarro, Battalion Chief, Fire Department

"I think Beverly Hills' faith in CalPERS is because of our longevity. Everyone's been in it a long time. It's like a partnership. CalPERS helps us out, we help CalPERS out. I think it's a great thing for both of us."
— Jeff Gettler, Street Maintenance Supervisor, Department of Public Works and Transportation

SERS made some modifications to its membership categories as new agencies contracted for coverage. The System continued to offer benefits for State employee
members under the categories of miscellaneous and patrol members and divided
contracting agency members into comparable categories.[29] Police officers, firefighters,
and county peace officers received patrol benefits similar to those of the California
Highway Patrol officers, while other public agency members were considered miscellaneous.[30] Also in 1939, the Legislature expanded the patrol category to include
employees of State prisons, and granted the widows and children of these workers
allowances comparable to those of the widows and children of State Highway Patrol
officers. Lawmakers in 1939 also extended SERS coverage to certain permanent part-
time employees for the first time.[31]

California correctional lieutenants from
San Quentin prison, 1949. The Legislature's
1939 expansion of the Patrol category allowed
prison workers to receive additional benefits
from CalPERS.

Restructuring Benefits

As both the SERS membership and Fund grew in size, some members began lobbying for changes in the benefit structure to provide for a larger retirement allowance that would be available to SERS members at an earlier age. The original act provided a $1/70$ at age 65 formula, meaning employees who retired at age 65 received monthly retirement benefits of $1/70$th of their monthly salary, multiplied by the number of years they had been in State service.[32]

CSEA also began to support calls for a more liberal benefits plan, following a study it conducted of the SERS benefits program. CSEA pressed for a new $1/60$ at age 60 formula. While this benefit formula offered a very attractive retirement benefit enhancement to SERS members, it also required increased funding. For SERS to offer such an improvement in benefits, the System and its members would have to fund it.

Legislation supporting this new benefit plan was submitted to the 1942 session of the State Legislature. The new plan, however, was referred to an interim committee for additional study. The Legislature did not want to reject the plan, but it was not in a position to approve it. The United States was then directly involved in World War II and the Legislature recognized that in a wartime economy when living costs and taxes were expected to increase, State employees were not likely to be able to afford the higher salary deductions necessary to fund enhanced benefits.[33]

State lawmakers did make one modification to the Retirement Law during the war to assist the war effort, passing a provision in 1943 that allowed employees to continue in service beyond their compulsory retirement age "if the appointing power so desired and the Board of Administration, after a medical examination, approved."[34] Legislators kept this provision in place only through World War II and for a brief time during the Korean War. During World War II, many State and public agency members left service to work for the federal government, in many cases joining the armed services. These members were allowed to return to their former positions at the conclusion of the war, with their SERS membership status reactivated upon their return to State or local service. They also had the option of continuing to pay their member contributions while away from their jobs or they could pay their contribution upon returning. Under certain circumstances, the State paid some members' contributions during their military leaves of absence.[35]

To Honor Those Who Serve

During times of national crisis, such as World War II, the men and women of California have proudly stepped forward to do their part by joining the armed services.

To do so, they left their jobs, families, and homes behind. In such a stressful time, the last thing these men and women should have to think about is their financial security when they return home. Yet time away from their jobs meant lost years of service to those public employees in the Retirement System—which impacted their future retirement benefits.

CalPERS and the State of California recognized this dilemma early on. In the 1940s, the Retirement System urged the California Legislature to pass laws allowing service men and women who returned to State employment after discharge from the military to not only return to their former positions with their membership in the System reactivated, but they could also purchase service credit for their time spent serving their country in the armed services.

As its membership grew and the country responded to new crises and military engagements, the Retirement System lobbied for bills that would respond to the needs of veterans. In 1949, the Legislature passed a law that allowed any member who had served in the military prior to 1932 and returned to State employment within six months of their discharge to have that time

credited for State service. Other bills extended the service credit to men and women who served in the Korean War.

Today CalPERS continues to recognize the difficult sacrifices that public employees make when serving their country. The ability to purchase military service credit protects their financial future just as they have protected the future for all Americans.

Midshipmen from the Sacramento Naval Academy, 1940. During WWII, CalPERS helped alleviate the stress of war by providing members involved in active military service more flexibility in their membership.

Investments

In the 1940s, the SERS Board gave increasing attention to the investment function, reconsidering both the administration of the SERS Fund as well as the types of investments it could make. As the SERS Board sought to exercise more control over the investment function, the Retirement System became an increasingly independent State agency.

As of the beginning of the 1940s, SERS invested only in U.S. and municipal bonds. Throughout the previous decade, a basic understanding between the SERS Board and the Department of Finance provided that the Director of Finance actually purchase these investments for SERS. This arrangement apparently satisfied both the SERS Board and the Department of Finance during the first several years of SERS operation. But as the Board gained a better understanding of their investment responsibilities and investment policy in general, it began to seek more authority to make investment decisions.

San Francisco Bay Bridge, 1936. The CalPERS Board approved the purchase of bonds from the San Francisco-Oakland Bay Bridge Authority in 1939. The Bay Bridge opened in 1936 and today is one of the busiest bridges in the United States.

General Bond & Corporate Stock Investments Approved by the SERS Board, 1939

1. United States Government

2. State of California

3. Counties of the State of California (with tax delinquency not to exceed 20 percent)

4. Municipalities of: San Francisco, Los Angeles, Sacramento, San Diego, Stockton, Fresno, Berkeley, Long Beach, Oakland, Pasadena, San Jose, and Santa Barbara

5. School districts, including within their boundaries the municipalities under the preceding line

6. Districts of: East Bay Municipal Water District, Golden Gate Bridge and Highway District, Los Angeles County Flood Control District, Marin Municipal Water District, Metropolitan Water District of Southern California, Colorado River Water Works, Santa Clara Valley Conservation District, Stockton Post District

7. Los Angeles Department of Water and Power Electric Plant Revenue

8. City of New York

9. San Francisco-Oakland Bay Bridge Authority*

*The Board agreed that SERS could purchase San Francisco-Oakland Bay Bridge Authority bonds after they had been offered on the open market "in the light of the conditions under which the bonds are offered."

Source: SERS Board Meeting Minutes, January 27, 1939.

During the SERS Board meeting of January 27, 1939, it was pointed out that "the Retirement Board from the inception of the Retirement System maintained that purchases should be made in the Retirement Office but that the Director of Finance at that time interpreted the law as giving him authority to purchase and that his desire[s] were followed for apparent reasons."[36] Thus, the Board began to challenge the Director of Finance's practice of purchasing bonds on behalf of SERS without direct involvement of SERS officers. At the same meeting, an even more pointed observation was made that "the Retirement Board repeatedly during the last few years has expressed certain policies it desired to be followed in purchases and that some of the policies were not followed because of the position of the Department of Finance in State Government."[37]

The Board then indicated its intention to exert authority over investment decisions and transactions in the future. Some Board Members conducted a conference call with Arlin Stockburger, Director of Finance, and reached an agreement with him that the SERS Executive Secretary, as the designate of the Board President, would "conduct the negotiations in connection with the purchase of bonds." The Board later indicated that proposed amendments to the State retirement law would place the purchase of securities for the Retirement Fund under the joint control of the SERS Board and a designated employee of the Department of Finance. However, the SERS Board would retain the authority to set investment policy and a designated SERS representative would approve each investment decision.[38]

The intricacies of investment policy continued to require an increasing amount of the Board's time. The amount of money available for investment was increasing dramatically, and the Board actively sought to enhance its ability to properly invest and otherwise manage these funds. During 1939, the Board considered the possibility of engaging the services of an investment counselor.[39] The Board considered, for example, using the investment service of Dun and Bradstreet, which, for $300, would "furnish a detailed report on 50 sources of issue followed by two supplementary reports per year."[40]

SERS continued to seek the employment of an investment adviser. This person would be responsible for purchasing bonds and examining the array of bond issues for possible purchase by SERS. The Board desired that this person be an employee of the

California Director of Finance Arlin Stockburger, date unknown. The CalPERS Board worked with Stockburger to sort out the details of the System's investment authority in 1939.

QUALIFIED APPLICANTS WANTED
FOR STATE EMPLOYMENT

Applications Will be Accepted Only If They Clearly Indicate That the Applicants Possess All the Entrance Requirements Listed Below

APPLICATIONS must be made out on official application blanks, procurable in Sacramento at 1025 P Street; in San Francisco at 108 State Building; in Los Angeles at 401 State Building; in San Diego at the San Diego Civil Service Commission, 453 Civic Center Building, or by writing to any of these offices.
CITIZENSHIP: All applicants must be full United States citizens.
RESIDENCE: Applicants must have resided in California for at least one year prior to the examination date.
VETERAN PREFERENCE: Proof of actual service must be submitted with application, but preferential credits will be allowed only if candidate qualifies in the examination. (Information and instructions on the back of the application form.)
FINGERPRINTING: The State Personnel Board may require fingerprinting of all applicants for the examination, either at the time of the examination or at the time of certification to the position.
MEDICAL and PHYSICAL requirements, as announced, must be met. Candidates may be rejected for any deficiency, abnormality, or disease that tends to impair health or usefulness such as defective vision, heart and lung diseases, uncontrolled hernia, paralysis and defective hearing.

NO SAMPLE QUESTIONS AVAILABLE

STATE PERSONNEL BOARD
The State Personnel Board is not connected with, nor does it recommend, any civil service coaching school.
LOUIS J. KROEGER, Executive Officer

INVESTMENT ADVISER
(Open to Men Only)

FACTS CONCERNING EXAMINATION

EXAMINATION DATE: May 27, 1939.
FILING OF APPLICATIONS: Applications filed at the office of the State Personnel Board should be filed not later than the close of the business day, May 20, 1939. Applications filed by mail must be addressed to the State Personnel Board, 1025 P Street, Sacramento.
PURPOSE OF EXAMINATION: To obtain eligibles to fill a vacancy in the Department of Finance; and to establish an eligible list from which to fill future vacancies.
LOCATION OF EMPLOYMENT: Sacramento.
NUMBER TO BE QUALIFIED: Under the authority of Section 89 of the State Civil Service Act the State Personnel Board reserves the right to limit the number of candidates to be qualified by this examination to 10 or such lesser number as may show by their examination ratings that they are able to successfully perform the duties of the position.
PLACE OF EXAMINATION: Sacramento, San Francisco, Los Angeles, San Diego, Fresno, and Eureka.

THE POSITION

DUTIES: Under the direction of the Director of Finance, to analyze security market conditions and make recommendations to the Director of Finance concerning the purchase and sale of securities by the State, including supervising the compilation of data concerning securities markets and values, appraising the value of bonds and other securities, maintaining records concerning securities purchased or sold, preparing reports concerning market trends, recommending the purchase or sale of securities, conducting negotiations in connection with the purchase and sale of securities, making regular reports concerning interest or premiums earned and the current status of investments, discussing investment policies with representatives of various state agencies, communicating with investment and financial agencies in the gathering of market data.
ENTRANCE SALARY: $320 a month. Employees maintaining an efficiency rating of 80% or better may

State of California's Investment Adviser position announcement, 1939. California employment law required all applicants to take a civil service examination before being considered for employment. In 1940, the Department of Finance hired Rene Rothschild to serve as the first Investment Adviser to CalPERS.

Department of Finance whose responsibility would be to "furnish the Retirement Board with information about various sources of issue of bonds in and out of California."[41] The person hired for this position would be required to take a civil service examination, so SERS could not simply hire an investment counselor of its own choosing, but rather would have to wait until after the exam for a list of eligible employees.

Late in 1940, the Department of Finance announced that it had hired an investment adviser. Rene L. Rothschild had taken the civil service exam and the State Personnel Board had placed him on the list of eligible candidates. Rothschild would "act as the designated employee of the Department of Finance, with the employee of the Board of Administration designated by said Board, in making purchases of securities from any list approved by the Board, all as provided in Section 60 (b) [of State Retirement Law]."[42]

Rene Rothschild:
Doing the Most … and Then Some

In the 1940s, a common slogan used to drum up support for war bonds asked Americans "Have you signed up for War Bonds? The MOST you can do is the LEAST you should do!"

For one person, the answer to this question was an easy one. Rene Rothschild, the System's innovative first investment adviser, played a seminal role in California's war loan effort and in the broader community.

Rothschild spearheaded a desk-to-desk campaign in State office buildings, engaging the community with events like Mexican-themed parties, meet and greets with Hollywood starlets, and charitable auctions. Through these and other efforts Rothschild garnered a great deal of praise and received accolades from the U.S. Treasury and California Governor Earl Warren.

He worked a great deal at general community outreach, as well—appearing on San Francisco's KFRC radio shows, speaking at the Public Employees' Speakers Club, and participating in question-and-answer sessions at his alma mater, Stanford University. All of these efforts did not go unappreciated. After a talk at the newly established Financial Women's Club of San Francisco, the members of the club sent Rothschild a letter effusively thanking him for "the most interesting talk … to an organization yet relatively small and new." They went on to credit his appearance with strengthening the club, writing that the "meeting had the largest number in attendance of any we have held and we are indebted to you for your responsibility in bringing them together."

Whether boosting the System's public profile or building its investment portfolio from $22 million to $1.2 billion in two decades, Rothschild took his successes in stride and was known for his unselfishness and kindness. His humility notwithstanding, those successes were vital in shaping what would become the nation's largest public pension system.

Rene Rothschild (*second from left*) with members of the Pacific Gas and Electric Company during a trip to the Moss Landing Steam Plant, 1952. Under Rothschild's guidance, the Retirement System broadened its investments, adding public utilities to the list of eligible corporate bonds in 1947.

Under Rothschild's guidance, the list of bonds in which SERS invested continued to grow in the early 1940s. The Board added the Port of New York Authority to this list in October 1941 followed within a year by the New York Triborough Bridge Authority, the Sacramento Municipal Utility District, and U.S. government bonds.[43]

World War II & SERS

When Japanese fighter planes bombed Pearl Harbor in Hawaii on December 7, 1941, the United States became directly involved in the military conflict already raging in Europe. World War II brought enormous change to the U.S. economy as emergency federal wartime agencies such as the War Production Board took control of the economy.

The U.S. government also issued war bonds to assist in financing the war effort, and the SERS Board began modifying its investment program in favor of U.S. bond purchases. By November 1942, SERS had already purchased $900,000 in such bonds.[44] Throughout the war, the majority of SERS bond purchases were U.S. government bonds.

Soon after the Pearl Harbor bombing, the State Legislature authorized SERS to become the designated agency to buy United States Savings Bonds with funds deducted from State employee salaries. SERS issued war bonds through a newly created business unit called the War Savings Bond Division, established on February 1, 1942.

California State war bonds, 1942. CalPERS supported the war effort through the sale and purchase of war bonds.

Opposite page
A Palo Alto city utility crew, 1950s. Employees of local public agencies could receive benefits through the Retirement System beginning in 1939. Palo Alto was among the first cities to contract for benefits for its employees; by 1946, 113 local agencies were doing so.

War bonds advertisement, 1942. CalPERS encouraged State employees to purchase war bonds through payroll deductions.

The California State Emergency Fund was tapped to pay for the initial expense of creating the new SERS division. As of June 30, 1942, more than 14,000 employees, or about one-half of SERS active members, had authorized payroll deductions and participation eventually exceeded that by several thousand members. The program ended with the issuance of the April 1947 payroll.[45] After the war, SERS temporarily served as the agent for employee purchases of U.S. Savings Bonds, though this function eventually moved to the State Controller's Office.[46]

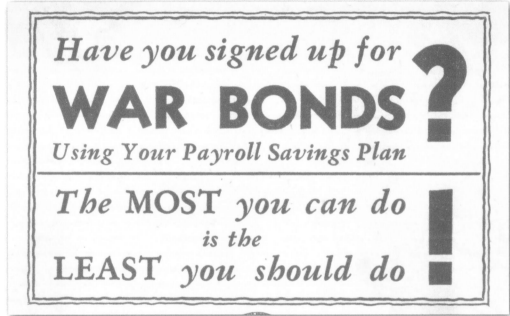

Have you signed up for **WAR BONDS**?
Using Your Payroll Savings Plan
The MOST you can do is the LEAST you should do!

SERS employee Marcella Weldon recalled that during the war, "It seemed to me that we were an office of women for an awful long time." Earl Chapman worked in the office, and actuary Ralph Nelson came to the office once a week. Later, Edward Coombs, who became SERS Assistant Executive Officer in 1947, returned from the service and worked regularly at SERS. Otherwise, the office consisted primarily of women.

When the war ended, "We closed the door, and everybody walked down K Street," Weldon recalled. "Everybody was walking down there and everybody was hugging everybody else. Everybody was happy."[47]

California's Retirement System emerged from the crises of the Great Depression and World War II a significantly bigger, more diverse, and more secure establishment. Its ability to thrive in these trying early years boded well for the era ahead.

In Recognition of Employment with the

State of California

for a Period of

Twenty-five Years

This Certificate is Presented to

Evelyn M. Buck

for Faithful Public Service

3: Investing for Life

When World War II finally ended, the nation entered a period of prosperity and growth—as did SERS. The System's membership continued to grow and diversify. Local public agencies joined at a particularly rapid rate, eager to offer their employees access to SERS benefits structure. And those benefits improved in the 1940s and 1950s, with the System offering new benefits and a more generous formula.

SERS investment portfolio also grew significantly in this time, especially after the Board broadened the pool of corporate bonds in which the System could invest. Another issue demanded much of the Board's attention during this era: coordination with federal Social Security.

At the close of World War II, SERS was well positioned to continue supporting its increasing number of members with enhanced benefits. One sign of the System's increasing size could be found in the 1947 Annual Report. From SERS inception through 1946, the Annual Report had listed the name, position, agency of employment, and date of retirement or death of every retired member in the System. In 1946, for example, the Annual Report listed by name 2,267 retired members and 138 deceased members. In the 1947 report, however, SERS began printing only aggregate information—a symbol of a new era for the System. SERS was no longer a fledgling institution by any means, but rather a complex and very large organization and a permanent and vitally important institution for thousands of Californians.

Retirement Law Changes in the Early Postwar Era

The push for a 1/60 at 60 retirement formula resumed in the final year of the war. Legislative hearings on the subject showed substantial political support existed for such a formula and during the 1945 legislative session, lawmakers passed a set of 10 retirement bills that covered the 1/60 at 60 formula and several other matters. Governor Earl Warren signed the new legislation in 1945 and the new benefits became effective on October 1, 1945, a month after the official end of World War II. The benefit increase applied to previously retired members as well as retiring members. Although not obligated by law to adopt the same formula, most of SERS public agency employers also adopted this new benefit formula.[1]

The 1945 retirement legislation also included a provision for a $300 death benefit for every retired member. SERS agreed to pay this benefit to the deceased member's designated beneficiary. The State funded these improvements, as well as the costs involved in applying the new benefit formula to members' service prior to October 1945.[2]

Perhaps the most significant issue the SERS Board confronted in 1945 involved the predictability of a retirees' pension. To address this matter, CSEA contracted a consulting actuary to survey and prepare an analysis of the Retirement System. The report, finished in June 1946, focused on the technical yet vital actuarial issue of the "money value formula" compared to the "guaranteed formula." Theodore H. Jenner, Chairman of the CSEA Retirement Committee was the principal CSEA representative who spoke in favor of the guaranteed formula to the State Legislature.[3]

Governor Earl Warren, 1950s. In 1945, Warren signed legislation providing key new benefits to CalPERS members, including enactment of the 1/60th at 60 formula, meaning members who retired at age 60 received monthly benefits of 1/60th of their monthly salary multiplied by their years in State service.

Theodore H. Jenner (*center*) with Stanley Fowler (*left*) and Joe Hislop (*right*), 1950. Jenner played an important role in the late 1940s advocating for retirement legislation to benefit workers. All three men served as President of CSEA during the 1950s.

Retirement booklet for State employees, July 1948. As the close of the 1940s brought increased benefits to CalPERS members, it also led to more outreach initiatives to inform members of all the System had to offer.

RETIREMENT INFORMATION

*T*HE PURPOSE *of this article is to provide the employees of the State of California with a concise analysis of their Retirement System. It is not intended that all provisions of the law be fully discussed or included herein; if more detail is desired, the law should be consulted. The benefits described in this article may not apply to employees of contracting public agencies, depending on the terms of the contract between the Agency and the Retirement System. This same material, prepared by the Retirement Administration Staff, has been published by the State for limited distribution.*

ADMINISTRATION

The following are members of the Board of Administration: Thomas E. Stanton, President, H. H. Benedict, John R. Cornwell, Vice-President, Donald Gallagher, Emery Olson, James Dean, Walter C. Kennedy, and Harold H. Robinson. In charge of the complicated day-by-day administration of the State Employees' Retirement System is Earl W. Chapman, Executive Officer. He is assisted by Edward K. Coombs, Assistant Executive Officer, and Lauren Haight, Assistant Actuary. The Actuary is Ralph R. Nelson.

MEMBERSHIP

1. All full-time State Employees, except as noted below, become members of the system after completing six months of state service which is uninterrupted by a break of more than one month. Part-time employees regularly and continuously employed likewise become members if they are working at least on a half-time basis. Elected officials of the State and appointees of the Governor voluntarily may become members under like requirements.

Twenty-one

Since the origins of SERS, the Retirement System had based its benefit payout on a money value formula. This formula was based on the combination of an employees' service retirement annuity, which was an annuity that the employees' accumulated contributions purchased by actuarial calculation, and the current service pension, which was a dollar-for-dollar matching annuity provided by the State. The combination of the service retirement annuity and the current service pension became the members' total benefit. While this formula was designed to provide an allowance equal to a ⅟₆₀ at age 60 retirement formula, it did not actually guarantee that precise amount would be paid.[4]

In response to the study, the 1947 Legislature switched from the money value formula to a guaranteed formula. The modification retained the actuarially figured service retirement annuity, but it required the State increase its own contributions when necessary to attain full benefit funding to the member under the ⅟₆₀ at age 60 formula.[5]

Two years later, the Legislature enacted another set of modifications to the State Employees' Retirement Law—modifications that adjusted how SERS calculated prior service. The original prior service formula calculated the average compensation earnable during the last three years of an employee's service prior to 1932. As salaries increased over the years, however, this strict formula produced a decreasing prior service credit relative to the times. The Legislature addressed this issue in 1949 by changing the prior service calculation so that the "highest five consecutive years" of a member's salary became the basis for the prior service contribution.[6] In a related change, the Legislature required that the calculation for determining an employee's final compensation take into account the average of the highest five consecutive years. Previously, final compensation had been based on the average of the last five years' compensation.[7]

The 1949 modifications also made it easier for a member who left the Retirement System to rejoin. Members who had left State service and withdrawn their contributions could now redeposit them, and the new legislation allowed them an extended period of time in which to do so.

Governor Earl Warren signing key retirement legislation, 1947. The 1947 measure enacted a "guaranteed formula" that changed how the System calculated the ⅟₆₀ at 60 benefit to better serve retirees.

Spotlight on the Legislators' Retirement System

In 1947, CalPERS began administering the Legislators' Retirement System (LRS) for Members of the State Senate and Assembly, Constitutional Officers, and certain legislative employees. With the passage of Proposition 3, these elected and appointed officials now had the right to vested retirement benefits after years of public service to the State of California.

In 1947, CalPERS began administering the Legislators' Retirement System (LRS) for Members of the State Senate and Assembly, Constitutional Officers, and certain legislative employees. With the passage of Proposition 3, these elected and appointed officials now had the right to vested retirement benefits after years of public service to the State of California.

Under the LRS, benefits are financed through member contributions, the State's contributions as the employer, and investment income. As a defined benefit plan, pensions are based on age, years of service, and salary. The plan also provides pre- and post-retirement death benefits, a disability retirement option, survivor benefits, and annual cost-of-living adjustments.

Enrollments of new Legislators were curtailed with the 1990 passage of Proposition 140. The ballot measure stipulated that California Senate and Assembly Members elected after November 7, 1990, participate in no retirement system other than the federal Social Security program. The proposition also imposed term limits on Legislators, which resulted in a significant turnover in elected representatives. Today, however, the LRS continues to benefit lawmakers elected before November 1990, Legislative Statutory Officers, and Constitutional Officers.

San Francisco Assemblymen filing for reelection with their families in tow, 1956. In 1947, CalPERS began administering the Legislators' Retirement System to provide benefits for retired State lawmakers and their families. Voters in 1990 approved a measure closing the System to new Legislators.

Broadening Investments

As the SERS membership base continued to grow in the years after the war, the System's investment policy evolved as well. Rothschild, the Department of Finance Investment Adviser for SERS, aggressively pushed SERS to broaden its investment policies. At a Board meeting in the summer of 1946, he urged the Board to include corporate bonds among its investment options. The Board rejected his proposal, stating that it would be "a radical change" in policy.[8] A year later, Rothschild recommended that SERS purchase World Bank bonds and the Board again rejected Rothschild's recommendation.[9] Nevertheless, Rothschild continued encouraging the Board to broaden its thinking in relation to investment opportunities. Finally, in the fall of 1947, the Board seemed persuaded by his position. After a convincing presentation by Rothschild, Board members agreed to add public utilities to the list of eligible corporate bonds. Within three years, SERS was investing approximately 40 percent of the Fund in public utility bonds.[10]

Rene Rothschild (*right*) at a California conference for investment policies of public retirement funds, 1962. Influential throughout his tenure, in the mid-1940s Rothschild urged CalPERS to expand its investment policies to accept corporate bonds.

SERS Investment in Bonds

Bonds	6/30/47	6/30/48	6/30/49	6/30/50
U.S. Treasury	96	77	61	47
Public Utility	0	18	30	41
Municipals	4	5	8	10
Equipment Trust Certificates	0	0	1	2

Source: Report of the Commission on Pensions of State Employees, December 31, 1928, p. 45.

1950s Prosperity & the Liberalization of Benefits

Military success during World War II and the transformation of the United States' economy from the financial distress of the 1930s to a surging economic powerhouse in the 1950s brought a new level of prosperity to the nation. As the standard of living in the United States rose, demands for more liberalized retirement benefits became more frequent and vocal. In California, the Legislature considered a retirement formula that would raise the retirement benefit from the existing 1/60 at age 60 to a 1/50 at age 60 formula. SERS actuaries performed a cost analysis of this proposal and found that it required an additional cost to the State of $7 million per year. The California Legislature did not act on this proposed amendment.[11]

The SERS benefits structure did undergo some significant changes, however. The death benefit increased from $300 to $400 during the 1950s. SERS also adjusted the formula for determining final compensation, using the highest average compensation for three consecutive years in the calculation. SERS previously had been using the highest average from five consecutive years. Members also gained the ability to receive credit for their first six months of service as well as past public service.[12]

California's Retirement Systems

By the 1950s, California was administering several retirement systems for different types of public employees, and each of these systems had reached a substantial size in terms of members, assets, and benefit liabilities. Early in the decade, the California Department of Finance investigated the idea of consolidating SERS with the State Teachers' Retirement System. SERS actuary Ralph Nelson met with a Department

CSEA Retirement Law booklet, 1947. CSEA distributed various publications to its members to educate them about key changes to retirement legislation.

Peace & Prosperity in the 1950s

The arrival of the 1950s gave Californians many reasons to celebrate.

Family approaching their new house, ca.1950. The prosperity of the postwar era allowed numerous young families to buy their first homes.

Not only did the decade mark California's Statehood centennial, it also heralded the beginning of a decade of economic prosperity and growth throughout the United States. World War II had finally ended, and thousands of servicemen and -women returned home to begin their search for the American Dream. Housing developments blossomed, young families burgeoned, and the rise of the suburbs changed the way Americans lived.

Televisions entered American homes along with new kitchen appliances, cars, and other consumer goods. Convenience foods, such as processed cheese slices, TV dinners, prepared cake mixes, instant oatmeal, and frozen fish sticks, appeared on store shelves for the first time. Shows like *Howdy Doody*, the *Ed Sullivan Show*, and *Ozzie and Harriet* entertained television viewers. Music by Elvis Presley, Chuck Berry, and Bobby Darin filled the airwaves while movie stars such as Marlon Brando, James Dean, and Marilyn Monroe smoldered onscreen.

The 1960s would bring a very different social climate, revealing that life in America was not as carefree as it appeared. But the decade that brought CalPERS its biggest growth spurt to date was a booming one indeed.

Girl watching television, 1951. A rarity in the 1940s, the television became a beloved fixture in American homes during the 1950s.

THE SACRAMENTO UNION
Sunday, June 12, 1949

State Employes Fund Has $140,000,000 in Reserve

of Finance official in January 1950, about the possibility of consolidating the two systems, and potentially the Judges' Retirement System as well, into one huge system. This was not the first time the State had considered such a consolidation. While the idea of having one administrative structure to oversee the State's several retirement plans might have seemed reasonable in theory, Nelson saw several potential problems with consolidation of SERS and STRS. Nelson pointed out that, if consolidated, the two systems' funds and accounts would have to be kept separate. SERS operated on a reserve basis in respect to both employee and employer contributions, he explained, while STRS functioned on a reserve basis only in respect to employee contributions.[13] The systems had other potential incompatibilities as well, including two very different sets of benefit formulas, governing systems, and bookkeeping systems.[14] Nelson seemed particularly concerned about the implications the consolidation could have for the respective Boards. If the Systems consolidated, the SERS Board of Administration would have to be reconstituted in order to provide representation for the State's teachers. Nelson worried this could spur demands for Board representation from other State employee groups as well.[15]

Headline about CalPERS from the *Sacramento Union*, 1949. State officials considered consolidating CalPERS with the State Teachers' Retirement System in 1950 but ultimately decided against it, in part because of the differences in how the two systems operated in terms of their reserves.

Ultimately, Nelson argued, "no savings would result from a merger for administrative purposes alone and my further belief [is] that any other kind of merger would be unwise and impractical." Nelson agreed to provide the Department of Finance with further information and he expressed continued interest in the consolidation study. Nevertheless, he said he was "not at all convinced that mergers and the resulting larger offices … result in any savings whatever to the State … I think we should get away from the idea that size means a greater production per employee, whether supervisory or not, and that is the real question at issue here."[16]

The Department of Finance was not the only part of California's government paying attention to the State's growing retirement systems. In 1953, the Legislature asked the Legislative Budget Committee to prepare a report and actuarial revision of all of the State's retirement systems. State Legislative Auditor A. Alan Post conducted a study of SERS and other retirement systems and prepared a four-part report of his findings, which provided lawmakers with the first comprehensive study of all retirement systems operating in California for which the State appropriated funds.[17] Part I covered the historical development of the State Employees' Retirement System, the Judges' Retirement System, the State Teachers' Retirement System, and the University of California Retirement System. It also included comparisons to other public and private systems. Part II focused on the issues involved in integrating SERS with federal Social Security; Part III reported on the actuarial valuation of California's public retirement systems; and Part IV contained analyses of proposed legislation that would affect SERS.

A New Building

State Legislative Auditor A. Alan Post, 1966. Post conducted an extensive assessment of CalPERS and other California retirement systems in the 1950s. His report was the first of its kind in California and an invaluable resource for lawmakers.

While State officials outside of SERS were analyzing how future laws could affect the System, Executive Officers within SERS had noticed a more tangible issue: space. The growing organization was clearly in need of larger office space than the leased quarters it was occupying in the Veterans Affairs Building in downtown Sacramento. The O Street building was one of several downtown sites where SERS had rented space during its first two decades in operation. Other addresses where the System had leased

State Resources Building, Sacramento, 1966.
After years of leasing offices in various downtown
Sacramento buildings, CalPERS employees moved
into the State Resources Building in 1965.

Bringing CalPERS to the Members

At its inception, the Retirement System served State employees only. These members lived and worked primarily in Sacramento, San Francisco, and Los Angeles.

In 1939, when local public agencies were able to contract with CalPERS for retirement benefits, the CalPERS reach began to expand—agencies from all parts of the State joined the System.

Soon the membership roster represented public employees from all kinds of employers located from North to South and from the Pacific to the State's eastern border. Today, CalPERS members live across the State, the nation, and the world.

As the Retirement System's world grew, so did the challenge of reaching members—making sure they had the information and the assistance needed to make the right retirement decisions.

A Retirement Planning Fair at CalPERS Sacramento Regional Office, 2006. Retirement Planning Fairs and other events at the eight CalPERS Regional Offices allow the System to assist members in person throughout the State.

A CalPERS employee helping a Retirement Planning Fair guest in Sacramento, 2006. CalPERS Regional Offices provide members with a wealth of services, resources, and information about CalPERS benefits and programs.

CalPERS employee Leroy Fitzgerald at his desk in the San Francisco Regional Office, 1974. Fitzgerald went on to head the San Diego Regional Office when it opened in 1974, the same year the San Bernardino Regional Office opened.

Today CalPERS operates eight Regional Offices located in San Francisco, Glendale, Orange, Fresno, Sacramento, San Bernardino, San Diego, and San Jose. But in the early days, special retirement specialists traveled the State, getting "out in the field" to conduct retirement interviews and group sessions at employer locations.

Ellen Baltezore, former division chief of the Contracts Office, often traveled four days a week when she worked as a retirement specialist. Retirement interviews were about 15 to 20 minutes. "You had estimates for their retirement [benefits] and you discussed what the procedures were," she explained. "Some of them were just there for information, not to actually retire. And, then answer questions and show them the various options they could take and what would be good for them."

But this one-on-one connection was more than just a convenience to members—for some it was the lifeline that ensured a financially secure future. "I had one time down in the valley, it was a little town, and the man worked for that county on the highways," Baltezore recalled. "He came in

and I was a bit late and said, 'Here's your estimate. Why don't you take a look at it while I unpack my things?' He hesitated just a minute and said, 'Ma'am, I can't read. I'll take it home for my wife.' ... So, I explained it to him so he could take it home."

Today, the Customer Service and Education staff still provide that personal touch. They continue to go the extra mile each year through:

- Approximately 11,000 one-on-one counseling appointments

- Nearly 1,000 employer location meetings

- Assisting approximately 60,000 customers at the eight Regional Offices

- Conducting nearly 2,000 retirement and financial planning seminar and workshop sessions

- Answering nearly 600,000 phone calls, with more than 525,000 resolved at the first point of contact

- Responding to 32,000 e-mail and 21,000 written correspondence

CalPERS still hits the road each year with the annual Benefit Resources Fairs. Thousands have attended these free, drop-in events at venues across the State, where they can meet with CalPERS representatives, as well as experts from related outside programs like the Social Security Administration; attend special workshops; get hands-on help with online Web services; and pick up publications or other information.

With members now all across the nation and the world, CalPERS is harnessing new technology to keep reaching out to members. Recently, the System premiered the first retirement planning workshops via video conferencing with members in Chicago, Texas, and New York. Adding to the "cyber connection" with members, CalPERS is also partnering with some contracting employers to Web cast other retirement educational events. And, with the CalPERS On-Line Web site, we can now bring CalPERS to members—wherever they are and whenever they want.

offices included the Library and Courts Building and 1320 K Street. By the early 1950s, SERS Board and Executive Staff felt the time had come for the System to build its own offices.

For this to happen, State lawmakers first had to pass legislation specifically permitting SERS to invest funds in an office building. In 1953, State Senator Earl Desmond introduced Senate Bill 474 to allow SERS to "invest the money in the Retirement Fund in real property or improvements constructed or to be constructed on real property when the real property or such improvements are acquired or made by the board for sale or lease to the State."[18] In the interest of both ensuring that SERS didn't lose money on any real estate investment and limiting SERS investments to office buildings used by the State, the bill required SERS to enter into a lease agreement with the state for the property prior to SERS investment in it. In addition, the lease agreement and any subsequent sale of the property had to be structured so that SERS was guaranteed the return of its original investment, plus applicable interest. The bill also authorized SERS to invest up to $300,000 to acquire a site for the building.[19]

Initial discussions indicated that the proposed building would cost about $2.5 million. At this price, the proposed building would have to house additional State offices as well; SERS Assistant Executive Officer Edward K. Coombs acknowledged in a memo that "it would be difficult to justify a $2,500,000 building solely for the use of the Retirement System."[20] Nevertheless, the Legislature in 1955 increased the amount SERS could spend on acquiring a location for the building to $700,000.[21] Officials eventually chose a site at 1416 Ninth Street.

The new building was ready for occupancy by the mid-1960s. Dedicated on January 8, 1965, as the Resources Building, the building was officially known as the Retirement Building since SERS funds financed its construction. The 16-story, 670,000-square-foot structure could accommodate 3,800 employees and included a 500-person cafeteria, 260-seat auditorium and various special facilities including a radar weather top on the roof.[22]

State Senator Earl D. Desmond, 1960s. In 1953, Desmond introduced legislation authorizing CalPERS to invest in real estate. The measure passed, allowing CalPERS to finance construction of the State Resources Building in Sacramento, the first offices built specifically for the System.

Growing Pains

From its inception, California's Public Employees' Retirement System has grown quickly—so quickly that the System has grown out of its office spaces numerous times through the years.

"We do not have enough space, machines, desks, equipment, or personnel to do the job facing us," Executive Officer Earl Chapman told the *Sacramentan*, a CSEA publication, in 1946. "We have borrowed and rented equipment wherever possible and … are now looking for a good wall stretcher to expand our floor space."

Until the mid-1960s, the System rented various office spaces in downtown Sacramento. One of its earliest moves was into 1320 K Street, above a See's Candies shop. "So … if you didn't take home a box of candy on pay day, there was something wrong," longtime employee Marcella Weldon recalled.

But over time, the System found itself in increasingly cramped quarters, as burgeoning file cabinets literally began weighing down the office. "The floors started sagging," recalled Ethel Johnson, who worked in Membership from 1947 to 1991. "They had to put boards underneath."

The Retirement System outgrew rented quarters in other ways, too. As the work became more complex and the System took on new administrative duties, employees increasingly needed their own space in which to conduct business.

Robert Walton, a former Assistant Executive Officer, recalled that when CalPERS began administering health benefits coverage in the 1960s, some employees were working in an open space in the Veterans Affairs Building basement. They were conducting sensitive negotiations with health carriers, and Bob Sanders, the division's first chief, felt they needed more privacy, Walton said. But the State wouldn't authorize any private space.

"So, Bob and Robert Wilson, his assistant chief, and several staff members came in on a Saturday with the appropriate amount of two-by-fours and sheetrock and built an office in the basement," Walton remembered. "Painted it, did the whole bit."

The Retirement System finally moved into the Retirement Building in 1965, a building it financed and had built. Since the Resources Building housed other State agencies, in 1985 the System once again had outgrown its available office space.

CalPERS had asked for more space and was denied by the Director of General Services, so CalPERS sued the Director. Under the settlement, General Services and the Department of Finance agreed to allow the System to build its own building and to select its own architect. Ironically, when the new building was completed, the State Architect moved into the building, leasing space for that Department.

For a second time, CalPERS financed and built new offices for itself, the spacious Lincoln Plaza—a Sacramento landmark, and its current home.

In 2005, CalPERS completed a two-wing, 560,000-square-foot building across the street from Lincoln Plaza to expand the workspace for both employees and the customers who use the System.

Veterans Affairs Building under construction in Sacramento, 1956. Retirement System employees moved into the 4th floor of the building, at 13th and O Streets, once it was completed. They had previously worked in offices a block away, and for a time, the sight of Retirement System employees pushing grocery carts filled with files back and forth on Thirteenth Street was a common one.

President Franklin D. Roosevelt signing the Social Security Act, 1935. A watershed measure of the New Deal era, the Social Security Act became increasingly relevant to CalPERS in the 1950s as the System considered coordinating benefits with the federal program.

State Retirement & Social Security

Changes to the Social Security Act in the 1950s made the landmark New Deal legislation a topic of intense interest for state retirement systems across the country. The act had created an unemployment insurance system that offered benefits to workers at age 65, as well as Old Age and Survivors' Insurance (OASI), which provided federally funded benefits to retired employees of privately owned businesses.[23] Congress had created OASI to function as a social welfare program for the majority of the nation's working population. The program essentially set a base income level for retired workers; Congress expected these workers also would have access to employer-provided retirement benefits, as well as personal savings to augment the base amount provided. In 1939, Congress extended benefits eligibility to the family members of retired workers, and provided for payment of survivor benefits to the spouses and children of insured workers who died either before or after retirement age.[24]

The same year, various state and local employee groups began to express interest in obtaining Social Security coverage. However, Section 218 of the Social Security Act required a voluntary agreement between the federal government and state or local employee groups before Social Security coverage could commence. This provision of the law prevented a close coordination of federal Social Security and state retirement programs.

A Constitutional issue also limited close coordination of federal Social Security with state systems. Under the Constitution, the federal government is prohibited from taxing the states and a coordinated system implied that federal Social Security would draw upon state funds. While this was perhaps more of an administrative and legal obstacle than a philosophical one, it required a solution before state or local retirement system members could become eligible for Social Security coverage. Some state retirement systems were also concerned about their prospects for independence if Social Security benefits were available to state and local employees. "There were fears of the retirement systems themselves," wrote one observer, "that they might be overtaken or overpowered by the Social Security program."[25]

During 1950, Congress began the process of expanding OASI coverage to include additional categories of employees. These included regularly employed farm and household employees and non-farming self-employed people. They also included employees of nonprofit organizations and public employees who were not covered by existing state retirement plans. State employees in this latter group could gain OASI coverage through a contract between the state that employed them and the Secretary of Health, Education, and Welfare. Such public employees entered OASI coverage through a federal-state contract.

Some state retirement system officials found this type of contract-plan coverage problematic because of issues related to state law and practice, coordination of staff retirement systems with Social Security and general worries about the possible intrusiveness of the federal government through Social Security.[26]

In 1954, further changes to the Social Security Act increased benefit amounts and also extended coverage eligibility to state and local workers who were covered by state or local retirement plans (except firefighters and police officers). This modification potentially increased the Social Security rolls by about 10 million new workers when it took effect on January 1, 1955.

San Mateo city officials, 1940s. Most of the Retirement System's local and State members became eligible for Social Security coverage under sweeping changes to the federal program in 1954. Police officers and firefighters were the only exceptions.

The Birth Date Discrepancy Desk

A member's date of birth is an essential piece of information for CalPERS—it's part of what determines the retirement benefit amount. Today, finding that information is simple, but it wasn't always that way.

For the first several decades of the Retirement System's operations, many workers didn't have Social Security numbers. Since birth certificates often got lost and years ago many were born at home and not in hospitals, reliable documentation was scarce, and mistakes about dates of birth were far more common.

To track down and verify correct dates of birth, the System had a Birth Date Discrepancy Desk. The staff there pored over family records, hunted down documents overseas, and scrutinized school records of those wanting to retire to confirm these members were indeed of retirement age.

A surprising number of people were wrong about their ages, recalled Ethel Johnson, who worked on the desk for years. Many had fudged their ages as teenagers to serve in the military or get a job, and then kept the new age for fear of being caught. Some middle-aged workers shaved years off when looking for work because of age discrimination issues.

"It was pretty rough back then," recalled Jean Turkalay, another veteran Retirement System employee. "If you were [too young], you couldn't get a job, and if you were too old, you couldn't get a job."

Some people genuinely didn't know their birthdays. These members were often particularly grateful for the Birth Date Discrepancy Desk's research efforts, which many times yielded information beyond dates of birth.

"I remember writing for school records [for] a policeman, and he thanked me for finding out who his relatives were," Johnson said. "He didn't know."

The desk had well-defined guidelines for what documents could serve as verification (with many of those rules still in place today when a birth or marriage certificate cannot be located). Life insurance policies, school records, and birth certificates were allowed; so were records from Masonic lodges and family Bibles.

Affidavits from family members, however, were not. At a 1948 meeting with members, Executive Officer Earl Chapman explained that these statements were often incorrect. His own mother, he noted, was wrong about his date of birth by two and a half years.

Such mix-ups grew less common as record-keeping grew more standardized, and eventually the Retirement System no longer needed a Birth Date Discrepancy Desk. According to Johnson, CalPERS ended the desk's operations around the 1970s.

Birth record in a family Bible, date unknown. In the 1950s, CalPERS allowed members to present family Bible records as proof of their birthdates.

The 1954 Social Security amendments did not mandate Social Security coverage for state workers however. Rather, they gave state workers the possibility of a choice. Workers covered by a state or local retirement program system could become OASI members if a majority of them by group voted in favor of OASI coverage. With an affirmative vote, employees could transfer membership from their state or local retirement system to OASI or from OASI to a state or local system depending upon their employment status.[27] The legislation also contained language that underscored Congress' intention that OASI coverage would not impair benefits allowable for eligible employees under state and/or local retirement systems.[28] The 1954 amendments called for computing taxes based on a salary up to $4,200 per year, or $350 per month. Benefits would be paid based on a formula that multiplied the first $110 of the average monthly wage by 55 percent, plus 20 percent of the remainder.[29]

While the 1954 amendments allowed public employees the possibility of participating in the OASI program, they could not participate in the federal program and their employer's program simultaneously. They had to decide to either continue in their respective public systems or switch to OASI. State and local government employees in California, like those in other states, vigorously debated the benefits and disadvantages of joining OASI.

Cover of *The California State Employee*, 1952. Through its periodic newsletters, CSEA kept its members informed of the issues, including the heated debate on OASI integration.

In 1954, California Legislative Auditor A. Alan Post prepared a comprehensive report on SERS. In it, he wrote that, "certain desirable features … are not included" in the State System, "and there has been considerable employee agitation in recent years to obtain new and expensive benefits." He cited as examples survivors' benefits, lifetime annuities for beneficiaries in lieu of death benefits, a ⅟50 instead of ⅟60 retirement formula for miscellaneous State members, an increase of disability retirement guarantees from one-fourth to one-third of average pay, and an industrial death and disability benefit provision for all members.[30]

Post recommended that SERS coordinate coverage with OASI. Noting that OASI covered 57 million U.S. workers by 1954, he wrote that "it becomes increasingly disadvantageous to both the employee and to the State to remain isolated from OASI" and that "employment patterns have been and continue to be fluid is further cause for participation in OASI, which provides a subsistence level of benefits of a continuous nature."[31]

"TWO-HEADED" MONSTER...

Cartoon published in CSEA publication the *Sacramentan*, 1959. CSEA opposed coordination between the Retirement System and federal Old Age and Survivors' Insurance (later renamed Old Age and Survivors' Disability Insurance, or OASDI), believing it would create an unwieldy system.

Opponents to OASI coordination worried it could allow the federal government to exert too much influence over states. Perhaps more important, Congress could increase the contribution rates required for OASI coverage. Some observers noted that if OASI increased both rates and benefits, OASI might supplant both public and private retirement systems, thereby granting the federal government complete control over U.S. citizens' retirements. The specter of a single federally controlled retirement program posed ideological problems for many opponents of SERS-OASI coordination.[32]

In 1955, the California Legislature passed legislation that allowed members of the State's several public retirement systems to obtain OASI coverage. This plan became known as the full offset plan. Under this plan, retirees would receive Social Security benefits, but these benefits would not supplement SERS benefits. Instead, the total amount of the retirement allowance would be the same under OASI coordination.

Before State retirement plan members could become eligible for both OASI and State retirement program benefits, State members and members under public agency contracts had to vote separately on the issue of whether OASI benefits should be included with those provided by SERS. An affirmative vote would require the integration of the two systems into one program; all SERS members would join the Social Security program under the full offset plan.[33]

Meeting organized by CSEA, 1954. State employees gathered at multiple meetings around California during the 1950s to learn more about potential coordination between the Retirement System and Social Security.

In response to widespread interest among State employees, California Governor Goodwin J. Knight ordered a referendum on the full offset plan in 1955. SERS staff initiated an impressive effort to educate public employees about the issues at hand. The System distributed to all State employees the official proclamation, as well as a booklet released in August that explained the benefits, liabilities, and rights of employees under the current Retirement System and under the proposed system integration with OASI. Between September and October, State and university employees organized about 270 informational meetings, which drew more than 35,000 people in all.[34]

Carl Blechinger, who became SERS third Executive Officer in 1975, recalled that in the mid-1950s, "There were four or five of us who went around explaining Social Security coverage to State employees. We worked days and nights." Explaining the complex issues of coordination to large numbers of people was often exhausting. "I know I got real tired," Blechinger said, "and so did [Earl] Chapman, because he'd go home and on a Sunday he'd dictate letters and do work at the office."[35]

Balloting on the referendum began on November 1 and lasted through November 25. More than 56,000 of the roughly 68,000 people eligible to vote on the issue cast ballots. When the votes were counted, the outcome was decisive: Only 12,860 people cast yes votes, compared to 43,203 nos. California's public employees had overwhelmingly declined to integrate the two systems.[36]

The effort to inform California's public employees about the coordination proposal taxed SERS Executive Staff. Executive Officer Earl Chapman had worked particularly hard on this matter. Less than two months after the coordination vote, on January 11, 1956, Chapman died. Chapman had worked for SERS since November 12, 1931— first as the Principal Accountant and later rising to Secretary, Executive Secretary in 1938, and finally Executive Officer in 1947. Before joining SERS, Chapman had served as the Principal Accountant in the Department of Finance, and had helped the State Employees' Retirement Campaign Committee raise and manage funds for Proposition 5.[37]

Edward Coombs, date unknown. As CalPERS Assistant Executive Officer in early 1956, Coombs temporarily headed the Retirement System after Earl Chapman's death.

Assistant Executive Officer Edward Coombs became the Acting Executive Officer upon Chapman's death. Coombs had worked at SERS since December 1941, leaving temporarily to serve in the military during World War II. He had served as SERS Assistant Executive Officer since returning from the war. His appointment to Executive Officer, however, was contingent upon the outcome of the civil service exam required for the position.

Coombs did not remain long as SERS Executive Officer. On August 27, 1956, the Board of Administration appointed William E. Payne to the post. A SERS publication from the next year noted that the System selected Payne "from the Civil Service list established by examination."[38]

William Payne brought significant organizational changes to SERS. The System's staff had consisted almost exclusively of female clerical workers during Chapman's tenure. They had worked under fairly strict guidelines. One employee recalled that Chapman "rang a bell for break time; he rang a bell for lunch; he rang a bell for when you get off work."[39] Payne was more forward-looking in his managerial style and more approachable personally; longtime employees often described him later as one of their favorite leaders.[40]

Every Time a Bell Rings …
It's Time to Get Back to Work

The workplace culture of CalPERS today has come a long way from that of the System's formative years.

The Retirement System's work week included Saturdays in much of the 1930s and 1940s, and female employees were required to wear skirts all six days, while men wore business suits. Staffers started work at the same time, stopped at the same time, and took breaks at the same time. And to announce those breaks, there was the Bell.

The Bell has become a famous—and, to some, infamous—story of CalPERS workplace. It's said that Executive Officer Earl Chapman instituted the bell system, and rang it himself to announce the 45-minute lunches and morning and afternoon breaks that Retirement System employees took at the same times each day.

Some say it was his executive secretary, Ismilda Brown, who controlled the Bell from her desk, which sat in a large room that housed most of the System's staff through much of the 1940s. Others claim it didn't exist at all.

"Seemed to me that one time somebody had a bell on their desk, but I think it was more for show than really using it," recalled Marcella Weldon, who began working for the Retirement System as a file clerk in 1943. "We would look at the clock. When it was 12 o'clock, we'd put our work down and take out our lunch and eat our lunch … We were on the honor system."

Other veteran employees have specific memories of the Bell, however. It was small and silver when Ismilda Brown controlled it, according to Ethel Johnson, who worked for the System from 1947 to 1991. Later, Johnson said, it was switched to a buzzer so employees working by the loud accounting machines could hear it.

And, according to Johnson and others, the whole system came to end when William Payne became Executive Officer in 1956. "That was one of the first things he did away with, the Bell," recalled Carl Blechinger, Payne's eventual successor.

Still, some insisted the Bell existed in some incarnation as late as the 1970s. When Robert Walton, a former Assistant Executive Officer, joined the System in 1971, "everybody had the same morning break, the same lunch, the same afternoon break," he said. "And our Benefits (department) … they actually had bells on the clock on when you go to break and when you come back."

Whatever the real story of the Bell is, it stands as a symbol to CalPERS employees today of the office mores of days past, which were reflective of general workplace standards across the country. While bells are no longer needed, CalPERS employees still work hard. You'll even find those who work that extra Saturday shift.

CalPERS employees, 1950s. In the Retirement System's early years, the mostly female workforce arrived, left, and took breaks at the same time every day. A ringing bell alerted them when lunch and other break times started and ended.

Lauren Haight, 1948. CalPERS Assistant Actuary since 1947, Haight replaced longtime Chief Actuary Ralph Nelson when he retired in 1954.

SERS had lost another key staff member less than two years earlier, when longtime actuary Ralph Nelson retired. Like Chapman, Nelson had worked with SERS since before its official creation, serving as a consultant to the original State Pension Commission as it drafted its report to the Legislature supporting the creation of SERS. He had also worked on the studies used to create retirement systems for the City and County of San Francisco. Upon formal establishment of SERS, Nelson began working for the System as a consulting actuary, a position he held until his retirement.[41] The Board of Administration appointed Lauren C. Haight, SERS Assistant Actuary since October 1947, as Nelson's replacement.

The loss of Chapman and Nelson constituted a profound change for the System. Both were founders of the organization and together they had managed SERS for more than 20 years. Their serious-minded dedication and conservative policies helped set a corporate culture that would remain for years to come.

A New Plan

Though SERS members had voted against the full offset plan for Social Security coordination in 1955, support remained strong for the idea of a coordination plan that would provide real benefits to public employees. In 1956 and 1958, Congress approved amendments to the Social Security Act that sought to further expand Social Security coverage and allow State Retirement System members who had voted against integrating with OASI another opportunity to coordinate.[42] As of May 1958, California was one of only eight states with a retirement system not coordinated in any respect with Social Security. Twenty-nine states had both Social Security and state retirement systems, eight had only Social Security, and three states had created retirement systems after adopting Social Security.[43]

The 1956 Social Security amendments also included a disability provision, which provided benefits to disabled workers aged between 50 and 64 and to disabled adult dependents of retired or deceased workers. President Eisenhower signed a law in 1960 that allowed benefit payments to disabled workers of any age and their dependents. By that year, about 560,000 people received disability benefits, with the average benefit amount about $80 per month. Reflecting this expanded benefit structure OASI became OASDI, or Old Age and Survivor Disability Insurance.[44]

Poster advertising Social Security disability benefits, 1962. In 1956, Social Security began providing disability benefits. Its OASI program became OASDI, Old Age and Survivor Disability Insurance, to reflect this change.

By the late 1950s, there was a renewed effort to coordinate California's State Employees' Retirement System with Social Security to maximize benefits for State workers. Though CSEA advocated giving California's public employees enhanced benefits, it remained opposed to coordination with OASDI. Instead, CSEA had been promoting the creation of a survivors' benefits provision for SERS members; Social Security already contained such a provision.

Survivors' benefits and OASDI coordination appeared to be separate issues, but they were in fact closely related. California's public employees keenly desired survivors' benefits and Social Security offered such benefits. In 1959, California's Legislature approved a bill—A.B. 2062—that established a survivors' benefits program for the State System. At the same time, the legislation also called for another election on the issue of coordinating OASI with SERS.[45] Under the terms of A.B. 2062, introduced by Democratic Assemblymen Thomas J. MacBride and Edwin L. Z'Berg of Sacramento, State employees could vote on the question of adding Social Security benefits. If a majority of State employees agreed to add Social Security coverage to their existing State coverage, the federal and state systems would be integrated. Employees not wishing to add Social Security could elect not to receive integrated coverage. The bill provided that the administrative costs for the integrated system would be paid from the interest of the SERS Fund, up to .1 percent of the total Fund.

Once again, SERS held a series of about 300 informational meetings throughout California to educate members on the issues. Each meeting included a 20-minute pre-recorded explanation with a slide presentation discussion of the relevant issues of coordination. The State University system conducted about 50 informational meetings as well. Most of these meetings took place between mid-August and mid-September.[46]

Balloting for the second election on coordination took place from the end of September to mid-October 1959. Except for California Highway Patrol members, all SERS members who were enrolled in the Retirement System as of September 30 were eligible to vote. A follow-up election was set for early to mid-November, during which SERS members would vote either to stay in the System with no changes or add survivors' benefits to the current System. If a majority of SERS members approved the coordination plan, the second ballot item asked members whether they desired coverage under the coordinated plan or preferred to remain solely under SERS.[47]

State Assemblyman Edwin L. Z'Berg, date unknown. The Sacramento Democrat co-introduced a bill in 1959 that gave State employees a survivors' benefits program.

Though CSEA opposed coordination, the organization did provide its membership with a substantial amount of balanced information about the coordination issue. In its monthly newsletters, CSEA strongly urged all SERS members to vote since the election results would not be valid unless a majority of the eligible voters participated.[48]

CSEA Education Committee, 1952. Much of the CSEA education outreach during the 1950s was devoted to Social Security coordination—an issue that members voted on twice in the 1950s.

Cover of the *Sacramentan*, September 1959. State workers followed the recommendation of CSEA, voting against Social Security coordination a second time in 1959.

Governor Edmund Brown, 1963. When the matter of OASDI coordination was ultimately brought before Brown in 1961, he diplomatically considered the overwhelming outpouring of feedback from constituents.

Shortly before the election, CSEA conducted its own non-binding poll on coordination. Detailing its results, the organization reported that "four out of every seven State employees voting in the 'division' election held by the State Employees' Retirement System last month said 'No' to the question of whether the System should be coordinated with Old Age [and] Survivors' Disability Insurance."[49] California's State workers, CSEA concluded, did not want Social Security.

When the Secretary of State's Office counted the official votes, CSEA officials were not surprised. About 57 percent of the nearly 76,000 voters who cast ballots (out of 100,000 eligible voters) opposed coordinating SERS with OASDI. The CSEA poll had indicated about 56 percent opposition to the measure. California's State employees appeared to have decided the matter once and for all. They would vote again in November only to request survivor benefits if they so desired.[50]

The coordination issue, however, would not go away. On June 16, 1961, the last day of the legislative session, the Legislature surprisingly passed a bill providing for the coordination of SERS with federal Social Security without a referendum. CSEA was not pleased by this development. In a memorandum, CSEA representative H. A. Allmendinger stated that, if signed by Governor Edmund G. Brown, the new law would divide the Retirement System. "This legislation," he wrote, "was passed as a result of extreme pressure of a minority group." He urged CSEA members to send telegrams to the Governor asking him to veto the bill.[51]

The new coordination plan provided for in the legislation, A.B. 873, made Social Security coverage retroactive to January 1, 1956. Under the coordinated plan, also referred to as the half-offset plan, the SERS benefits structure retroactively became a $\frac{1}{90}$-$\frac{1}{60}$ plan. SERS contributions and benefits based on an employee's compensation up to $400 per month would be reduced by 30 percent. Contributions and benefits on an employees' salary of about $400 per month would remain at the $\frac{1}{60}$ formula. Those members selecting OASDI coverage would begin receiving survivor's protection—available through SERS since 1959—through OASDI, which offered a similar plan for $2.00 month. While employees' contributions to SERS on the first $400 of their salaries would drop, they would begin paying for Social Security coverage at the rate of $3\frac{1}{2}$ percent of the first $400 of their salary per month.[52]

The plan was controversial, perhaps more so for the way lawmakers enacted it after State employees already had rejected it. Responding to the intense interest in the matter, California Governor Brown agreed to hear from parties on both sides of the issue. On July 13, 1961, about 750 State employees congregated in an Assembly Committee hearing room and an adjacent overflow room in the East Wing of the State Capitol. When Governor Brown entered the room, the attendees gave him a standing ovation.[53]

His opening statement must have been sobering to people on both sides of the issue. "I am completely open-minded," he stated. "I have made no commitments. But I can't please both sides. I have received 13,000 letters on this bill, more than on any other piece of legislation." Of those letters to Brown, 7,495 favored A.B. 873 and 6,679 opposed it.

At the hearing, CSEA Chief Counsel John W. McElheney and CSEA President Albert C. Ricksecker gave forceful statements in opposition to the bill. McElheney argued the current law essentially violated procedure. "It has consistently been the position of our association," he stated, "that the bill should provide a referendum vote which would require majority approval by employes [sic] before the state employes' [sic] retirement system be coordinated with the federal Social Security system."[54]

Repeating one of the powerful arguments successfully used against the full-offset plan proposed in 1955, McElheney and others also warned against sending California's employees' funds to Washington, D.C.—funds that under the SERS program went directly to the System and stayed in the State. Under the coordinated plan, California employees' funds would flow to Washington, 3,300 miles away. Governor Brown was not impressed with the argument. Referring to Washington, D.C., he said, "They're not a foreign potentate, you know."[55]

Representing SERS, Executive Officer William Payne fully endorsed integration with Social Security. He stated that California would simply find it increasingly difficult to remain outside the federal system, pointing out that state retirement systems throughout the country were integrating with Social Security. If California bucked this trend and stayed out of the federal program, he argued, the State would find it increasingly difficult to recruit employees.[56]

CalPERS Executive Officer William Payne, 1975. Payne strongly believed in the potential merits of an integrated system and endorsed the coordinated OASDI plan.

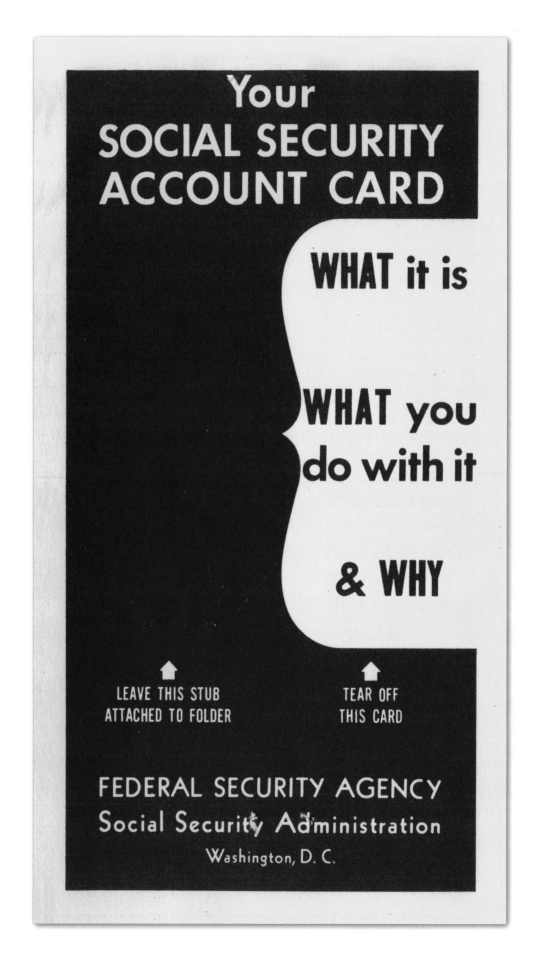

Pamphlet on Social Security, 1953. Retirement System members, like people across the country, became increasingly familiar with Social Security during the 1950s, when use of the program was far less prevalent than it is today.

Governor Brown made his decision and signed A.B. 873 on July 17, 1961. "One fact emerges clearly from my investigations of this measure," the Governor stated in signing the bill. "It will help many thousands of State employees and harm none. On that basis alone, I would be obligated to sign A.B. 873 to permit those who wish to take advantage of its benefits to do so." He said he would resist "with all the resources at my command, both here and in Washington, any impairment of the level of benefits now offered to members of the System."[57]

With Governor Brown's signature, SERS members were able to select coordination with SERS on an individual basis. This included school and local public agency members, whose benefits would also be administered by SERS. Voting on the individual selection option took place between November 6 and November 20, 1961, and coordination would begin January 1, 1962. CSEA leadership was not pleased that Governor Brown signed the legislation, but they accepted the new development. CSEA President Ricksecker said that the "decision of the Governor to provide coordination, hard as it may be for a great number of employees to accept, is nevertheless law and CSEA will do all in its power to provide employees with a complete understanding of the new system."[58]

Social Security coordination would continue to be a contentious issue within SERS for some time. But the System would soon become immersed in administration of another form of benefits as well—an entirely new one for the System, and a crucial one for its members. SERS would also increasingly turn its attention in coming years to its investment practices and fund operations, as the federal government began scrutinizing and regulating pension funds more than it ever had before.

4: New Benefits. New Leadership. New Name.

The State Employees' Retirement System changed its name in 1967 to the Public Employees' Retirement System. Though not earth-shattering, the change reflected some important aspects of the System's development in the 1960s and 1970s. The System clearly was no longer only—or even mostly—a State employee institution, but rather had an increasingly broad reach and membership.

By this time, PERS was the nation's largest public pension fund, encompassing thousands of members from hundreds of public agencies. It took on an enormous new responsibility in the 1960s, when it began administering health care benefits to these public employees. It broadened its investment portfolio significantly and increased its Fund assets, despite a recession in the 1970s. And PERS made these strides while going through key leadership changes.

2,000 May Retire From State Jobs

SACRAMENTO (P)--Some 2,000 state employees are expected to retire during the first month of 1962 when a bolstered retirement program takes effect.

William E. Payne, executive officer of the State Retirement Board, said Tuesday the number retiring as the result of a law merging state retirement with federal Social Security could go as high as 3,000.

After the integration of SERS with Social Security, some State employees who had recently retired decided to return to State service so that they could qualify for higher benefits. At least 20 retired State workers took advantage of the opportunity to take what amounted to short-term positions with the State. Retired workers were eligible for reinstatement, said Executive Officer William E. Payne, as long as they were not within six months of the mandatory retirement age of 70. Other conditions of reinstatement included a job opening, passing a physical exam, and having been retired for a minimum of one year. Many retired workers had a strong financial motive to take a temporary State job. As long as the reinstated employees' names appeared on the State payroll by year's end, they became eligible for the coordinated benefits. One department head who had rehired some of the retired workers said, "It was the human thing to do."[1]

These returning employees, as long as their names appeared on the employee roster as of December 31, 1961, were eligible for as much as $100 per month more than they received during their first retirement. "It was the difference between living on Cockroach Alley and moving into one of the new developments for senior citizens," one employee stated. The new short-term hires benefited SERS as well. They were able to help staff complete a variety of temporary assignments.[2]

Not all State employees believed the coordination with OASDI was a good thing. Throughout much of the early 1960s, there was a simmering of discontent among large numbers of State employees. Many were concerned that coordination resulted in lower benefits and an uncertain retirement future.

The CSEA monthly newspaper, for example, reported on the continuing controversy within its own membership surrounding the "long-time issue" of Social Security coordination. "A movement to take State employees out of OASDI … was launched with zestful force and very nearly won a policy victory on the spot," the paper reported. Arguing that the cost of coordination was too high for young employees and that coordination offered lower benefits than straight SERS coverage, opponents of OASDI participation claimed that employees would be better off without it.[3]

At the CSEA General Council held during November 1966, some delegates argued forcefully against continued coordination with Social Security. They passed two resolutions that were referred to the CSEA Board of Directors. The resolutions called upon CSEA to conduct a formal poll of State employees to determine if a majority of them desired to terminate the coordinated plan. Delegates at the General Council pointed out that there was a provision allowing for the termination of coordination after five years and that the CSEA should fully consider whether to support such an action. In order to terminate coordination, the Legislature would have to pass, and the Governor sign, legislation mandating the end of coordination.[4]

CSEA subsequently published in its monthly newspaper a detailed comparative analysis of the SERS program and the coordinated program. The article noted, among other things, that Social Security was a "pay as you go" system and therefore substantially underfunded. Opponents of coordination seemed to distrust federal involvement in the State program.[5]

CSEA began conducting its Statewide poll on coordination during the Summer of 1967. The organization mailed ballots on July 20 along with stamped, return-addressed envelopes to its 114,000 members.[6] Arguments pro and con were provided to CSEA members. One opponent, M. Van Schaik of Sacramento, argued that a vote to retain the coordinated system might result in a total loss of SERS benefits. He chided the "unfunded" Social Security plan and warned, "When you retire they tax our children to pay you a pension." He concluded by stating, "Social Security is okay for those who can't take care of themselves. The State employee can and does!"[7]

Supporters of coordination touted the benefits of both programs. They pointed out that benefits in both programs were being increased and the increases were supplementary. By terminating coordination, State employees would lose disability benefits up to $368 per month and survivors' benefits up to the same amount, as well as the death benefit provision and Medicare. These supporters also reminded employees that as much as 35 percent of their Social Security contributions were applied to non-retirement benefits and that Social Security benefits were tax free.[8]

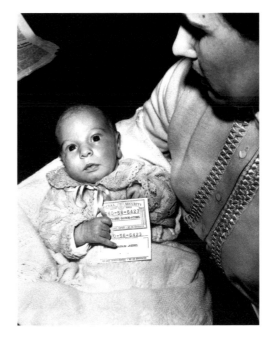

Fifteen-day-old Philippe Mitchell Gaspard-Michel, the youngest person in California to have a Social Security card, 1958. Though Social Security became an increasingly common part of American life in the 1960s, some CalPERS members continued to have doubts about coordinating benefits with the federal agency.

Social Security Administration poster publicizing the Medicare program, 1968. CalPERS members who supported continued coordination with Social Security pointed out that termination would end their benefits from Medicare, a program established in 1965 to help elderly Americans with medical expenses.

After the conclusion of the poll, CSEA published the results. Only 50 percent of eligible voters cast ballots, and of those cast, approximately 51 percent, or 29,372 CSEA members, voted to terminate coordination. About 50 percent of those who voted in the poll were in the coordinated plan and 62 percent of those CSEA members voted against coordination. However, the results were neither overwhelming nor conclusive. Indeed, CSEA members who voted against coordination represented only about 10 percent of the total SERS membership of approximately 409,000.[9]

The CSEA General Council subsequently adopted a resolution that called for termination of the coordinated plan only if members currently covered by Social Security received the same benefits under the SERS plan alone. Apparently, CSEA leadership understood that the coordinated plan offered benefits that SERS alone did not provide.[10]

The Heart of CalPERS

CalPERS has changed enormously during its 75-plus years in operation, but its founding principle has never wavered: CalPERS exists to provide comfort and security for its members. They are the System's entire reason for being. William Payne, CEO from 1956 to 1974, aptly summarized CalPERS regard for its members in a welcome message to new employees during his tenure:

"What is a Member? A Member is the most important person ever in this office—in person or by mail. A Member is not dependent on us—we are dependent on him. A Member is not an interruption to our work— he is the purpose of it. We are not doing him a favor by serving him—he is doing us a favor by giving us the opportunity to do so. A Member is not an outsider to our business— he is a part of it. A Member is not a cold statistic—he is a flesh-and-blood human being with feelings and emotions like your own. … A Member is not someone to argue or match wits with. Nobody ever won an argument with a Member. A Member is a person who brings us his wants. It is our job to handle them."

Though the System's membership has grown exponentially, exceeding 1.5 million today, CalPERS employees have never lost sight of the fact that each of these members is an individual—and a vitally important one to CalPERS. They prove their commitment to members constantly, whether through small kindnesses in their day-to-day service or more extraordinary actions in times of crisis.

Even employees who don't normally deal with members on a one-on-one basis understand that, ultimately, their job is to help members—and to help them through complicated and difficult times. In November 2006, Anita

Lee, an Information Technology Services employee with the Management Support Office at CalPERS headquarters, received a call late one afternoon from an official with the State Water Resources Control Board about an employee who was dying of cancer.

The employee was slipping in and out of consciousness at a hospital, and he needed to retire immediately so that his family could be provided for and his finances could be in order after his death. Lee managed to reach Denise Hilson, a Retirement Program Specialist in the CalPERS Glendale Regional Office, near where the man was hospitalized.

Hilson immediately contacted the family by phone, and offered to go to the hospital that evening to go over the man's retirement paperwork. She spent more than two hours with the member and his family, explaining his retirement options and enabling him to retire.

Lee and Hilson provided exceptional service during a highly stressful situation—not unusual for CalPERS employees, who often answer the call to provide personal assistance in emergency situations.

But it was of great note to the member's employer at the State Water Resources Control Board, who was so touched by the efforts of CalPERS staff that he wrote in a thank you letter to CalPERS CEO Fred

Buenrostro, "This amazing service gave the employee and his family great comfort during a very difficult time. Your staff, particularly Ms. Lee and Ms. Hilson, should be commended for their dedication and service to CalPERS members."

The qualities reflected in the actions they took—care, dedication, competence— perfectly embody the service CalPERS employees have given members from the start.

CalPERS employees helping members at a Retirement Fair in Sacramento, 2002. Meeting the needs of members is the top priority of every CalPERS employee, just as it has been since 1932.

Advertisement in a CSEA publication, 1946. Before CalPERS began administering health benefits to members, CSEA offered various benefit plans for State workers, sponsoring its first group plan in 1939.

Medical & Hospital Care

The first major new benefit for SERS members came in the early 1960s. The State Employees' Medical and Hospital Care Act of 1962, also referred to as the Meyers-Geddes Health Benefits Act, dramatically increased SERS responsibility for providing health care services to eligible State employees. Later amended as the Public Employees' Medical and Hospital Care Act, the act marked the origins of the SERS health care program, which moved SERS into a very different and volatile arena.

There had been earlier efforts to provide health benefits to State workers. CSEA offered health benefits to State employees beginning in early 1939, when it sponsored a group health plan underwritten by Pacific Employers' Insurance Company headquartered in Los Angeles, California. This plan apparently lasted for less than one year, and CSEA continued to seek health benefits for CSEA members.[11]

Only one day prior to the termination of CSEA existing group insurance policy, a new agreement was signed with California Physicians' Service (CPS). CPS agreed to serve as the CSEA Statewide health benefits plan administrator. As the CSEA master policy holder, CPS administered "all physician and physician-related charges and [administered] the hospital benefits provided by several hospital and/or insurance services operating in California."[12]

The original CSEA policy through CPS became effective on August 13, 1939. CSEA members had the option of enrolling in either the high or the low plans. The high plan cost each member $2.50 per month in return for:

- Surgical care
- Home, office, and hospital visits
- X-ray and lab services
- Hospitalization for a maximum of 21 days.[13]

The low plan differed from the high plan in that the beneficiary's premium was reduced to $2 per month, and the beneficiary was responsible for paying for the first two physician visits.[14]

The arrangement with CPS proved problematic. The Sacramento County Medical Society (SCMS) refused to do business with CPS. SCMS objected to CPS payment schedule, claiming that it did not offer adequate payments for SCMS medical services. In addition, CPS was an untried and new organization, although its President was Dr. Ray Lyman Wilbur, who was also President of Stanford University and a past president of the American Medical Association (AMA). The organization's unanticipated action left about 6,000 Sacramento-area CSEA members without health services. CSEA then sought to negotiate a new contract with another firm to provide coverage to Sacramento-area members.[15]

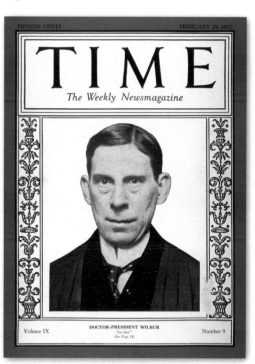

Cover of *Time* featuring Ray Lyman Wilbur, 1927. A nationally prominent doctor, Wilbur headed the California Physicians' Service in 1939, when CSEA began contracting with the organization for health benefits.

Doctors posing with a new ambulance in front of the Central Emergency Hospital in San Francisco, 1938. Ambulance service up to $10 was among the benefits offered in a group health plan CSEA negotiated in 1939 with California Western States Life and Occidental Life Insurance Companies.

Sacramento-area CSEA members did receive coverage under a new contract. In 1939, CSEA President Roy P. Womack negotiated and signed a contract with California Western States Life and Occidental Life Insurance Companies of California (CWO), effective November 25, 1939. This agreement, however, required that CWO "enroll at least 75 percent of predetermined sub-groups of employees working within the Capitol area."[16] This requirement evidently was met.

Since CSEA had to negotiate a new plan through CWO, there was also a new benefits structure. For the CWO plan, there was a basic $1.60 monthly premium, increasing to $3.00 for optional home and hospital calls, or $2 for office calls. The original policy provided the following benefits:

- Up to $5 per day for the cost of hospital room and board, limited to 70 days

- Special hospital services such as anesthetics, laboratory analysis, and operating room fees up to $25

- Ambulance service up to $10

- Surgical benefits fee schedule to $150 maximum

- Up to 14 days of pregnancy-related care

- A non-occupational accidental death and dismemberment benefit of $1,000

- A unique feature in case of non-work-related injury: " … an identification card will be issued to each insured employee providing expenses up to $50 necessary to put insured in care of friends in the event of accidental injury, not in the course of employment …"[17]

From its inception in 1939 through the early 1960s, only State employees who were also members of CSEA had the option of enrolling in the medical and hospital benefits program. During the late 1950s, a new movement promoted enactment of legislation that would provide such benefits to all State employees regardless of their membership in CSEA.

California Division of Highways employees, 1956. Until the early 1960s, CalPERS State members also had to belong to CSEA to be eligible for group health benefits.

The U.S. Congress debated proposed legislation during 1958 that would provide health benefits for both active and retired federal employees. During the same year, two California congressmen proposed State legislation for the same purpose. Charles W. Meyers, chairman of the Assembly Committee on Civil Service and

State Personnel, and Assemblyman Samuel R. Geddes introduced two bills, A.B. 2315 and A.B. 2699, respectively, to establish a health benefit program administered by a commission operating under the organizational structure of the State Personnel Board. During the next two years, the Meyers Committee conducted a series of hearings on this issue throughout the State. However, the Legislature did not pass either bill.[18]

The seed had been planted though, and efforts to establish a health care benefits program for State workers continued. CSEA was also a strong supporter of a State-supported health plan for employees. The association lobbied Governor Edmund G. Brown in 1960 for his support. The Governor indicated that he did support such a plan, stating in early 1961 that, "I feel that the time has come for the State to participate in the cost of adequate health plans for all State employees. I urge the Legislature to approve a measure authorizing such participation and I plan to earmark an appropriate amount in the 1961-62 budget for that purpose."[19]

The State Legislature, 1959. California lawmakers in 1958 began considering two separate bills to establish a health benefits program for State employees. They held hearings on the issue over the next two years, but did not pass either measure.

Assemblymen Charles Meyers (*left*) and Samuel Geddes, date unknown. Geddes and Meyers championed the establishment of a State employees' health care program. In 1961, the Legislature passed the State Employees' Medical and Hospital Care Act, also known as the Meyers-Geddes State Employees' Medical and Hospital Care Act, which created a program under CalPERS administration.

One of the important issues was determining the agency or commission that would ultimately administer such a program. In the original legislation, the State Personnel Board assumed this responsibility. Subsequent discussion generated interest in granting oversight to the California Department of Public Health and even the Department of Finance.

It became increasingly clear to supporters of a Statewide health care program that SERS provided a virtually ready-made organizational structure for administering a health care program. As Robert Wilson, head of the System's Health Benefits Division, noted later, SERS had an existing Board comprised of both elected and nonelected State officials that could oversee the plan, as well as a competent actuarial and investment staff that could more easily accommodate administration of a health care program than would be the case by creating a new organization. In addition, newly proposed legislation included a provision for increasing the SERS Board size from eight to 11 members, with the three new members voting only on health care issues.[20]

The State Legislature passed a compromise bill establishing a State employees' health care program under SERS administration in 1961. The State Employees' Medical and Hospital Care Act, also known as the Meyers-Geddes State Employees' Medical and Hospital Care Act, became operational on September 15, 1961. Enrollment and coverage began on January 1, 1962.[21]

Triumph & Tribulation

In the early 1960s, California officials considered the creation of a Statewide health care program for State employees and identified SERS as the best administrator of such a program.

The SERS organizational structure and staff resources—its Board, actuarial staff, and investors—rendered the System well-equipped to take on the task. Some familiar with the events surrounding the creation of the program, however, suggested an alternate explanation for the Legislature's selection of SERS.

SERS Executive Officer, William Payne, represented the Retirement System at meetings with lawmakers and other officials. On one memorable occasion, the Legislative committee held an important final meeting on the administration of the new health care program. It was at that meeting that the crucial question of which State agency would oversee the program was to be officially decided. Yet Payne was notably absent. The committee proceeded without him and decided, as expected, that SERS would be the administering agency.

So what kept Payne from this important meeting? It turned out that an axle on the Triumph sports car Payne was driving broke on the day of the meeting, leaving him temporarily stranded. Later, Payne suggested—mostly tongue-in-cheek—that

he had actually been planning to submit the names of other agencies to take on the administrative health plan duties, but his car troubles thwarted his efforts.

A Triumph TR3, 1960. A broken axle on CEO William Payne's Triumph kept him from making it to the meeting in which it was decided that SERS would administer the State's health benefits program, which began in 1962.

The Meyers-Geddes Act authorized SERS to offer voluntary group coverage of medical and hospital benefits excluding life insurance. The new health plan offered health coverage for all State employees. Local public agencies would be allowed to contract for health program benefits with SERS beginning in 1967. The health plan for State employees called for the State to contribute up to $5 per month for each employee's health insurance coverage beginning in 1962.

Now that SERS had become the central administrative agency for State employee health plans, it also acquired the authority to approve the existing health plans offered by CSEA and other agencies. SERS began reviewing the CSEA health plan and other public agency health plans that offered coverage of specific groups of public employees.[22]

During November 1961, State employees began to enroll in a health plan of their own choice. The new health care legislation required even those employees already covered by an existing plan to enroll in one of 10 plans in order to be eligible for the $5-per-month State contribution. All enrollment plans had to be completed and submitted by December 5, 1961, in order for coverage to begin on January 1, 1962. CSEA sponsored two plans (California Western States-Occidental and California Physicians Service-Blue Shield) and the State offered two as well (California Western States-Occidental and Blue Cross-CPS Blue Shield). Some of the other plans were available only in certain parts of the State.[23]

The CSEA and State health plans had significant similarities and in 1966, State representatives and CSEA agreed to combine them. Effective January 1, 1967, the respective health plans offered by California-Western States and Occidental Life Insurance Companies merged. The new plan was more expensive than either of the existing plans, although SERS explained that rising health care costs, not administrative expenses, produced the increase. The new plan also offered enhanced benefits including higher benefits for outpatient diagnostic work and maternity allowances.[24]

Headline from the *Los Angeles Times*, January 8, 1961. The health care plan the Legislature approved authorized CalPERS to offer State employees group coverage for hospital and medical benefits. The State contributed $5 per month for each employee's insurance.

Health Plan for State Employees Proposed

Program Advocated by Assembly Group Would Provide Medical Care for 115,000

Upgrading Retirement Benefits

During 1968, California Governor Ronald Reagan signed legislation that added annual cost-of-living increases to the System's retirement allowances. Assemblyman E. Richard Barnes had submitted the original bill, Assembly Bill 508, to the Legislature. A.B. 508 provided for annual increases up to 1.5 percent for current retirement allowances. This increase would be pegged to the cost-of-living index for the previous year up to 1.5 percent.[25]

Assemblyman E. Richard Barnes, 1967. Barnes submitted a bill adding annual cost-of-living increases to CalPERS members' retirement allowances that became law in 1968. He later authored the bill that allowed the System to invest in common stock.

Assemblyman Barnes was particularly pleased that Governor Reagan had signed this legislation. "This is a modest start toward the elimination of the present costly approach of one-time increases at sporadic intervals," Barnes stated. "It is an orderly and realistic solution to the problem of needed annual adjustments in retirement allowances due to the spiraling, inflationary costs of living increases as recorded annually by the Department of Labor Cost Index."[26]

Retirement benefit enhancements had to be funded. In this case, Assemblyman Barnes had initiated a change for the Retirement System's investment policies to provide a mechanism for funding these enhancements. Barnes supported a change in law to provide the Retirement System the authority to invest its funds in common stocks, or equities. By expanding its investment options, Barnes believed the System could fund the cost-of-living increase without increasing either the employee or employer contribution rates.

Investing in Equities

During 1960, the SERS Board of Administration considered a proposal for reorganization made by John E. Carr, the California Director of Finance. Carr believed that transferring the Investment Officer, who had previously been a Department of Finance employee, to SERS was organizationally appropriate, as it placed the investment function closer to the interested agency and would bring added efficiency. SERS officials also wanted to reorganize the Investment Office so that the Investment Officer reported directly to the Board and worked more closely with the Executive Officer, in the same manner that the SERS actuary functioned. The SERS Investment

Officer would continue to be responsible for investing funds of the Teachers' Retirement System and other State agencies.

Discussion of reorganizing the Investment Office came amid important personnel changes. In August 1961, SERS longtime Investment Adviser, Rene Rothschild, resigned. Rothschild had served as SERS investment adviser and Investment Officer since 1940 and his departure marked the end of an era of investment policy limited primarily to government, municipal, and utility bonds.[27]

Staffing of the Investment Office remained in a certain amount of flux over the next several years. On February 7, 1964, William Payne reported to the Board that he had assigned Edward Coombs as Acting Chief of Investments. Coombs would be responsible for overseeing the SERS investment program, including a new mortgage loan program, while developing a list of candidates for a permanent chief of investments.[28] Later that year, Charles B. Blank was promoted from Investment Officer to Chief Investment Officer and Ernest O. Ellison was promoted from Assistant Investment Officer to Investment Officer, effective November 1, 1964, and December 2, 1964, respectively.

The new mortgage loan operation began with a small staff. SERS hired Carl Halterman, formerly with California Department of Veteran Affairs, as its mortgage loan officer. Jim Smith, one of the first new employees hired to work with mortgages, recalled that originally there were about seven staff members, including the secretary. Several of the mortgage investment officers also came to SERS from the Department of Veteran Affairs.

Initially, the mortgage group's investments were limited to FHA and VA loans purchased only from mortgage bankers and banks. "We inspected each and every property, no matter where they were in California," Smith recalled. "We would only buy loans in California at the time."[29] SERS later moved into commercial mortgages.

Rene Rothschild, ca. 1940. CalPERS first Investment Adviser, Rothschild left the System in 1961. During his two decades of service, he advocated broadening the System's investment options—a strategy the Investment Office continued to promote after his departure.

When SERS began to purchase mortgages directly rather than through banks, it became the System's responsibility to make sure that each property was in good condition and accurately represented in the mortgage documents. Therefore, one

Laying the Foundation:
CalPERS Member Home Loan Program

CalPERS understands that the dream of homeownership is one shared by many of its members and retirees. To strengthen its support of members through mutual investment opportunities, CalPERS initiated its Member Home Loan Program in 1981.

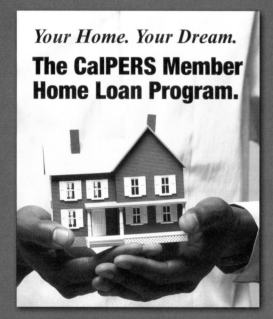

Ad from CalPERS *PERSpective* newsletter, Spring 2006. CalPERS keeps members abreast of new ways the Member Home Loan Program can benefit them through publications, a toll-free phone number, and a section of the CalPERS On-Line Web site devoted to the program.

The idea for the program grew out of a conversation Board Member Charles Valdes had with one of his staff at the Department of Transportation. The employee, a single mother, had just been informed by her landlord that her rent was increasing to a rate she couldn't afford. After examining her finances, she realized that the best long-term option for her and her family was purchasing a condominium, but without money for a down payment or the possibility of a loan from a bank, it seemed impossible.

Valdes was sympathetic to her situation and wondered whether there might be a way CalPERS could help. He brought the issue to the Board, and Board Members determined that by getting into the residential mortgage financing business, CalPERS could capitalize on a good investment opportunity while also helping thousands of public employees. Such a venture would help stimulate jobs, thereby strengthening California's economy.

Since this idea came to fruition, thousands of members of CalPERS, the Legislators' Retirement System, and the two Judges' Retirement Systems (JRS and JRS II) have taken advantage of the many benefits offered by the Member Home Loan Program, including competitive financing on a variety of loan options, free 60-day interest rate locks, and low- or no-down-payment options, among others. Managed by CitiMortgage, the program is efficient and user-friendly, allowing homeowners peace of mind during one of life's more complicated, yet exhilarating transitions. Whether it's buying a new home or refinancing an existing mortgage, CalPERS members enjoy the extra benefits of controlled closing costs, reduced mortgage insurance premiums, and 100 percent financing options.

Since its inception, the Home Loan Program had made more than 128,000 real estate loans, with a total dollar volume exceeding $20 billion. The impact on California's economy has been tremendous; the effect on thousands of members' lives immeasurable.

CalPERS member Rey Pena realized his dream of owning his home on two acres in 1997, and has refinanced through the program twice since then—with no red tape or headaches. "My role was pretty minimal," he said. "My CalPERS-approved loan officer picked up the ball and just ran with it."

of the most important functions of the mortgage staff was property inspection. Smith recalled that there were times when an inspection revealed that "there wasn't any property. I mean, there wasn't any improvement on the property, I'll put it that way. Obviously, we wouldn't be buying anything like that, but we were glad that at that point in time we were looking at them."[30]

The new mortgage investment operation and the ongoing bond investment operation worked within the same division. "We were combined, but we were departmentalized," Smith said. "We were always kind of fighting to see who would get the most money to invest to keep going, but bonds outdid us at the time."[31]

Executive Officer Payne was particularly interested in developing SERS investment operations. He recognized that SERS needed additional investment options and he had promoted the idea since at least the late 1950s that SERS should invest in common stocks.[32] At the February 10, 1961, Board meeting, Payne presented a recommendation that the Board seek legislative authority to invest SERS funds in common stock. To do this, legislation would be required to amend the California State Constitution. Payne explained that the Legislature would also have to pass specific legislation allowing the Board to invest in common stock. He proposed the following language for such a law:

The Board may invest moneys in the retirement fund in an amount determined on a cost basis, not exceeding 25 percent of the assets of such fund in common or preferred stock of any corporation. In making each and all of such investments, the Board shall exercise the judgment and care under the circumstances then prevailing which men of ordinary prudence, discretion, and intelligence exercise in the management of their own affairs, not in regard to speculation, but in regard to the permanent disposition of their funds, considering the probable income therefrom as well as the probable safety of their capital.

The Board unanimously agreed to initiate the legislation required for SERS to invest in common stock.[33] At the same meeting, the Investment Committee requested that SERS staff "secure an opinion from the Attorney General in order to clarify the Board's present authority to invest in mortgages without additional legislation."[34]

First, California's voters would have to approve an amendment to the California Constitution. Proposition 1, the measure providing for the amendment, enjoyed

Common stock certificates, 1960s. A 19th-century provision in State law prohibited CalPERS from investing in common stock for its first three decades in operation, placing a severe limitation on the Retirement System's investment capabilities.

Stock Purchases by State Pension Funds Supported

BY ARELO SEDERBERG
Times Staff Writer

Representatives of industry and government spoke enthusiastically here Monday in behalf of a proposition on the November ballot which would grant authority for California public pension funds to invest a portion of their assets in stocks.

widespread support. Many, if not most, newspapers in California published editorials supporting the proposition. There was general agreement that the 94-year-old provision in the Constitution that prevented investment in stock was well out-of-date. The *Oakland Tribune* noted that 30 states "already permit pension funds to invest in professionally selected stocks, and private pension funds allot 40 percent of their money to securities."[35] After conducting an analysis of SERS investments, the First National City Bank of New York stated that, "The total absence of common stocks is the major shortcoming of the SERS portfolio."[36] *The California State Employee* published an interesting analogy:

If any single individual had as much as $3 billion in his investment portfolio without a cent of it in common stocks, he would be considered as not only rich but very much on the balmy side, a person whose will would be certainly open to question and on the highly logical grounds of his sanity.[37]

In September, Payne spoke publicly in favor of Proposition 1. The results of investing in high-yield blue-chip stocks, he said, would be increased retirement benefits and lower costs to both employees and taxpayers. Payne was well aware of SERS potential marketplace clout. Even in 1966, SERS was the largest public pension fund in the nation. "We have a real desire to promote California's economy," Payne stated, "and we should stay here if we can."[38] Payne explained that SERS was investing about $22 million per month in bonds and mortgages. These included major utility, municipal, water, and irrigation district bonds, as well as FHA-VA mortgages.[39]

Supporters of Proposition 1 maintained that improving SERS investment options was a necessity in order to enhance member benefits. CSEA reported that if California's voters approved Proposition 1, then the State would consider legislation providing for automatic cost-of-living adjustments for retirement benefits. Similar legislation had been defeated in 1965 because an additional $35 million would have been required to fund the increased benefits.[40]

In the 1966 general election, California's voters approved Proposition 1, granting SERS the authority to invest Fund assets in common stocks. First, however, the Legislature had to change State law. This was accomplished with Assembly Bill 913,

Men reading stock prices off a ticker at the San Francisco Stock Exchange, 1961. Proposition 1, which California voters passed in 1966, allowed the Legislature to amend the State Constitution to allow CalPERS to invest in common stocks. This gave the System far more latitude in building its portfolio.

a measure authored by Assemblyman E. Richard Barnes, which passed in 1967.[41] Governor Ronald Reagan signed A.B. 913 into law in September 1967.[42]

Ernest Ellison, the SERS Investment Officer at the time, said that the measure would have "no impact initially, but over a period of years, we anticipate a rather substantially higher increase [in stocks] than from bonds."[43] SERS hired Lionel D. Edie and Company to serve as its investment counsel. With an office in Los Angeles

Old California State Fairgrounds on Stockton Boulevard in Sacramento, ca. 1960. Among CalPERS real estate investments in the 1960s were the former State Fair site and the surplus land for the State Fair's "Cal Expo" site, which opened in 1968.

and headquarters in New York City, Lionel D. Edie offered advice principally in regard to investment in common stock.[44]

While Governor Reagan approved SERS authority to invest in common stock, he vetoed other bills that would have increased member benefits. In 1967, Reagan vetoed Assembly Bill 740, which would have increased retirement benefits by 2 to 10 percent. This bill passed the Assembly 75-2 and the Senate 28-6. Reagan, however, said funds were not available for cost-of-living increases for retired State employees. "Provision will be made in the 1968-69 budget for these needed cost-of-living increases," he said. CSEA expressed great disappointment in Reagan's action.[45]

SERS also increased its position in real estate investments. The SERS investment in the Retirement Building at Sacramento was the first of many office buildings in which SERS invested. Though the costs associated with constructing this building continued to increase, real estate proved to be a good investment. The Board considered purchasing building certificates for other State office buildings as well. During the spring of 1960, the Board agreed to purchase building certificates for a State office building in Colton. In late 1962, the SERS Board authorized investment in building certificates up to $1.5 million for constructing a State office building in Stockton.[46] Another bill, A.B. 601, authored by State Senator Albert Rodda, allowed SERS to purchase the existing California State Fair site and the surplus land for a new State Fair location.

A New Name

Reflecting SERS overall expansion during the 1960s, SERS upper-level organizational structure and name changed as well. During late 1967, the State Personnel Board formally created four new Division Chief positions at SERS. These Division Chiefs managed four major functions: legislative, contracts, information, and policy development and evaluation.[47]

Governor Ronald Reagan speaking at a CSEA event, date unknown. Though Reagan signed into law some key measures benefiting State workers, he vetoed others, including a 1967 bill that would have provided cost-of-living increases to employees retired from State service.

More noticeable to the public, SERS changed its name in 1967, becoming the Public Employees' Retirement System, or PERS. Though the name change may have seemed inconsequential to some, it reflected the broad growth of the System's membership. By 1967, SERS contracted with 585 public agencies for retirement benefits. With a membership that extended well beyond the ranks of State government employees, the new name more accurately described the System's diverse membership.[48]

Downtown Monrovia, California, 1950. Monrovia was among 585 local public agencies contracting with the Retirement System by 1967, when the System changed its name to the Public Employees' Retirement System (PERS).

Changing from Chaindex

By 1960, CalPERS had more than 257,000 members and its assets had passed the $1.2 billion mark. The massive filing system that kept track of the necessary information for all these members was called Chaindex.

Employees of the Retirement System (then known as the State Employees' Retirement System, or SERS) had relied on the manual system since its inception.

The Chaindex system was comprised of small cards that linked together on a chain and were housed in a giant cabinet. When a member joined, SERS employees typed up a detailed record on that person and assigned them a Chaindex number, which served as the person's unique identifier.

The Chaindex number was used to access member correspondence and other records, which were kept in other filing systems. "That little Chaindex, which was maybe one-by-three inches, or something like that, would have an entire employment history on it," longtime Membership Division employee Roberta Cournoyer recalled. "Everything you needed to know about an employee ... as far as tracing his employment from one State employer or agency employer to another, it was all right there on that little Chaindex."

Eventually, SERS intricate and voluminous filing systems got so unwieldy that at one office, on Thirteenth and K Streets, the floor started sagging beneath the files and workers had to put boards underneath it for stabilization.

Employees remember using Chaindex well into the 1970s. When SERS finally made the switch to computers, some of the new computer staff seemed intimidated by the massive Chaindex system. "I think we frightened all of the computer people when they'd look at what was on [the Chaindex]," recalled Cournoyer. "There was just so much."

Conversely, some of the old guard were a bit intimidated by the new computer technology, as well as the wave of "high-tech" workers it brought. These employees learned programming languages such as COBOL and Fortran and talked to each other in—or about—"code."

Nevertheless, the Retirement System successfully completed the Chaindex-to-computer transition. And it continues to update its business technology, moving increasingly to paperless systems. In the early 2000s, the System embarked on an ambitious project to convert tens of millions of papers from its files to digital images, allowing these records to be accessed far more efficiently and creating huge savings in operating and storage costs. In 2006, CalPERS kicked off its most significant technology initiative to date aimed at developing a consolidated pension information system that will harness the power of the Internet and ultimately provide for faster, more reliable, and more cost-effective service to members and employers.

Drawers of CalPERS Chaindex cards, 2007. The Retirement System has hundreds of drawers of Chaindex files stored at its headquarters, though it began using a more efficient computerized system for maintaining member information in the 1970s.

Regulating Private Pension Funds

Before World War II, relatively few American workers in private business received pension benefits and few pension plans existed. During the war, however, businesses increasingly offered pension benefits to attract employees. By 1946, approximately 7,000 private pension funds existed, covering 3.3 million employees. Pension fund growth slowed briefly following the war, but high taxes and organized labor's continued strong support boosted pension fund growth. In 1950, private pension plans covered 9.8 million workers, or about 23 percent of the private workforce. By 1960, private pension fund coverage included 21 million workers, or 37.2 percent of the workforce. By 1970, these numbers reached 30 million and 42.1 percent, respectively. Private pension fund assets grew from $12 billion in 1950 to $137 billion in 1970.[49]

American Express building in New York, 1917. American Express established the nation's first formal private pension plan in 1875. Such plans were a rarity, however, until World War II, when American businesses began offering pension benefits to attract employees.

Changes in Membership
Public & Private Pension Systems, 1950-1970

Category			Membership
	1950	1960	1970
Private Plans			
Active	9,805,000	21,235,000	30,354,000
Pensioners	405,000	1,780,000	4,726,000
Government Plans			
Active	5,793,000	7,550,000	10,566,000
Pensioners	662,000	1,343,000	2,266,000
TOTALS			
Active	15,598,000	28,785,000	40,920,000
Pensioners	1,112,000	3,123,000	6,982,000

Source: Securities Industry Association, State and Local Pension Funds, 1972.

The rapid growth of pension plans in the postwar era, however, was accompanied by numerous cases of mismanagement and abuse. In 1958, Congress passed the Welfare and Pension Plans Disclosure Act to force pensions to register, report, and disclose various aspects of their operations to the federal government. However, the act apparently did little to bring stability to the rapidly growing pension business.[50]

Suffering from "growing pains," the pension fund industry seemed to require reform. According to Historian William Graebner, "By the late 1970s, about two decades after the institution reached its peak of influence and acceptance, retirement was in retreat. At every level of government, legislatures and commissions reviewed the complex web of retirement institutions. Pension plans, mandatory retirement, early retirement, retirement on disability, even Social Security were all weighed and evaluated."[51]

While some observers believed that the careful inspection of pension funds was part of the overall reform movement in the United States that began in the 1960s, others pointed out that many pension funds were confronting significant managerial, actuarial, and general policy-related problems. Some critics contended that forcing elderly workers to retire and promising them a pension in return was at the root of the pension fund problem. More likely, the culprit was not the concept of retirement plans, but rather the uncontrolled growth of such plans and the opportunities for mismanagement and abuse such growth created. This was the issue that needed to be studied and managed more efficiently and in the public interest.

Both public and private pension funds had their share of problems in the 1960s and 1970s. Perhaps the most nationally publicized pension fund debacle occurred in New York City. For as many as 10 years, New York City's government reported that the city's budget was balanced when it was actually being "balanced" with funds from the city's retirement fund. The city went bankrupt in 1975, leaving its retirement system entirely without funding. By 1976, New York City's unfunded past-service liability reached an estimated $5.5 to $6 billion and possibly substantially higher.[52]

Part of New York City's pension fund problem related to actuarial computations. The city based its pension-funding requirements on actuarial calculations devised in 1918. The average life expectancy at that time was less than 55 years. By the mid-1970s, average life expectancy had increased to about 70. Thus, New York City's pension fund was unprepared to pay retirement benefits to retired employees who lived into their 60s and beyond, regardless of external economic conditions.[53]

PENSIONS EXPAND AS RULES TIGHTEN

More Funds, More Benefits More Employers Pick Up Check, More Red Tape

By J. E. McMAHON

Pension funds achieved a peak in 1957, as states adopted more laws to regulate them. The number of pension plans increased and benefits under them in many instances were improved.

Excerpt from a *New York Times* article, January 6, 1958. With numbers of private pensions growing rapidly, Congress in 1958 passed the Welfare and Pension Plans Disclosure Act, a measure intended to make the funds more accountable for their operations.

Though New York City's was among the most publicized pension fund crises, it was not the first. Federal lawmakers had made efforts in the late 1960s and early 1970s to bring about pension fund reform. Between 1967 and 1973, U.S. Congress debated and considered many pension reform bills. The Labor Subcommittee chaired by Representatives John Dent and John Erlenborn sponsored many of these bills in the House. In the Senate, Senators Vance Hartke, Jacob Javits, and Gaylord Nelson led the pension reform movement.[54]

The movement gained momentum in the early 1970s. In January 1973, several Congressional leaders of the reform efforts introduced bills in both the Senate and House. Almost two years later, the U.S. Congress passed the Employees Retirement Security Act (ERISA), also known as the Pension Reform Act of 1974. President Gerald R. Ford signed the act into law on Labor Day, 1974. Upon signing it, Ford said that under the law, "the men and women of our labor force will have much more clearly defined rights to pension funds and greater assurances that retirement dollars will be there when they are needed." He also noted that employees without access to company plans would have greater tax incentives to provide for their own retirements under the law. An editorial in *Pension & Welfare News* called the legislation "the most important legislation affecting retirement of employees in the United States since the passage of the first Social Security Act in the 1930s."[55]

Although ERISA set standards for private pension funds as opposed to public funds, it marked an important change in the way that the federal government viewed pension funds generally. The ERISA legislation contained seven significant provisions. These provisions included standards for employee participation, standards for vesting retirement benefits, requirements that pension fund fiduciaries act in the interest of the beneficiaries, requirement of full disclosure, tax law modifications to provide more equal treatment of various pension plans, and establishment of the Pension Benefit Guaranty Corporation to back up pension plans and provisions for transferring pensions.[56]

Under ERISA, private pension funds began to diversify their fund assets. Prior to the legislation, private pensions typically invested their funds in fixed-income securities such as government bonds. ERISA, however, granted private pension plan sponsors

New York Senator Jacob Javits, 1966. Javits was among the U.S. senators leading the charge for pension fund reform in the late 1960s and early 1970s. Their efforts were instrumental in the passage of the Employees Retirement Security Act (ERISA) in 1974, also known as the Pension Reform Act of 1974.

the fiduciary responsibility to invest funds as they saw fit. Pension funds quickly began diversifying into stocks and other investment instruments and returns increased. In addition, the legislation allowed pension funds to invest internationally.

Not everyone was pleased with ERISA. Some critics charged that it unnecessarily complicated an already complex pension fund sector. ERISA, they said, added administration, communications, and benefit-related costs, without improving employee benefits.

President Gerald Ford after signing the Employees Retirement Security Act of 1974 (ERISA) on Labor Day of that year. Many considered the landmark legislation, which defined and protected the rights of employees who held private pensions, the most significant retirement legislation since the establishment of Social Security.

Nevertheless, the impact of ERISA on the overall pension fund business environment in the United States was considerable. Some supporters called for the government to extend the ERISA standards to cover public pensions at all levels: municipal, county, state, and federal; though public pensions generally opposed any attempt to impose federal regulation on them.[57]

Thus, the ERISA legislation marked both the beginning of federal regulation of private pensions and calls for closer oversight of public systems. The New York City pension system debacle provided substantial fuel for those critics who believed that public systems were in need of oversight as much, if not more, than private systems. By the very nature of their public function, the leaders of public pensions noted that their systems were already subject to a great deal of oversight and inspection. However, a report by the federal Pension Task Force found otherwise:

Public (pension) plans in general do not appear to be operated within the general financial and accounting parameters established by custom and practice in the private retirement plan field. The absence of any external independent review has perpetuated a level of employer control and attendant potential for abuse unknown in the private sector.[58]

Excerpt from a *New York Times* article, March 28, 1976. After ERISA began regulating private pension funds in 1974, many critics turned their gaze to public pensions, faulting some for being underfunded and politically controlled.

Pension Fund Risks for Public Employees

By LOUIS M. KOHLMEIER

WASHINGTON—In a room in the Cannon building, one of the House office buildings on Capitol Hill, a small task force is quietly investigating the thousands of pension funds that cities and states have created for the benefit of millions of public employees.

One of the cases that fascinates the task force involves the Police Pension and Relief Association of Erie, Pa., which has, or had, assets of $1.5 million.

The association hired as its investment adviser Francis J. Pilewski, a retired Erie police sergeant, and invested $340,000 in unrated bonds of two medical facilities in Arizona and Michigan and $260,000 in unrated bonds of a medical facility in Georgia. The association agreed to invest another $125,000 in the New Jersey ski resort of Playboy Inc.

The Arizona and Michigan medical facilities subsequently fell into receivership, the Georgia facility went into reorganization and the Erie police pension fund may have lost as much as $600,000. Mr. Pilewski was fired before the Playboy investment was completed.

"I don't think that example will be atypical of smaller public pension funds," says Russell J. Mueller of the Congressional pension task force staff.

If the Erie case is typical of smaller public pension plans, larger state and municipal plans have different problems of greater magnitude.

tion and it is liable to the funds for certainly more than $2 billion because of past underfunding. Additionally the city will be indebted to the funds for at least $4.1 billion more.

"Incredible," declares another member of the Congressional pension task force.

As cities and states have found it an increasing struggle to meet current pension costs, public employees have become frightened that there may not be enough money to pay all the benefits promised. The employees, and their unions, therefore have gone to court in Illinois, Detroit, Philadelphia and other states and cities to force state and local governments to begin meeting unfunded liabilities.

While New York State pension funds also have been obligated to the rescue of the city and of state agencies, no other major city or state so far has fallen back on its own pension funds to avoid bankruptcy. Many cities and states, however, for years also have had underfunded pension costs by billions of dollars.

As the Kinzel Commission said, New York City "chose to use pension underfunding as one method of balancing its operating budget." Other cities and states did the same.

Congress nearly two years ago overwhelmingly passed the Employee Retirement Income Security Act, known as ERISA, to reform the funding, fiduciary and other practices of private employers' pension plans.

A critic finds plans 'inadequately funded, poorly designed and subject to political manipulation.'

Professor Don M. McGill of the University of Pennsylvania, Wharton School of Finance, and chairman of the University's Pension Research Council, provided an even harsher commentary on public pension funds. Testifying before the United States Subcommittee on Labor in 1972, two years prior to Congressional passage of ERISA, McGill characterized public employee retirement funds collectively as "inadequately funded, poorly designed, and subject to unsound political manipulation." People knowledgeable about retirement systems, he said, generally agreed "that retirement systems for public employees are much more in need of regulation than the plans of private employees."[59]

California's political leadership and PERS officials alike recognized the potential for the emergence of serious problems in the State's public pension system. After enactment of ERISA and the related public debate about the health and security of the nation's pension systems, the California Senate Committee on Public Employment and Retirement, chaired by Newton R. Russell, contracted with Bill Horne Associates to prepare a three-volume study of public retirement systems.

The report echoed the cautionary tone of McGill's congressional testimony and the federal Pension Task Force report. Indeed, it indicated that California's own public retirement systems lacked both uniformity in the vast number of plans offered in the State and, perhaps even more important, clearly defined policy objectives for public retirement in California.[60]

The growth of pension plans spawned a variety of pension fund research groups and institutes that offered research services, plan analysis, and policy work. A group of consultants founded the Employee Benefit Research Institute (EBRI) in 1978, for example, to provide information on pension funds and pension fund issues. EBRI and other associations, combined with the nation's many public and private pensions, created a pension industry in the United States that controlled a vast amount of the nation's wealth, as well as maintaining responsibility for the retirement funds of a majority of the nation's workers.[61]

Founders and leadership of the Employee Benefit Retirement Institute (EBRI), 1988. The growth of pension plans nationwide spurred the creation of organizations like EBRI, which was formed to study the industry and provide information to the public.

Leadership at PERS

The momentous changes in the pension fund industry required ever-vigilant leadership at PERS. In early 1975, months after the passage of ERISA, a new leader took the reigns at PERS. Carl Blechinger, a veteran employee who had served as legislative representative, Social Security Division Chief, Accounting Division Chief, and Assistant Executive Officer of the System would guide PERS through some of its most formative years.

Blechinger replaced William Payne, who had served as the Executive Officer since 1956, when he succeeded Earl Chapman to become the System's second Executive Officer. Payne left the System unexpectedly late in 1974, reportedly after a meeting with Governor Reagan. Board Member Bob Carlson recalled that Payne met with Reagan in the morning and then "came over to our Board meeting and announced his resignation." At the time, PERS had almost 600,000 members and assets of $6.8 billion.

Bob Carlson, who was then President of CSEA, reported having great success with Governor Reagan himself. For example, the Governor was poised to veto a bill on a CalPERS recommendation that would have allowed unused sick leave hours to be converted to service credit for retirement. Carlson paid a call to the Governor. The

Governor said if Carlson could convince his four cabinet secretaries this was in the best interest of the State, he would remove his opposition. Carlson visited each secretary and received their agreements. The law went forward and was signed in 1974.

With support from staff and others, Carl Blechinger stepped in to fill this unanticipated opening and became PERS third Executive Officer. Born in Massachusetts, Blechinger trained early as a machinist, served in the military, and made his way west, where he graduated from California State University, Sacramento with a degree in Business Administration. He went to work for PERS in 1955 after running the Social Security Program in the California Department of Employment's accounting section.

CEO William Payne (*third from left*) with CalPERS employees at a holiday party, 1971. Payne, a respected and well-liked leader within CalPERS, resigned unexpectedly in 1974.

He became instrumental in running the Social Security program at PERS as well—at a time when the program was undergoing significant change and controversy.

One of Blechinger's first actions as PERS Executive Officer was to remove himself from the System's Investment Committee. Both Earl Chapman and William Payne had served on this Committee, but Blechinger felt the Executive Officer did not need to be a member. Later, however, he did attend the Executive Sessions of the Investment Committee for informational purposes.[62]

Carl Blechinger, 1983. Blechinger, a CalPERS veteran who guided the System's Social Security program through profound changes in the late 1950s, became CalPERS third Executive Officer in 1974, replacing William Payne.

Blechinger also committed much energy to staff development, which he later identified as his greatest accomplishment at PERS. "For the first time, I had women working first as Assistant Division Chiefs, then as Division Chief and than as Assistant Executive Officer."[63] He instituted a sort of affirmative action policy at PERS before such programs became commonplace in corporate America. "He was affirmative action," Board Member Carlson recalled. "There was no policy on that. He did it."[64]

Health Benefits & a Changing Environment

The Meyer-Geddes Health Benefits Act of 1961 put PERS into the business of managing its members' health care. The health care business, perhaps even more so than the pension fund business generally, underwent rapid change and volatility during these years. Robert Wilson, former Chief of the PERS Health Benefits Division, commented in 1982 that the PERS health benefits program "has been in a continuing state of flux, ever-growing and responding to major changes in the provision of health care [such as] federal Medicare and Medicaid in 1966 and the federally created Health Maintenance Organizations (HMO Act) in 1973."[65]

Certainly, the PERS health care program was more complicated to administer than its retirement program. The variety of health care choices, as well as the multitude of health issues, created a complex program subject to ever increasing costs. The emergence of Health Maintenance Organizations, or HMOs, in the mid-1970s added an additional administrative challenge to the PERS health care system. At the same time, dealing with HMOs allowed PERS to create more unified and standardized health care benefit rates.

IMPLEMENTING MEDICARE

1. Getting the People 65 or Over Ready
2. Getting Hospitals and Other Institutions Ready
3. Arranging for Participation of Physicians
4. Tooling Up for Internal Operations

CASH BUDGET
CALENDAR 1966 ESTIMATE

U.S. Secretary of Health, Education, and Welfare John Gardner, outlining the newly enacted Medicare program, 1966. The emergence of Medicare, Medicaid, and Health Maintenance Organizations added complexity to the administration of CalPERS health benefits program, as Retirement System officials navigated rising insurance costs and a changing national health care scene.

Modifications to the Benefit Structure

Even as PERS was developing a major new benefits program in the area of health care, it was also making significant actuarial changes to its basic benefits structure. In 1977, PERS officials decided to abolish separate male and female benefit factor rates in favor of a single one. The creation of a uniform rate represented a momentous change in both policy and practice—a "political change," according to former Health Benefits Division Chief Wilson.[66] Indeed, PERS abandoned the gender-based benefit factor rates at the height of the women's movement in the United States, as women were seeking equality in all arenas. Some questioned whether PERS decision stemmed more from politics than actuarial science, but others heralded it as a judicious decision both actuarially and politically.

Investment Income Growth

The 1970s marked the start of several decades of dramatic growth in the PERS Fund. With its newfound ability to invest in stock and an increasingly sophisticated investment

Annualized Time-Weighted Rate of Return

	December 1971-1980	December 1975-1980	3 Years Ended June 1981
PERS Stocks	5.2%	14.8%	14.8%
Salomon Brothers Bond Index	4.2	4.3	3.1
Dow Jones Index	6.4	13.7	12.7
S&P 500 Index	8.5	17.6	7.1

Source: Adapted from the Public Employees' Retirement System, Fiftieth Annual Report, June 1981, p. 26.

Opposite page
Female Palo Alto city worker shoveling by a sign announcing men at work, 1970s. The push for gender equality in every aspect of society in the 1970s played an important role in CalPERS decision to make its benefit factor rates gender neutral.

apparatus overall, CalPERS enlarged its Fund assets from approximately $4 billion in 1970 to more than $11 billion in 1979, despite a recession in the early 1970s. With the assistance of highly trained consultants and its own experienced staff, PERS reaped above-average returns on its investments as well as an ever-increasing asset base.

In 1972, PERS added "Ginnie Mae" (GNMA) securities to its real estate investment portfolio. Comprised of FHA-VA loans for single-family homes pooled into a security, the federal government backed these investments through the GNMA Corporation. In an expanding economy, these were both safe and secure investments.[67] By the end of the decade, PERS was investing about one-half of its Fund in bonds, with the remainder split evenly between stocks and real estate mortgage loans.[68]

The PERS Board of Administration also modified the relationship between the PERS investment staff and its outside investment consultant in the 1970s. Until about 1977, the PERS investment staff had the responsibility for making investment decisions and the outside consultant was available for consultation and review of those choices. In the 1970s, Lionel D. Edie and Company, a New York-based investment firm with offices in Los Angeles, was CalPERS outside consultant. But the Board switched these roles so that Lionel D. Edie made the investment decisions in consultation with PERS investment staff and a PERS employee still actually placed the trade order. At that time, PERS employee Jim Graham had this responsibility. After receiving a list of securities for trading from Lionel D. Edie, Graham decided on the best time to make the trade. It sometimes required an entire month to complete the list of trades.[69]

CalPERS Growing Duties

In the beginning, CalPERS administered one retirement system only—the State Employees' Retirement System, as it was known in its early decades. CalPERS took responsibility for a second system, the Legislators' Retirement System, in 1947.

Then, in the course of two years, CalPERS gained responsibility for two additional systems: the Judges' Retirement System in 1979 and the Volunteer Firefighters' Length of Service Award System (VFLSAS) in 1980.

The Judges' Retirement System (JRS) was established in 1937 for Supreme and Appellate Court justices, Superior Court judges, and Municipal Court judges. For more than 40 years, the State Controller had administered the JRS, so its move to CalPERS was a momentous one.

San Francisco Superior Court judges being sworn into office, 1954. CalPERS started administering the Judges' Retirement System (JRS) in 1979. The State Controller's Office previously ran the JRS, which began in 1937.

It also proved a challenging one. The JRS plan was structured as a "defined benefit" plan, providing benefits calculated under a defined formula rather than contributions to a savings plan. Judges can work as long as they want under this plan and receive their full pension of either 65 percent or 75 percent, based on years of service. Unfortunately, the policies and structure of the JRS were not actuarially sound.

To address this situation, CalPERS began administering a second system for judges—the Judges' Retirement System II (JRS II)—in 1994. The JRS II was set up to be a fully funded, actuarially sound plan for judges who were appointed or elected on or after November 9, 1994. It offers a combination of two types of retirement benefits: a defined benefit plan and a monetary credit plan. The latter plan allows for a refund of member contributions, a portion of employer contributions, and interest. Unlike the original JRS, judges must be at least 65 years old with 20 years of service, or 70 with five years of service, to receive the defined benefit plan.

A year after taking over administration of the first JRS, CalPERS gained responsibility for the Volunteer Firefighters' Length of Service Award System. The program provides a reward for volunteer firefighters throughout the State. In its February 1980 *Retirement Newsletter*, CalPERS announced its part in

Crowd gathered at the dedication of a memorial to volunteer firefighters in San Francisco, 1933. CalPERS began administering the Volunteer Firefighters' Length of Service Award System in 1980—a program that rewards the service of these volunteers throughout California.

bolstering the program's effectiveness as it gave "cities, counties, and districts … the opportunity to offer an award for life as an incentive for the volunteer to respond to emergency calls, attend approved formal study courses, and attend official department training drills and meetings."

As of 2006, the VFLSAS had about 4,300 active members and firefighters receiving awards, and had made payments totaling more than $102,000. The JRS had 825 active and deferred members and had made more than $133 million in payments to approximately 1,600 retirees and beneficiaries, while the JRS II had almost 875 active members, retirees, and beneficiaries and had made nearly $860,000 in payments.

New York Stock Exchange telephone clerks, 1967. Throughout the 1970s CalPERS investment portfolio continued to expand dramatically. The New York firm of Lionel D. Edie and Company provided consultation on the System's investment decisions, while CalPERS employee Jim Graham placed the trade orders.

PERS entered the 1980s with a strong and growing investment portfolio, important new investment capabilities, a host of new programs and benefits systems to administer, and a new name to reflect the broad scope of its membership. The System was very healthy by any standard and its position as the country's largest public pension system was well established. At the same time, the nation increasingly was taking notice of public and private pension funds—recognizing their growing prominence and their potential to impact their beneficiaries and society as a whole. The convergence of these circumstances pointed to big developments ahead for PERS, though the System's evolution in the coming years would be stunning even to those most familiar with PERS and its potential.

5: Influence & Integrity

CalPERS celebrated its 50th anniversary in 1982, and as the System matured, its vitality and confidence clearly showed. PERS, long the nation's largest pension fund, emerged in the 1980s and 1990s as a leader in the growing corporate governance movement. Spurred by the philosophies and charismatic presence of Jesse Unruh, PERS became an active investor, wielding enormous influence in boardrooms of the world's most powerful corporations.

CalPERS also became more autonomous with the passage of Proposition 162. This momentous 1992 ballot measure put an end to State attempts to take from the CalPERS Fund, and bolstered the System's control over its own destiny.

Jesse Unruh (*left*) being sworn into office as the Speaker of the California House of Representatives, 1967. With his enormous political influence and charisma, Unruh played a pivotal role in making CalPERS a national leader in the corporate governance movement.

Among the most towering figures in PERS history was Jesse Unruh. Known as "Big Daddy," Unruh was large in both physical size—weighing in at about 300 pounds—and political stature in California. He achieved renown as the speaker of the California Assembly, a position he held from 1966 until 1969. After an unsuccessful run for Governor against incumbent Ronald Reagan in 1970, he ran for State Treasurer in 1974 and won. He stayed in the position until 1987. This also gave him a seat on the PERS Board beginning in 1982, when the State Treasurer and Controller were added to the CalPERS Board. By then, the 62-year-old Democrat had significantly reduced his weight, but he remained a heavy hitter in State politics. Indeed, Unruh then participated on more than 30 commissions and boards that managed State funds. Many in California politics considered him to be the 81st member of the 80-seat California Assembly.[1]

Political observers had already credited Unruh with turning the California Legislature into a more politically active body. *New York Times* reporter Fred R. Bleakley said that Unruh "transformed the Legislature from a part-time, ill-informed body that rubber-stamped the Governor's wishes—and paid too much heed to lobbyists—to one that did its own research, passed a raft of liberal legislation, such as civil rights and education reform, and became a model for other states."[2] The mark Unruh made on PERS was equally profound.

When he took the Treasurer's seat on the PERS Board, Unruh immediately understood the financial stakes involved, and he took an active role in implementing new policies. He was responsible for two innovations at the Retirement System. First, he led the way in transforming it into an activist investor, thereby instituting its "corporate governance" program. Almost simultaneously, Unruh mobilized many of the nation's large pension funds into a shareholder organization that U.S. corporations could not ignore: the Council of Institutional Investors.

Jesse Unruh's high-profile political persona attracted a great deal of attention, positive and negative, to himself as well as PERS. Many observers publicly questioned Unruh's intentions. In detailing his power and influence at both PERS and as California's Treasurer, Bleakley of the *New York Times* suggested Unruh could have a conflict of interest. Unruh, he wrote, "is responsible for supervising the raising of billions of dollars for the State through the sale of California's notes and bonds on Wall Street—not to mention having a strong hand in controlling billions of dollars that are invested annually for the pension funds."[3] But Unruh was both upfront and candid about his political power and influence. Indeed, he seemed to relish his power and made no apologies for it. Never one to shy away from controversy or politically sticky issues, Unruh was always open about demanding money—and lots of it—from Wall Street. But he argued that because he took from everyone, it didn't influence his decisions, and his openness and characteristic bluntness often seemed to defuse his critics.[4]

Council of Institutional Investors

During most of the 20th century, U.S. pension funds—and public ones in particular—remained passive in their investment strategies, even as they grew exponentially in total assets and percentage of corporate stock ownership. Traditionally, pension funds

Excerpt from an article in the *Los Angeles Times*, July 27, 1984. Among the takeover tactics that proliferated in the 1980s, Jesse Unruh took particular issue with "greenmail"—in which a company pays an inflated price for a block of its own stock to avoid a hostile takeover.

Unruh Urges Fight Against 'Greenmail'

By KATHRYN HARRIS,
Times Staff Writer

Alarmed by the tactics being used in corporate takeover battles, California State Treasurer Jesse Unruh has begun a nationwide campaign to urge pension funds to flex their muscle as investors if they object to "greenmail" or some of the other devices used to repel unwelcome takeover bids.

The "Big Daddy" of California Politics

Jesse Unruh was known for his larger-than-life personality, straightforward nature, dislike of corruption, and inimitable way with words.

Two of the most famous quotes attributed to California's "Big Daddy" aptly illustrate both his personality and his politics: "Money is the mother's milk of politics," and, referring to lobbyists, "If you can't take their money, drink their booze, eat their food … and still look them in the eye and vote against them, you don't belong here."

Unruh reached the height of California's power structure from very humble origins. The son of Kansas sharecroppers, he once said that he never wore socks before age 12, but his feet were so dirty, no one could tell. When he arrived in California in the early 1940s to work as a riveter, he slept in a chicken coop on a mattress stuffed with newspapers.

His personal knowledge of what it meant to be powerless showed in his politics. In 1959, he authored the Unruh Civil Rights Act, which became a model for national civil rights reforms. Unruh managed Robert F. Kennedy's presidential campaign in California and was with Kennedy when he was assassinated.

After Unruh left California's Legislature in 1970, becoming State Treasurer in 1974, he became known as the 81st Assemblyman— a nod to his lasting influence within the 80-member body. When he died of prostate cancer in 1987, then-Assembly Speaker Willie Brown placed in the Assembly chamber an 81st desk draped in black.

Jesse Unruh, 1970. The charismatic Jesse Unruh became a legend in California politics, both for his personality and his emphasis on both social and corporate reform.

invested under the basic "Wall Street rule," which posited that institutional investors voted for, and with, management. If an institutional investor disagreed with management, it simply sold its shares and invested in another corporation.

In the 1980s, many argued this approach no longer made sense as institutional shareholders had an increasingly large stake in the market. "If a number of large institutional shareholders don't like the management, to whom will they even be able to sell their shares, and at what price?" Robert A. G. Monks, head of the U.S. Department of Labor's office of pension and welfare benefits, pointed out. "The rule doesn't work anymore now that institutions dominate the market." If walking away was no longer a viable option for institutional investors like PERS, forcing management to change its policies was the only alternative. That meant taking a more aggressive stance against corporate policies that did not benefit the pension fund's investment.[5]

By the early 1980s, however, much of PERS stock was invested in indexed funds. Of the $6.6 billion PERS invested in stock, about half was invested in a Standard and Poor's index fund managed by Bankers Trust of New York. This meant that PERS owned stock in each of the corporations that were part of the Standard and Poor's 500 in the same proportion that these firms' stocks were represented in the index. As an investor in an index fund, PERS did not buy and sell stock immediately upon market changes, but rather held on to its stock for the long term.

Unruh realized that pension funds had to take a more active and aggressive stance in order to exercise their fiduciary responsibility both for the short term and the long term. In particular, he believed that the ongoing intense merger and takeover activity of the 1980s was wreaking havoc on pension fund investments. He was particularly concerned about the use of a practice called "greenmail" in takeover attempts.

Corporations trying to fend off a potential hostile takeover sometimes offered to purchase back any stock the corporate raider had already purchased. The takeover target typically paid the raider a higher price for the stock than the stock's public trading price. After the stock buyback, however, the stock price typically fell, resulting in a loss of value to the shareholders. This buyback practice left the target corporation independent, but it reeked of blackmail to Unruh and others since in the end, only the corporate raider ended up receiving a premium for the targeted firm's stock. Thus, investors began referring to it as greenmail.

Portrait of Robert A. G. Monks, 1993. Corporate governance advocate and former Administrator of the Office of Pension and Welfare Benefit Program for the U.S. Department of Labor, Monks believed that institutional investors like CalPERS should hold corporations accountable for actions and policies that harmed investors.

Herb Block cartoon from the *Washington Post*, April 21, 1985. Dubious corporate practices spurred Jesse Unruh in 1985 to form the Council of Institutional Investors (CII). Originally comprised of 21 pension funds, CII seeks to protect shareowner interests through education and advocacy.

Desiring to put an end to the practice, Unruh joined with John Konrad, Chairman of the Wisconsin State Investment Board, and Harrison J. Goldin, Comptroller for the City of New York, during the Spring of 1984 to discuss how pension funds could mobilize efforts against what they believed to be destructive corporate practices.[6]

Unruh also challenged his colleagues at other pension funds to join in the effort after a series of greenmail incidents drew his ire.[7] In 1984, for instance, Disney Productions paid New York corporate raider Saul P. Steinberg greenmail in order to avoid a take-over by him. Disney's stock price fell by 15 points, resulting in a $7.5 million loss for one of California's public pension funds, which had a significant investment in Disney. A greenmail case later that year involving Texaco gave Jesse Unruh the ammunition he needed to mobilize the nation's pension funds.[8]

Texaco's management had successfully avoided a hostile takeover attempt by the Bass Brothers Enterprises, retaining Texaco's independence by purchasing the Bass Brothers' 2 million shares of stock for 12 percent more than the stock was trading on Wall Street. No other investors, including PERS and STRS, which together owned about 1 percent of Texaco's stock, received such a buyback offer. Rather than file a lawsuit against Texaco, PERS sent its Chief Counsel, Gerald R. Adams, to Texaco's annual meeting. Adams spoke out against Texaco's "improper expenditure of corporate assets" at the meeting and also voted PERS shares against management proposals designed to give management more freedom. Although the management's proposals passed, PERS was making its mark as an active institutional investor.[9]

Unruh went to Wall Street to seek support for his plans for creating an organization to represent the rights of institutional investors. He made it clear that the group he wanted to form would not be anti-management, but rather pro-shareholder—a way of ensuring management acts in the best interest of shareholders.

On January 24, 1985, he and his partners formed the Council of Institutional Investors (CII). The CII's stated aim was acquiring information and developing policy to help its members protect their fiduciary interests and responsibilities. The CII had an initial membership of 21 pension funds representing more than $100 billion in assets.

Saul P. Steinberg, 1985. In an infamous example of greenmail, financier Steinberg forced Walt Disney Productions to pay him $325 million to avoid a hostile takeover in 1984. The ramifications were harsh for Disney's shareowners, as the stock fell by 15 points.

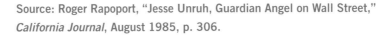

PERS Stock Portfolio, March 1985			
Company	% of Portfolio	Book Value (millions)	Market Value (millions)
IBM	4.8%	$215	$376
Exxon	2.2	94	173
GE	1.7	60	134
Standard Oil	1.2	40	97
ARCO	1.0	42	81
3M	1.0	61	79
AT&T	.9	52	68
DuPont	.9	58	67
GM	.8	52	61
Phillip Morris	.8	43	60

Source: Roger Rapoport, "Jesse Unruh, Guardian Angel on Wall Street," *California Journal*, August 1985, p. 306.

Phillips Petroleum Chairman and CEO William Douce, 1985. Phillips Petroleum Company became the first target for CII in 1989, when the investor group organized a meeting to discuss the company's recapitalization plan that Douce attended. The plan was ultimately modified and won shareowner approval.

By late 1985, the CII had 30 members representing $132 billion in assets. However, it had only one corporate member, US West, Inc. The other members were state and local pension funds and labor groups.[10] In order to become a member of CII, institutions paid annual dues of $100 per $100 million in assets, with minimum annual dues of $1,000 and maximum of $15,000. The group remained loosely organized for several years, with no permanent office or staff until 1988.

In 1989, the CII adopted a "Shareholder Bill of Rights" to emphasize its solidarity with all shareholders. The original bill of rights contained four basic provisions: One-Share, One-Vote; Equal and Fair Treatment for All Shareholders; Shareholder Approval of Certain Corporate Decisions; and Independent Approval of Executive Compensation and Auditors. In February 1985, CII representatives tackled their first big corporate issue: the Phillips Petroleum Company recapitalization plan. The CII invited the major players to a meeting at the office of Harrison J. Goldin, co-chairman of the CII and Comptroller of New York City, to a meeting. Realizing the significance of CII in the corporate market, arbitrageurs Carl Ichan and Ivan Boesky, both of whom held a substantial amount of stock in Phillips Petroleum, attended, as did T. Boone Pickens and Phillips Chairman and CEO William Douce. This was the first time that major arbitrageurs had met with representatives of a block of institutional shareholders. The CII members subsequently rejected the Phillips recapitalization plan. But because of that rejection, the plan was modified enough to win shareholder approval.[11]

PERS had to deal with another takeover battle a few months later, when T. Boone Pickens instigated a hostile takeover of Union Oil Company (Unocal), a California corporation. Before the takeover effort, Unocal shares were selling for $38 per share. The price surged to $53 per share after Pickens began purchasing the stock, but it fell to less than $30 per share when the takeover effort ended unsuccessfully.

Rather than attempt to sell its Unocal shares at $53, PERS held on to them. Unruh defended the pension fund's decision to retain its 630,000 shares of Unocal as the share prices went up and then down, "You don't sell index funds because the price goes up; you don't buy because it's going down. You look at the long-term of a company." PERS actions made a powerful symbolic statement of support for Unocal's management. (As it turned out, the PERS Board had agreed to sell 400 so-called "discretionary" shares in Unocal during the takeover battle.)[12]

Though its first high-profile encounter with T. Boone Pickens suggested the CII had a glowing future, some questioned the viability of the organization early on: how could the CII represent public pensions, labor groups, and corporate members at the same time when each of these groups could be expected to have different agendas? Would the CII remain as an information clearinghouse or would it seek to promote policy?[13]

Nevertheless, in December 1985, the Securities and Exchange Commission invited the CII to its December 1985 meeting in Atlanta, a gesture that acknowledged the CII was a significant voice in the financial marketplace. At the meeting, CII presented its Shareholder Bill of Rights as a proposal and promoted the position that corporate management should be restricted in its use of anti-takeover devices, such as poison pills and greenmail payments. John Shad, then-chairman of the SEC, was impressed. He proclaimed that the organization "may prove to be the most important development in investor representation since the creation of the SEC." Still, in response to the CII opposition to anti-takeover devices, Shad and SEC Commissioner Joseph A. Grundfest suggested that not all anti-takeover devices worked and that the market should be allowed to function without undue government interference.[14]

Unocal Chairman Fred L. Hartley announcing the end of a takeover bid, 1985. When entrepreneur T. Boone Pickens initiated a hostile takeover attempt of California-based Unocal, CalPERS refused to sell its 630,000 shares, making a strong statement of support for the company.

SEC Commission (*from left*) Joseph A. Grundfest, Charles C. Cox, John S. R. Shad, Aulana L. Peters, Edward H. Fleischman, 1986. The SEC invited the Council of Institutional Investors to its 1985 meeting in Atlanta—an action that reflected CIIs growing influence in the financial world.

Unruh remained strongly opposed to greenmail and other corporate practices that benefited only management. Management ousted by a successful takeover sometimes received extremely high bonus payments known as golden parachutes. These payments in theory compensated executives for their work, but lower-ranking employees who lost their jobs often received very little severance pay. He found the golden parachute agreement to be "particularly odious." Unruh was not alone in believing that these payments were unnecessary, financially unsound, and detrimental to shareholders' interests.[15]

The CIIs most high-profile encounter with corporate America came in 1987, after General Motors (GM), the nation's largest automaker, paid Board member H. Ross Perot $700 million for his GM securities when the Board ousted him from his seat. Perot had also founded and headed the GM Electronic Data Systems unit, which the corporation acquired in 1984. To Unruh and CII, the $700 million payment looked like "a tinge of greenmail."[16] CII members, who owned a total of 6 million shares of GM common stock and 1.2 million shares of its Class E stock, asked for an explanation.[17]

On December 17, 1986, Harrison Goldin, CII co-chair, waited with other CII members for GM chairman Roger Smith to show up for a meeting in New York City. Instead, Smith sent four deputies, which didn't please the CII representatives. The following month, Smith agreed to meet with the same group. This time, he came in person. He explained the Perot buyout in a closed-door meeting of about 30 people around a large table at Harrison Goldin's Manhattan office. Smith promised the group a big improvement in GMs performance. During the next two months, he participated in about 22 meetings with investor groups across the nation, clearly recognizing the burgeoning power of such groups.[18]

Still, by the late 1980s, it wasn't clear whether the tactics of shareholder groups were entirely effective. Pension-fund-sponsored proxy resolutions were costly and time consuming. PERS itself began to focus more on director relationships and specific corporate governance issues in the late 1980s, such as the poison pill, a device that greatly increased the purchase cost of a corporation that desired to remain independent.[19] An in-depth study of PERS shareholder activism, however, determined that its actions did indeed produce positive financial results.[20]

H. Ross Perot and GM Chairman Roger Smith at an Economic Club of Detroit luncheon, 1986. Recognizing the growing power of shareowner groups, Smith agreed to meet with CII in 1987 to discuss GM's $700 million payment to Perot when he was ousted from its Board.

Leadership Changes

Jesse Unruh's arrival on the Board wasn't the only significant leadership change at PERS in the early 1980s. In 1983, Carl Blechinger, the System's third Executive Officer, announced his retirement. A venerated figure within PERS, Blechinger had worked for the Retirement System for nearly three decades, including nine years at the helm. During that time, the public pension, Social Security, and health care fields all changed dramatically, as Blechinger noted in a parting column in PERS *Update* newsletter, describing his tenure as "hectic but fulfilling." [21]

PERS conducted a nationwide search for Blechinger's replacement, but ultimately chose Deputy Executive Officer Sid McCausland to fill the post. McCausland joined the System in 1981 as its first Deputy Executive Officer, to help Blechinger as PERS operations

Big Bear Airport, date unknown. The Big Bear City Airport District was one of 28 local agencies that joined CalPERS in 1980-81, bringing the number of contracting employers to 1,068. CalPERS growth and rising public profile in the early 1980s brought new challenges to the Board.

became increasingly large and multifaceted. A Petaluma, California, native, McCausland attended Occidental College in Los Angeles and UC-Berkeley and earned a graduate degree in public affairs. He served in a number of high-level State positions before joining PERS, including Director of CalTrans, Deputy Director of Finance, and Assistant State Treasurer. While at the Department of Finance, he also served as the Director's representative on the PERS Board.

The Board was also undergoing significant changes in the mid-1980s. Board Members increasingly were dealing with several controversial and very public issues. Many of these involved how to invest the Fund's money, particularly in regard to current social concerns. Should PERS, for example, invest in companies that did business with South Africa's apartheid regime? Also, should PERS investment staff, which was responsible for investing a huge sum of money, receive salaries more closely aligned with those of investment managers in private industry? Finally, and perhaps most important, PERS in the 1980s and 1990s would have to actively seek to redefine its relationship to the State.

The salary disparity between PERS investment staff and their counterparts in private industry reportedly caused some personnel problems. In 1984, the System's chief investment manager, Mel Peterson, left PERS. His salary was $48,000 at the time, but he reportedly received about twice that in his new job with a Seattle bank.[22] PERS then hired Greta Marshall, who had been president of Bay Banks Investment Management in Boston. Marshall's starting salary was $125,000, with the possibility of additional income in performance bonuses. Simply stated, her job was to outperform the market. If money managers could not attain the PERS Board's objectives, Marshall said, "You will see this Fund indexed in a few years, totally across the market."[23]

Lincoln Plaza

PERS emergence as a powerful force in the investment world found physical expression in 1986 with the completion of its new corporate headquarters, Lincoln Plaza, in downtown Sacramento. Named after the Lincoln Elementary School that once occupied the same site, Lincoln Plaza was a two-block complex bounded by Third and Fifth Streets and P and Q Streets.

For the previous 20 years, PERS had occupied the Resources Building on Ninth Street. PERS had provided the financing to construct the building, which was commonly known

Sid McCausland (pictured in a CSEA newsletter), 1984. McCausland was CalPERS first Deputy Executive Officer, joining in 1981 to assist CEO Carl Blechinger with the expanding administrative duties of the growing System. After Blechinger retired in 1983, McCausland took over as CalPERS fourth CEO.

Illustration of Lincoln Plaza, date unknown. In 1986, CalPERS completed construction on its stunning new headquarters in downtown Sacramento.

as the Retirement Building, and then leased office space there from the State. PERS paid for the construction of Lincoln Plaza and had the option under legislation that Congressman Robert Matsui introduced in 1984 to sell the building to the State and then lease it back.[24]

Both PERS and STRS had originally intended to occupy Lincoln Plaza. However, STRS decided to purchase and occupy its own building. For $18 million, STRS bought a three-story building on Folsom Boulevard and leased the empty space to other tenants.[25]

With a cost of $72 million, Lincoln Plaza was reportedly among the biggest and most expensive buildings in Sacramento's downtown.[26] The five-story structure included extensive exterior and interior foliage and a waterfall in an outside courtyard. While the building attracted some criticism, it was built with foresight: Lincoln Plaza would not quickly become outdated or outmoded. For example, it included raised floors in order to allow for easier wiring and reconfiguration of offices. PERS Executive Officer Sid McCausland was quoted in the *Golden State Report* stating that Lincoln Plaza "is going to be a building that will win a lot of architecture awards and will probably be as attractive 50 years from now as it is on the day it opens."[27]

While the building was both very large and architecturally stunning, it fit well with the surrounding neighborhood, which was mostly residential. Shaped as an irregular pyramid, the building's five floors each physically stepped back from the floor below it. The environmentally friendly building design included extensive terracing and utilization of as much natural light as possible.[28]

Growing Pains

The emergence of PERS onto the national investment scene and the participation of powerful political figures such as Jesse Unruh in PERS operations led to a number of controversies in its new Board room. Assemblyman Louis Papan, who sponsored much PERS-related legislation in the early 1980s, championed a bill that would have placed new retirement funds into a Pooled Money Investment Account under the control of the State Treasurer—at that time Jesse Unruh. Some observers feared that the account would be subject to undue political influence and voters rejected the plan.[29]

Soon after, another issue arose regarding political influence on PERS investment strategy. In 1986, the California Legislature adopted a bill that called for divestiture of stock in companies that did business in South Africa as a protest against apartheid, a system of racial segregation and discrimination. As of January 1, 1987, the Legislature prohibited the State's pubic pension funds from making new investments in companies or financial firms doing business with South Africa. By January 1, 1988, the funds had to begin a three-year divestiture of stock in all companies doing business in South Africa. The law made an exception for companies that adopted resolutions against expanding operations in South Africa.[30]

Protestors in Los Angeles rallying against South African apartheid, 1985. CalPERS and other California public pensions divested stock holdings from companies that conducted business in South Africa as a protest against its racist political system.

From Learning to Earning:
Award-Winning Lincoln Plaza Makes the Grade

After decades of squeezing into various cramped office spaces throughout downtown Sacramento, in 1986, the employees of CalPERS finally moved into a space of their own—the beautiful, modern, and environmentally friendly Lincoln Plaza complex. It was a momentous occasion—and it took a tremendous effort on the part of CalPERS officials to make it happen.

The State Department of General Services, which handled facilities for State employees, did not want the Retirement System to build a new structure, but CalPERS contended it was not General Services' decision. When General Services would not relent, CalPERS Board President Bob Carlson suggested suing the agency, and his fellow Board Members agreed.

The action was unprecedented for CalPERS, and it was a difficult legal battle. In the end, however, CalPERS won not only permission to build the facility but Carlson insisted on writing the statute that would provide for its construction. He explained in a 2000 interview that he didn't want "any other controls … on the building of our new building, because it was going to be an investment for us, and we were going to pay for it."

More than 20 years after Lincoln Plaza's construction, CalPERS staff and Executives continue to take pleasure in their stunning home. "It's one of the finest public buildings in all of the United States to house public agency workers," Carlson said. "I'm very proud of it. I think the members of our staff are very proud of it, and every Board Member that's ever been on our Board is very proud of this facility we now have here."

Lincoln Elementary School, 1915-16. CalPERS headquarters, Lincoln Plaza, takes its name from the school once located on the site.

Former Lincoln Elementary students at the groundbreaking for the Lincoln Plaza building with Board Member Bob Carlson (*far left*), 1983.

Article in the *Sacramento Bee*, July 8, 1984. More than 4,000 yards of concrete went into construction of the building, which spans two city blocks.

A building with 'PERS-onality'

It may not be the tallest one around, but the Lincoln Plaza building under construction at 4th and P streets is certainly one of the biggest office buildings in Sacramento. Covering a two-block site once occupied by Lincoln School, the five-story, battleship-sized structure will provide approximately 500,000 square feet of usable space. Work was started last summer, and the job is expected to take about two years to complete.

Like mother birds giving nourishment to their young, above and right, giant cranes feed heavy structure supports for the building to assembly workers. The complex is designed to accommodate 2,200 employees, including 750 from the Public Employees Retirement System (PERS) and 350 from the State Teachers Retirement System. Space that could house another 1,100 employees will be leased.

The general contractors are Nielsen, Vasko & Earl Inc. (NVE) of Sacramento and M.M. Sundt Construction Co. of Phoenix, and Dreyfuss & Blackford of Sacramento is the architect. Coldwell Banker Commercial Real Estate Services is handling the leasing.

The PERS-owned building will have five terraced levels and a six-story atrium in the center. The ground level will include a 250-seat auditorium and dining area surrounding an open courtyard, complete with a two-level waterfall.

Bee photos/Morgan Or

Lincoln Plaza atrium, ca. 1980s. The stunning design of CalPERS headquarters made it an instant Sacramento landmark.

Exterior of Lincoln Plaza, 1990s. The building's concrete exterior and surrounding landscaping serve to stabilize temperatures inside throughout the year.

presented by the
Northern
California
Chapter

American
Society of
Landscape
Architects

1988

award of excellence

Lincoln Plaza
Sacramento, CA

Danielson
& Associates

Award of Excellence presented to Lincoln Plaza by the Northern California Chapter of the American Society of Landscape Architects, 1988. CalPERS headquarters has won numerous accolades, both for its physical beauty and its environmentally conscious design.

Lincoln Plaza expansion, 2005. In 2005, CalPERS completed a two-building winged addition to its headquarters. The elegant buildings became known as Lincoln Plaza East and West, while the original building was called Lincoln North.

Governor George Deukmejian, 1983. Governor Deukmejian proposed to the PERS Board in 1986 that the State's contribution to the Fund be reduced in order to help balance California's State Budget deficit. While Jesse Unruh supported the proposal, CEO Sid McCausland adamantly opposed it.

CalPERS Board Member Charles Valdes, 1979. Valdes supported CEO Sid McCausland, whom Jesse Unruh wanted to fire. Though many people involved with CalPERS shared Valdes' support, Board Members ultimately voted 7-6 to fire McCausland in June 1986.

The South African divestiture brought to the surface some key issues that would continue to churn in the 1990s. Should PERS not invest in firms that conducted business deemed socially destructive or irresponsible, or should PERS invest in companies that provided a reasonable return on investment regardless of their lines of business? Inside and outside the PERS Board room, experts and interested parties made strong arguments on both sides of the issue. With billions of dollars to invest, some argued, the ramifications of every investment should be thoroughly addressed.[31]

PERS huge pool of money also attracted California Governor George Deukmejian's attention. In 1986, the State Budget was running a deficit and Deukmejian wanted to balance it with help from PERS.[32] A similar attempt had failed in 1982, when Assemblyman Papan introduced a bill providing for a three-month suspension of all employer contributions to PERS to assist in balancing the State Budget. Assemblyman Papan apparently submitted the bill, A.B. 1253, at the request of Governor Jerry Brown's administration. Governor Brown signed the bill, but the PERS Board voted against transferring funds to cover the State contributions due PERS. Ultimately, the State did make its $187 contribution to PERS.[33]

Deukmejian was more successful. With Unruh's assistance, he gained support of the PERS Board for a $404 million reduction in the State's contribution to PERS during the following fiscal year. PERS Executive Officer Sid McCausland actively opposed the arrangement, however, and tension mounted between McCausland and Unruh.[34]

At one Board meeting, Unruh and another Board Member, Charles Valdes, had a verbal sparring match on the subject, which the *Sacramento Bee* chronicled the next day. "We were yelling and screaming at each other," Valdes later recalled. "He wanted to fire Sid McCausland … The advantage I had was that every time I spoke, the audience would cheer and clap and when Jesse spoke, they'd boo. It was quite a thing … It was even broadcast all over the Capitol, so everyone was listening to it and knew about it." After the tumultuous Board meeting, Unruh told Valdes in private that he would continue with his effort to oust McCausland.[35]

Unruh and Deukmejian had strong views and both wanted to promote their agendas at PERS. While Deukmejian wanted to utilize PERS funds to help with the California Budget, Unruh wanted McCausland out of the PERS administration. There was talk of a conspiracy between Unruh and Deukmejian. Together, they managed to get the votes they needed to oust McCausland. "That was a very cold morning," Valdes recalled. "Everyone knew what was happening and why and so on, and so I didn't say much about it at all."[36]

In 1986, the Board of Administration voted 7-6 to fire McCausland. The vote split along political interests. The Board Members who represented State and public agency employees cast the six votes in favor of McCausland, while the seven opposing votes came from the elected State officials and State appointees.

In 1987, it became clear that Jesse Unruh was not well. He made what turned out to be his last public appearance at the third annual CII meeting in Santa Monica during April 1987. Already, many members of the CII and others had been questioning the organization's effectiveness and Unruh's illness clearly meant the CII would soon be lacking his strong leadership skills. At the meeting, Unruh gave a bluntly realistic assessment of the organization he had worked so hard to create. "We have learned that concerted action is virtually impossible, given our fiduciary obligations and divergent interests," he said. "We have learned not to move too fast or expect too much. As an organization, our value has been to share information and let members make their own decisions." Some observers interpreted these remarks as a reflection of Jesse's own state of health.[37]

Unruh died of prostate cancer in 1987. Governor Deukmejian then nominated U.S. Representative Daniel Lungren as California's next Treasurer, and therefore, a new Member of the PERS Board. While the California Assembly confirmed the appointment, the Senate rejected Lungren's nomination. Lungren appealed to the State Supreme Court, and the Supreme Court sided with the Senate. Consequently, California lacked a Treasurer for several months. In the meantime, however, Elizabeth Whitney, an Unruh protégé, served as Acting Treasurer.[38] Perhaps not surprisingly, after Unruh's death, during the June 1988 primary, voters approved a measure that imposed limits on campaign contributions to Statewide candidates.[39]

Soon another political figure began encroaching upon the territory formerly occupied by Unruh. California Controller Gray Davis, who had made an unsuccessful run for Treasurer in 1974, became one of three co-directors of CII in 1988, taking Unruh's former seat. Some suspected that Davis was now preparing a run for Governor as early

The Jesse Unruh Office Building, Sacramento. Formerly "California State Office Building No. 1," the State building on the Capitol Mall, renamed after Unruh's death in 1987, is one sign of his lasting influence in California politics.

Dale Hanson, 1991. In April of 1987 Hanson stepped up to fill the CEO position vacated by Sid McCausland. A tireless and charismatic proponent of corporate governance reform, Hanson raised CalPERS national profile significantly.

PERS logo (*left*), 1985, and CalPERS current logo (*right*), 2007. The Retirement System changed its name in 1992, adding a "Cal" in front of PERS in reference to its home State.

as 1990. One of Davis' agenda items at CII, as well as at PERS and STRS, was making sure that the pension funds enforced the investment restrictions against South Africa.[40]

While the Treasurer's Office remained without a permanent replacement, PERS soon filled its top spot. In April 1987, a new Executive Officer came to PERS. Dale Hanson, formerly the Wisconsin Retirement System's Chief Operating Officer, took the helm.[41] Hanson later recalled that one of his first impressions of PERS was the lack of high technology in the workplace. "When I came here in 1987, we had one personal computer in the entire organization, in this marvelous organization. For the most part, the entire System was using dummy terminals connected to a big, blue box downstairs."[42] In the new computer era, this would soon change.

Not long after moving into its new headquarters, Lincoln Plaza, modern technology did take hold at PERS. Soon, most staff had their own personal computers. One of the major changes new technology brought to the System was the move toward the so-called paperless file, which increasingly made the computer system the primary location for the System's records. This allowed PERS to implement new customer service programs for its growing membership. PERS set up a Telephone Information Center, where staff could pull up callers' information based on their Social Security numbers and answer specific questions using manuals, including online manuals.

CalPERS & the State of California

In 1992, the Retirement System changed its name from "PERS" to "CalPERS," distinguishing the System from public employees' retirement systems in other states, which often used the same acronym. For years, officials within the Retirement System expressed concern over confusion that sometimes arose because of this. A Retirement System newsletter item from October 1983 noted that an Associated Press article about a casino hotel that owed money to Nevada's retirement system "referred to 'PERS' without noting that it was Nevada's PERS, not California's." This and similar news stories "continue to confuse PERS members, retirees, and employers," the article noted. "Board members and staff receive many phone calls every time a new story hits the papers." The name "CalPERS" solved this problem at a time when the Retirement System's public profile was rising rapidly.

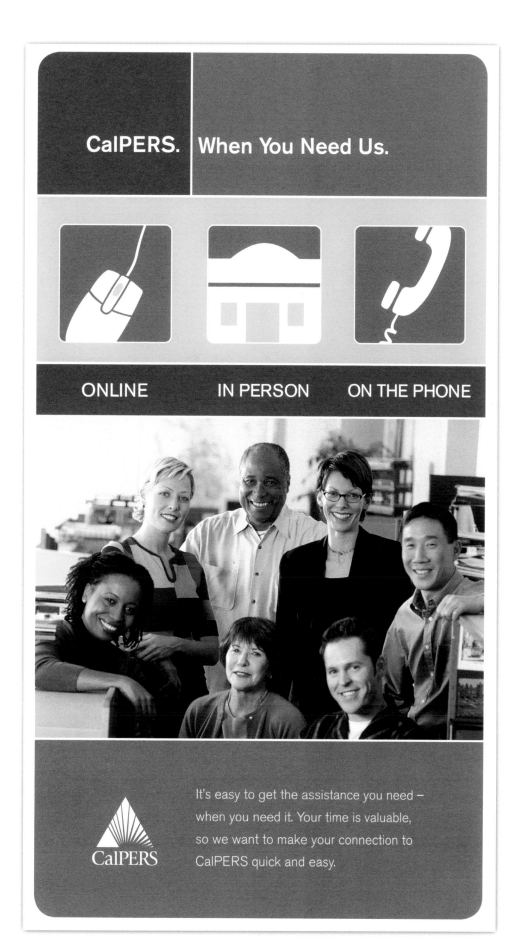

Pamphlet on CalPERS customer service outreach efforts, 2006. CalPERS increasing use of computers instead of paper files in the mid-1980s boosted its ability to serve members more quickly and effectively.

Drawing Attention: CalPERS in Cartoons

As CalPERS has grown over the decades, so has its public profile. One vivid indicator of this is the frequency with which CalPERS has served as fodder for editorial cartoonists. While it made the occasional appearance in cartoons in its early decades, by the 1990s, CalPERS was a regular subject of cartoonists' pens. Following are just a few of those depictions from the last two decades.

Cartoon published in *Pensions & Investments*, 1991.

Cartoon published in *Pensions & Investments*, 1992.

Cartoon published in *Pensions & Investments*, 2004.

Cartoon published in *Pensions & Investments*, 2004.

Cartoon published in *Pensions & Investments*, 2005.

Cartoon published in *Pensions & Investments*, 2005.

At the outset of the 1990s, CalPERS was one of the largest pension funds in the United States, with substantial assets invested in corporate America. But it was also subject to California State government jurisdiction. In the 1990s, tension mounted between California's Governor and CalPERS over control of the Fund and its accounting operations.

The 13-Member CalPERS Board of Administration set policy for the System's 800 employees and Executive Staff. State and public agency employee groups elected six of the Board Members; the Governor appointed four Members; the State's Treasurer and Controller served as Ex Officio Members; and the California Legislature appointed one Member to represent California's citizens. The Board of Administration's major responsibilities included overseeing management, setting investment targets and asset allocation goals, devising corporate governance policy, and making recommendations to the State Legislature on bills affecting CalPERS and retirement issues.[43]

While the CalPERS Board did make recommendations to the Legislature on particular pieces of legislation, some Legislators had their own ideas about the best policies for CalPERS. During the Spring of 1991, for example, the Legislature considered several proposals that sought to set guidelines for, or otherwise restrict, CalPERS investment policy. Legislation aimed at limiting CalPERS ability to invest in companies doing business in the People's Republic of China or Northern Ireland was defeated, as was another bill designed to require CalPERS to invest a particular portion of its assets in small businesses, primarily in California.[44]

CalPERS Investment Guidelines by Asset Class

Asset Class	June 1990	Range Guidelines
Domestic Equities	39.50%	30-50%
Domestic Fixed Equities	39.60	30-50
International Equities	6.30	5-15
International Fixed Income	3.90	2-10
Real Estate	8.90	5-15
Alternative Assets	0.03	0-2
Cash Equivalents	1.90	2-10

Source: Harvard Business School, "California PERS," Harvard Business School case N9-291-045, July 10, 1991.

Governor Wilson Seeks Control of CalPERS

The State of California confronted a weak economy in the early 1990s and Governor Pete Wilson increasingly viewed the CalPERS Fund as a means to balance the State Budget. The Legislature passed a $56.4 billion spending plan in 1991, but balancing the Budget required about $14 billion in cuts plus tax increases. The Budget crisis prompted Wilson to propose a controversial plan to make up for the shortfall.[45]

Wilson called for restructuring the CalPERS Board by decreasing it from 13 to nine members and granting the Governor authority to appoint five of those Board members. The Legislature would appoint the remaining four members. Steve Olsen, the Deputy Director for the California Department of Finance, stated that Wilson's rationale for this proposed change was "to make the makeup of the Board a little more balanced in terms of Constitutional obligations." In other words, the *Sacramento Bee* reported in June 1991, the Wilson administration "believes the Board heavily favors the CalPERS members at the expense of the State."

Cartoon published in the *Sacramento Union*, May 17, 1991. Legislative proposals to use pension fund money to help alleviate the State's Budget crisis provoked sharp response from critics.

Dedication. Vision. Heart. The CalPERS Story

He also proposed using $1.6 billion from CalPERS accounts to help alleviate the State's Budget crisis. Wilson wanted to close two Retirement System reserve accounts the Legislature established in 1982 to protect retirees against inflation. His plan evoked quick opposition from Yolanda Solari, President of CSEA and Jake Petrosino, a CalPERS Board Member who represented public agency members.[46] "We have struggled to build a solvent retirement system for 60 years that will provide retirees a decent pension," Solari said in a prepared statement. "Gov[ernor] Wilson wants to disband it with a nod."

California lawmakers also worked on plans designed to alleviate the Budget crisis that involved use of CalPERS funds. The CalPERS budget was running a surplus and the premise of these plans was that these surplus funds would be best utilized in balancing the State Budget. One of these potential compromises devised by Senator David Roberti, Governor Wilson, and Senator Ken Maddy called for $7 billion in tax increases, welfare payment reductions, and appropriation of $1.2 billion of CalPERS Retirement Fund earnings. State employee groups strongly opposed this plan as well.[47]

The Wilson Administration warned that without such a change in the fiscal relationship between CalPERS and the State, as many as 22,100 State jobs could be eliminated—about one-fourth of California's State employees, excluding those employed by the California State University, University of California, the Department of Motor Vehicles, and CalTrans, all of which were financed through special funds. Administration officials said Wilson needed up to $1.6 billion from CalPERS to avoid the massive layoffs. Wilson also wanted greater control over the CalPERS Board to increase his influence over the System's Fund.[48]

The CalPERS controversy attracted national political attention. U.S. Congressman Edward R. Roybal announced in June 1991 that a Congressional committee would investigate the situation. Roybal, chairman of the House Select Committee on Aging, had strong words about the various proposals involving CalPERS funds. If implemented, he said, "the proposals before the California Legislature … would mirror the actions of corporate pension plan raiders who divert the retirement savings of workers and retirees and leave them with empty promises."[49]

CSEA President Yolanda Solari (*center*) with past Presidents Frances Dillon (*left*) and Margaret Dean, 1990. Solari and other CSEA leaders and members strongly objected to Governor Pete Wilson's proposal to take $1.6 billion from CalPERS funds to help balance the State Budget.

Governor Pete Wilson, 1991. Among the reasons groups cited for opposing Governor Wilson's plan was the idea that by appropriating money from the CalPERS Fund for the State Budget, Wilson would violate a central tenet of pension tax law.

CII pointed out other problems in Wilson's plan to take funds from CalPERS to balance the State Budget. "There is one basic of pension tax law: the fund must be for the exclusive benefit of employees or their beneficiaries," CII's Sharon Cayelli stated. "By messing with that formula *and* taking money from the pot at the same time, Wilson is definitely risking [CalPERS] tax-exempt status." Phyllis Borzi of the U.S. House of Representatives' Education and Labor Committee expressed similar sentiments, remarking that it was "hard to imagine any interpretation of the IRS exclusive benefits rule that says taking money from the fund will benefit employees."[50] Opponents to Wilson's plan also had an overarching concern about its potential repercussions across the country. "We don't want a precedent to be set through this type of legislation," Cayelli said. "Other states could look to solve their fiscal problems the same way."[51]

In the days leading up to the vote in the California Legislature on Wilson's plan to use CalPERS Funds to balance the State Budget, the level of rhetoric ratcheted up. Board Member Jake Petrosino called it "a despicable act to garner short-term gain." But Wilson didn't back down. He responded sharply that the CalPERS Board intentionally "frightened retirees in California. I really think that's contemptible … We're not going to let them suffer any cut in their benefits. What we are trying to do is reduce the taxpayers' contributions by excessive earnings."[52]

CalPERS Board, 1991. Standing (*from left*): David Woods, Bill Crist, Madale Watson, Charles Valdes, Jake Petrosino, Kurato Shimada. Seated, middle row (*from left*): Bill Ellis, Tom Clark, Lorrie Ward. Seated, front row (*from left*): Lillian Rowett, Bob Carlson, Kathleen Brown. Many CalPERS Board Members sharply criticized Governor Pete Wilson's plan to dip into CalPERS accounts and tried to compromise with him. Wilson refused, and the Legislature passed a bill containing his proposal in 1991.

State Controller Gray Davis also opposed Wilson's plan, calling it "naked aggression." State Treasurer Kathleen Brown, a CalPERS Board Member, remarked that under Wilson's proposal, he would be "one person in charge of $63 billion of assets," and asked him rhetorically, "Isn't the job of governor big enough?"[53] CalPERS Executive Officer Dale Hanson called it his "first hostile takeover."[54]

In an attempt to resolve the dispute through compromise, CalPERS Board President Bill Ellis wrote to Governor Wilson and offered the State access to the $1.6 billion in reserves held in two accounts. CalPERS, however, would retain the two accounts and guarantee that retirees continue receiving benefits that remained equivalent to 75 percent of the purchasing power of the retirement benefits at the time of retirement. Wilson said the offer was "too little, too late."[55]

Even Cal-Tax, the California Taxpayers Association, took sides in the matter. Cal-Tax had commissioned a study that supported Wilson's plan on the grounds that current pension benefits were too rich and cost the State too much money. The organization particularly opposed CalPERS cost-of-living-allowances, believing they were too high. Some CalPERS members, however, struck back.

On June 24, Governor Wilson formally outlined his public pension plan. Contained in Assembly Bill 702, the measure allowed the State to use $1.7 billion from CalPERS reserve funds to reduce the State's contribution to the pension fund. Wilson said this would bring $560 million in savings to the State Budget. The bill also proposed that the Governor have the authority to appoint the entire CalPERS Board.[56]

Despite CalPERS best lobbying efforts, the California Legislature passed A.B. 702 on June 30, 1991. This legislation allowed the State to eliminate the two accounts the Legislature created a decade earlier to fund cost-of-living increases and other benefits for CalPERS members. These special reserve accounts, the Investment Dividend Disbursement Account (IDDA) and the Extraordinary Performance Dividend Account (EPDA), had been left largely untapped by CalPERS because the investment returns from its fund were sufficient to pay the required member benefits. A.B. 702 also repealed the additional benefits allowed under the 1982 legislation that created the IDDA and EPDA reserve accounts, thereby allowing for permanent liquidation of these accounts. The legislation directed that these funds be used to reduce employer

HANDS OFF

OUR BENEFITS

California State Employees Association
SEIU LOCAL 1000

contributions to CalPERS, including a $727 million allocation to the State in order to offset pension contribution costs.[57] In addition to the legislated "raid" on CalPERS funds, A.B. 702 granted actuarial control of CalPERS to a Governor-appointed actuary. (Subsequently, the State Legislature rejected the actuary that Wilson nominated on three occasions.)[58]

Opponents to A.B. 702 mobilized their forces quickly and soon presented voters with Proposition 162, a Constitutional amendment counteracting the bill. Opposition to Proposition 162 came primarily from Cal-Tax. In November 1992, California voters passed the measure—but just barely. About 5 million voters supported the measure, while approximately 4.9 million voted against it, making the split about 51 to 49 percent.

Proposition 162 essentially overturned A.B. 702 and amended Article XVI, Section 17 of the California Constitution. While it neither returned any of the raided funds nor restored the IDDA and EPDA reserve accounts, the measure did return to the CalPERS Board the "plenary authority and fiduciary responsibility for investment of monies and administration of the System." Proposition 162 also added wording in the Constitution that precluded the Governor and Legislature from changing the number of members, their terms, and the method of selection or removal of members of the Retirement Board.

A labor union rally in support of Proposition 162, 1992. Unwilling to accept defeat, CalPERS supporters quickly united around Proposition 162—a ballot initiative designed to counter the damage done by A.B. 702. Voters approved the measure in November 1992, restoring to the Board investment and administrative authority of the CalPERS Fund.

Proposition 162: A Grassroots Effort

Once Proposition 162 became a ballot measure, California law prohibited CalPERS from actively campaigning for the proposal or spending any money or resources in its support. The System could take a formal position on it—which, of course, it did—but that was about as far as CalPERS involvement could go.

That is not to say that the proposition lacked organized support—quite the contrary. Public sentiment had been building against Governor Pete Wilson's attempts to access CalPERS funds to balance the State Budget. CalPERS members and retirees felt the government "should not be able to take or

put their hands on money that belongs in the trust, money that is really deferred compensation of the employees," recalled Board Vice President Bob Carlson some time later.

Newspaper editorials echoed the sentiment, along with private and union pension groups.

"If this happens to State employees, it could happen to any other employee that belonged to any other type of pension plan," Carlson explained.

CSEA and numerous other labor, employee, and retiree organizations and State groups banded together to mount a formidable grassroots campaign. The organized effort that emerged was reminiscent in many ways of the campaign for Proposition 5, which paved the way for the Retirement System's creation. In fact, in a show of support, retirees formed a human chain around the CalPERS headquarters building's four-block site, demonstrating solidarity and protection of their benefits.

Once again, an organized and dedicated group rallied on behalf of the State Retirement System. What they lacked in entrenched political power, they made up for in spirit and tenacity, organizing marches, letter-writing campaigns, and informational workshops. Their perseverance paid off with the narrowest of victories—a 51 percent margin—as yet again, a groundswell of grassroots support clearly illustrated that Californians believed in the concept of a public employee retirement system devoted to providing security to its members.

Proposition 162 supporters gathering signatures during their campaign for the measure, 1992. Dedicated groups of volunteers worked diligently across the State to rally support for the ballot measure, which passed with a narrow 51 percent margin.

Proposition 162 brought important and far-reaching changes to CalPERS. Effective July 1, 1992, CalPERS gained authority to appoint its own actuary and prevent future raids by the State. In addition, CalPERS received budgetary autonomy so that it was no longer required to receive State approval of its budget. Richard Koppes, CalPERS General Counsel, said in *Pensions & Investments* that the measure would "give us a lot more flexibility to hire and compensate people and to really make them accountable." This was particularly true of CalPERS investment staff.[59]

Proposition 162 also effectively shielded CalPERS corporate governance policies and practices from State meddling. David Felderstein, Chief Consultant for the Senate Public Employee and Retirement Committee, noted that Proposition 162 acknowledged that CalPERS has "adopted policy which says it's within the best interest of the System for them to do the kind of corporate governance efforts they do, and Proposition 162 insulated them from legislative interference."[60]

The voter-approved measure also reoriented CalPERS relationship with the State. While the proposition granted CalPERS plenary authority over the administration of the System, it actually provided this form of independence to every public retirement system in California. This meant that CalPERS was no longer required to receive State approval for new positions or expenditures. CalPERS gained budgetary control, but remained a State agency with obligations to the State. CalPERS still could not set retirement benefits, which as a product of Retirement Law, can only be changed legislatively. CalPERS then administers those benefits. While the System has independence over its budget and investments, it still submits investment reports to the Legislature.[61]

CalPERS exercised its new budgetary autonomy in an open forum. CalPERS Board Member Robert F. Carlson described the budget-setting process at the pension fund thusly: "We hold hearings. We invite the Legislature. We invite the Budget Committees in both houses of the Legislature. We invite the State Treasurer and the State Auditor General to comment on our budget and they don't respond. But we do a great job in amending and changing and justifying our budget as it goes through each year."[62]

The Wilson Administration, however, did not relinquish its attempt to extract funds from CalPERS to tend to the Budget crisis. In 1992, another piece of legislation, S.B. 1107, gave the State authority to delay its share of employer

States Seeking Aid on Budgets From Pensions

By RICHARD W. STEVENSON

Growing numbers of state and local governments are drawing money from or slashing contributions to their pension funds, raising concerns about the funds' ability to pay retirees decades from now.

Excerpt from an article in the *New York Times*, July 21, 1991. Governor Pete Wilson's attempts to use CalPERS Fund to balance the State's Budget reflected a growing trend that alarmed public pension funds, labor groups, and lawmakers alike.

contributions due to the pension fund. Previously, the State made its contributions quarterly. The new schedule permitted semi-annual payments, six months in arrears. Before the State made any payments under this schedule, however, another law, S.B. 240, established yet another guideline for the State contributions to CalPERS. Under S.B. 240, the State could make its contributions annually and one year in arrears. The State sought to make payments under this arrangement into 1997.

The CalPERS Board of Administration sued the State to overturn the laws that permitted the delayed payments. In 1997, the California Supreme Court ruled in favor of CalPERS and ordered the State to pay CalPERS $1.36 billion. The State argued unsuccessfully that the delayed payments did not materially impair the Retirement System because all payments due would be made. CalPERS successfully argued that delayed payments reduced earnings, compromising the Fund's actuarial soundness. [63]

Council of Institutional Investors founding members, ca. 1994. After a slow period for the corporate governance movement in the late 1980s, institutional investors made significant strides in their efforts in the early and mid-1990s.

Even before CalPERS had successfully restored its Fund, a new type of threat to public pensions in California emerged. Assembly Bill 3252 provided public employees with the opportunity to establish their own alternative defined contribution (DC) retirement plans. The bill, sponsored by Assemblyman Howard Kaloogian, would permit CalPERS and CalSTRS members to establish a DC plan as an alternative to their current defined benefit (DB) plan. Mutual fund companies, brokerage firms, and insurers stood to gain a tremendous amount of new business if public pension fund members began to create their own alternative retirement plans.

Both CalPERS and CalSTRS opposed the Kaloogian proposal. CalPERS suggested that the plan had been drawn up too hastily and that it was flawed. More important, it wasn't clear that Kaloogian's bill would protect State employee retirement funds. The State Senate rejected the bill in July 1996.[64]

Corporate Governance in the 1990s

After Jesse Unruh helped establish the Council of Institutional Investors, pension fund-sponsored corporate governance became a fact of life for corporate America. Despite some early successes at Texaco and General Motors, corporate governance activism seemed to wane during the late 1980s. Sarah Teslik, CII executive director during this time, compared getting the attention of corporate managers to "trying to take a bone from a dog."[65]

Beginning in 1989, however, the tide began to turn. Pension funds successfully turned back corporate measures deemed to restrict share value. They defeated anti-takeover measures promoted by Honeywell, Inc. The Wisconsin public employee pension fund sponsored shareholder resolutions that limited management's ability at Kmart and Champion International to implement poison pill defense programs. Both resolutions passed with shareholder approval.[66]

CalPERS also initiated a discussion with the SEC in 1989 that would allow shareowner groups to become significantly more effective in their attempts to take on underperforming companies. Executive Officer Dale Hanson sent a letter to Linda C. Quinn, director of the SEC's division of corporate finance, in November asking the commission to review the proxy voting process. The SEC's proxy rules were created in the 1940s, when shareowners were mostly individual investors. Such investors traditionally voted with management or, if they did not agree with management, sold their shares.

By 1990, institutional investors owned an estimated 45 percent of all corporate stock.[67] As such investors became more prominent, rules on shareowner communications with one another increasingly seemed outdated. Institutional investors did not want to simply sell their holdings if they were unhappy with management; they wanted management to change. As Dale Hanson put it in a 1993 column he wrote for *Financial Executive*, "If we buy an office building and the property manager isn't properly maintaining it, we don't sell the building—we change the property manager."[68] But proxy rules made it difficult for shareowners to communicate with one another if they had concerns about a mutual investment. Institutions had to immediately disclose their talks if the sum of shares they owned of a company's stock exceeded 5 percent. If the conversations involved a certain number of owners, proxy rules could compel them to obtain SEC clearance for mailings.[69]

In his letter to Quinn, Hanson outlined 48 specific proposals for proxy changes that addressed shareowner communication restrictions and other issues. Other institutional investors voiced support for the changes and offered proposed reforms of their own, sparking a national debate among investors and corporations. SEC officials soon made it clear that they were considering changes to proxy regulation, though corporate board rooms urged against it. The Business Roundtable, an organization representing major companies, issued a statement contending that the "exercise of ... concentrated voting power" of institutional shareholders could hurt the interests of individual shareowners and damage corporate competitiveness. [70]

Nevertheless, in 1992, the SEC issued proposals for sweeping reforms, including the removal of limitations on communications between shareowners. In his 1993 *Financial Executive* column, Hanson praised the changes the SEC ultimately made, noting that "the SEC has adopted some rules with which we're fairly satisfied that give owners a little more freedom to communicate with each other, or a 'safe harbor.'" [71] Years later, *Pensions & Investments* credited the proxy rule changes with "transform[ing] pension funds into powerful corporate governance players." [72] Anne Hansen, then-Deputy Director at the Council of Institutional Investors, recalled in the article that when "the boards of directors saw that shareholders were allowed to communicate with each other about what was wrong at these companies, they fired their underperforming CEOs." [73]

More than a century ago, Georg von Siemens, a founder of the Deutsche Bank, said that, "If one can't sell, one must care." This dictum was truer in the 1990s than ever before. [74] CalPERS, as a major stakeholder in many of the United States' largest and most important corporations, had a fiduciary responsibility to "care" about the viability of its holdings. The concept of corporate governance by this time reflected the idea that shareowners had the right to protect their investments. Economist Peter Drucker of the Claremont Graduate School took note of this in an article published in the *Harvard Business Review* in early 1991. He called the emergence of pension funds as corporate watchdogs "one of the most startling power shifts in economic history." [75] Drucker also predicted that pension fund activism "and government efforts to raid public pension funds are going to be the hottest subjects of the next 10 years." [76]

Certainly, CalPERS activism grew more intense in the early 1990s. Dissatisfied with previous attempts to effect change by meeting with a particular corporation's CEO, CalPERS decided during this time to bypass the CEO in favor of direct contact with a corporation's outside directors. This more aggressive stance toward corporate governance underscored CalPERS commitment to supporting efforts to improve the financial performance of firms in which it invested. "We tried a kinder, gentler approach," then-Executive Officer Dale Hanson said in 1993, "but we concluded that wasn't working."

Excerpt from an article in the *New York Times*, December 18, 1990. CalPERS request that the SEC reform its proxy rules to allow more communication among shareowners sparked a heated national dialogue within the investment and business communities.

A Debate Grows Over Proxy Rules

SAYING that insurgent shareholders already score at least partial victories in three-quarters of proxy fights, America's largest corporations asked the Securities and Exchange Commission yesterday to turn aside pleas from institutional investors to change the system.

The Business Roundtable, which represents most major companies, warned against corporate policies being set in "back-room negotiations" among a handful of institutional shareholders.

● ● ●

The S.E.C. has let it be known that its staff is considering changes in proxy voting rules, and some institutions hope the changes will make it much easier for them to gain influence over corporations. Until now, much of the debate has been dominated by big institutions, mostly those representing public pension funds.

CalPERS Largest Corporate Holdings, 1991

Company	Shares	% of Company	Market Value	% of Portfolio
General Electric	6,684,300	.72%	$478,762,987	2.1%
IBM	4,232,500	.74	471,923,750	2.1
Exxon	8,455,100	.68	438,608,312	1.9
Philip Morris USA	7,972,700	.85	381,693,012	1.7
AT&T	7,365,893	.67	272,538,041	1.2
Merck & Company	2,933,400	.64	261,439,275	1.1
WalMart Stores	7,833,200	.68	245,766,650	1.1
Proctor & Gable	2,745,876	.75	238,204,743	1.0
Coca-Cola Company	4,771,800	.57	216,628,650	1.0
General Motors	4,560,400	.75	212,628,650	.9

Source: Harvard Business School, "California PERS," Harvard Business School case N9-291-045, July 10, 1991, p. 17.

Corporate CEOs typically were not fond of CalPERS new approach—perhaps because the approach seemed quite effective in forcing corporate responsiveness.[77]

In the early 1990s, CalPERS identified 12 firms in which it held substantial equity positions that could benefit from improved financial performance. CalPERS called it the "Focus List." By early 1993, CalPERS representatives had met with outside directors of seven of these corporations, including Boise Cascade Corporation, Champion International Corporation, and Time Warner, Inc., among others. CalPERS saw results from this effort.[78] At Boise Cascade, for instance, management agreed to implement corporate governance principles that CalPERS had drafted. Champion International agreed to consider appointing outside directors nominated by shareholder groups. In a prepared statement in 1993, Hanson said CalPERS was "enormously pleased" with the response the list garnered.[79]

To increase its effectiveness as an activist shareholder, CalPERS also considered increasing its stock holdings of particular companies. In 1993, about 80 percent of CalPERS $25.5 billion investment in equities was invested in index funds. CalPERS owned less than 1 percent of the outstanding stock in more than 1,500 firms. Although

Huge Fund Turns Up Proxy Heat

Criticizes Policies At 10 Big Companies

Excerpt from an article in the *New York Times*, March 21, 1992. CalPERS unveiled a new tool in its corporate governance efforts in 1992—its yearly "Focus List" of companies in which the System invested that it felt were underperforming.

CalPERS investment in these firms represented a substantial sum of money, a holding of less than 1 percent did not provide CalPERS with clear leverage over management. Even with this level of investment, however, CalPERS had been able to influence change. "Imagine the effect we could have if we owned say 3 percent" of a firm's outstanding shares, Dale Hanson told *USA Today* in 1993.[80]

The approach Hanson was considering was a relatively new strategy known as relationship investing. In relationship investing, the investor raised its stake from, for example, less than 1 percent of a firm's outstanding stock to 3 percent, thereby dramatically increasing its influence over the firm's board and management. According to one study, corporations subjected to relationship investing outperformed the Standard & Poor's 500 index by 30 percent during the previous six years.[81]

Not surprisingly, CalPERS approach encountered some criticism and opposition. John Budd, chairman of the New York consulting firm the Omega Group, said CalPERS had "gone too far. They're investors, not managers."[82] Yet, some of the very corporations on CalPERS Focus List acknowledged that CalPERS approach was effective and beneficial.

New Investments

Around the same time that Hanson was spearheading CalPERS effort to reform governance at targeted corporations, some critics pointed out that CalPERS own management and investment structure needed attention. On the investing front, CalPERS real estate portfolio was not performing well. With $5 billion invested in real estate, the pension fund experienced negative performance results during 1992. While CalPERS management continued to support a 10 percent fund allocation in real estate, Board Member Jake Petrosino called for a reduction in the pension fund's real estate exposure.[83] Even CalPERS chief of investments, DeWitt Bowman, admitted the pension fund's real estate holdings were underperforming. With property prices nationwide declining 5-10 percent per year, real estate was not a good performer. Bowman noted that in relative terms, real estate was not doing that badly. But "on an absolute basis, it's been a disaster," he told The *Wall Street Journal*.[84] Clearly, the real estate market statewide was suffering, but this did not mean investors should simply pull out of this market.

Entrance to the Las Flores community in Orange County, date unknown. Las Flores was among the communities in which CalPERS invested after launching a single-family housing development program in 1992. The program stimulated the State's economy while offering CalPERS attractive investment opportunities.

CalPERS found a new way to achieve positive returns from investment in real estate: It expanded into single-family homes. During the early 1990s, CalPERS and its real estate partners had started 36 housing projects valued at about $670 million. CalPERS projected a 20.3 percent return from this investment. CalPERS program focused primarily on the first-time homeowner and the system made a significant contribution to this market. The Construction Industry Research Board estimated that CalPERS and its partners would initiate 5 percent of all housing starts in California during 1993. CalPERS continued to invest in housing throughout the 1990s.[85]

CalPERS also decided to enter the private equity market in 1991, earmarking about $2 billion—or 3 percent of its more than $63 billion in assets—to buy direct stakes in companies, as opposed to stocks or bonds.[86] The System did not make any private-equity investments for more than a year, however, as it examined its options and familiarized itself with the arena. In 1993, CalPERS entered into its first private-equity deal, when it teamed up with Houston-based Enron Corporation to form a natural gas partnership. The agreement called for CalPERS and Enron to each contribute $250 million for three years; CalPERS agreed to invest cash in the partnership while Enron invested stock. The partnership, Joint Energy Development

Investments L.P., or JEDI, planned to invest in natural gas assets including pipelines, gas storage facilities, and other investment opportunities, as well as Enron stock.[87] Dale Hanson said in a prepared statement that the deal "should generate a very favorable rate of return to the partners."[88]

CalPERS also entered the media industry. During December 1994, the pension fund announced a plan to purchase cable television networks with Comcast Corporation. Comcast would own and operate the venture; CalPERS would have a 45 percent stake in the partnership.[89]

Comcast sign outside of its customer care center, 2004. In December of 1994, CalPERS planned to work with Comcast Corporation on a project to purchase cable television networks. This venture marked one of CalPERS first direct partnerships with a corporation.

Direct partnerships such as those with Enron and Comcast offered CalPERS the opportunity to take a more active role in managing its investments. However, even in these ventures, CalPERS typically took a subordinate role, leaving actual management and operation responsibility to the experts.

Personnel Issues

Corporate governance may have been the hot topic for pension funds in the 1990s, but this was only one of several important pension fund tasks. Hanson acknowledged that Board Members and others wanted him to pay more attention to CalPERS functions other than corporate governance. "A lot of people think this is my single crusade," Hanson was quoted saying in a 1993 *Wall Street Journal* article. "It isn't … The board has said to me, 'You're spending a lot of time on the asset side. Spend more time on the liability side.'" In other words, the Board wanted him to pay more attention to the benefit side of the system.[90]

As Hanson pressured corporate CEOs to link their salary to performance, CalPERS was linking a portion of the Executive Officer's salary to performance. As of January 1, 1994, Hanson was eligible to receive an incentive bonus, or merit pay increase, based on his overall performance. The *Wall Street Journal* noted that Hanson's regular salary was equivalent at that time to those of the top officers at smaller state pension funds, even though he was heading the nation's largest public pension.[91]

Despite the dramatic growth in the CalPERS fund, pressure on top management seemed to increase. In late 1993 DeWitt Bowman, CalPERS chief investment officer, retired after five years with the fund. A seven-month search for his replacement ensued. CalPERS hired Sheryl Pressler, formerly the director of retirement funds at

A Healthy Regard for CalPERS

If people outside of California started hearing the CalPERS name on the news in the mid-1990s, it was most likely for one of two reasons: the System's influential corporate governance efforts or President Bill Clinton's frequent accolades for its health care program.

As President Clinton lobbied in support of his plans for national health care reform, he often cited CalPERS as a model for his envisioned health care purchasing cooperatives. Every year, CalPERS negotiates contracts with HMOs and PPO health plans on behalf of its members—a system similar to the regional alliances Clinton was advocating nationwide.

Yet Clinton was not alone in watching the CalPERS program. Numerous media outlets marveled at CalPERS success in using its purchasing power to negotiate manageable rates for its members. *Washington Post* columnist David Broder noted that CalPERS was able to negotiate "miniscule" rate increases in 1992 and 1993; in 1994, he wrote, CalPERS "actually got the insurers and health maintenance organizations it deals with to reduce their rates."

CalPERS made several important strides in its health benefits program during the early and mid-1990s, including the introduction of standardized benefits, the creation of the PERS Choice PPO self-funded health plan, and the publication of its first *Health Plan Quality and Performance Report* to help members make health care choices. Many of its accomplishments remain rooted in CalPERS approach to negotiating on behalf of its members.

Attendees at a rally outside the White House supporting health care reform, 1994. President Bill Clinton frequently cited CalPERS successful health benefits program as a model for the national reforms he advocated.

Ironically, Clinton's proposal, which required all public employees and retirees to join regional alliances, would have put CalPERS health benefits program out of business had it passed. CalPERS officials were not shy about making their position clear. Then-Board President William Crist said CalPERS supported the objective of Clinton's proposal, but "We have concerns about the impact of his reform proposal on our successful, cost effective health program, and the almost 1 million Californians it represents."

McDonnell Douglas Corporation of St. Louis. Described by a former colleague as "very smart and very cautious in her comments," Pressler's talents and abilities received wide praise. With a starting salary of $175,000 plus incentives, Pressler was expected to deal immediately with money management marketers. Board Member Petrosino said he expected that she would "be inundated with business people who swamp her like a cloud of locusts—taking her to lunch and dinner. She will be lucky if she can turn around without being bumped into. The marketing people are going to be making a full-court press." Pressler's job security, however, was not guaranteed by contract. Rather, she served at the pleasure of the Board.

Pressler quickly proved her investing acumen. Soon after joining CalPERS, she recommended the System invest much more of its money in stocks. The Board agreed, and stock allocation rose from 49 to 63 percent of CalPERS total assets.[92] Industry watchers considered this shift in distribution a bold move, but it was a successful one. CalPERS became one of the best-performing public pension funds in the nation. The System's assets more than doubled during her six-year tenure, growing from $78 billion to $168 billion.[93] Her leadership within the CalPERS Investment Office won accolades for the value it brought investment operations; in the broader investment community, she led efforts to improve the terms and conditions of private equity deals so that pension funds could make better-informed investment decisions. Pressler moved back into private industry in 2000, accepting a position heading Atlanta-based Lend Lease Real Estate Investments. "The value she and other members of the investment staff have added has been literally in the hundreds of millions of dollars a year," then-Board Member Michael Flaherman said upon Pressler's departure. [94]

Change also came to CalPERS top position. Dale Hanson resigned from CalPERS in May 1994 and announced that he was becoming CEO of American Partners Capital Group, a new organization that would focus on private equity investing, including single-family housing in California. A widely recognized pioneer in the corporate governance movement, Hanson raised the system's profile and influence in the movement both nationally and internationally. Under his leadership, CalPERS saw its assets increase from $44 billion in 1987 to more than $80 billion. Although there was some speculation that Board tension over Hanson's focus on investments hastened his departure, Hanson was ready at that point to pursue other opportunities.

Chief Investment Officer Sheryl Pressler (*third from left*) with (*from left*) Robert Aguallo, Assistant Executive Officer for Investment Operations; Bob Boldt, Senior Investment Officer, Global Equity; and Charles Valdes, Board Member, date unknown. Pressler joined CalPERS as Chief Investment Officer in 1994 and significantly expanded the System's assets with bold investment strategies.

CalPERS General Counsel Richard Koppes served as interim Chief Executive while the system searched for a new Executive Officer. Within two months, CalPERS announced the hiring of its sixth permanent CEO: James E. Burton, who had served as a top aide to several former California politicians, including Jesse Unruh. After his appointment, Burton said he would project "a less strident voice for change," reflecting a similar toned-down climate within the larger pension fund industry.[95]

New Directions for Corporate Governance

With Burton at the helm, CalPERS corporate governance program evolved and expanded. The system began placing more emphasis on structural change in the corporate boardroom. During 1994 and 1995, CalPERS sent letters to the largest 300 firms in the Standard & Poor's 500 requesting that they prepare written guidelines for their board practices. The requested guidelines would cover procedures for appointment of board members, holding of meetings, and choosing of outside directors. CalPERS reported that 53 percent of the companies that received letters had already prepared such guidelines or were in the process of doing so. CalPERS General Counsel Richard Koppes disclosed that 86 companies had provided exceptional responses.[96] Several firms, however, declined to provide any response.

CalPERS also turned its attention to boardrooms outside the United States. With the system's stake in foreign corporations growing, CalPERS decided to launch an international corporate governance program. The system planned to focus its international program on countries where it had substantial equities investments. By the summer of 1994, this included Japan, France, Germany, and Great Britain.

CalPERS had to balance political, economic, and cultural concerns when investing overseas. In Japan, for example, company boards tended to be controlled by a relatively small group of influential businessmen. Shareholder rights were not well protected and corporations typically paid out small dividends. This, of course, conflicted with CalPERS mission to promote shareholder rights. While CalPERS didn't "want to be seen as the Ugly American," Richard Koppes said, the firm anticipated "actively voting. And not always with management."[97]

In its first venture into international corporate governance, CalPERS opposed a merger of two French firms in which it owned stock. Matra S.A., an industrial

CEO Dale Hanson at his CalPERS retirement party, 1994. Popular and respected within CalPERS, Hanson was regarded as a powerful foe by many business leaders because of his unrelenting corporate governance efforts while heading the Retirement System.

Jim Burton, date unknown. Two months after Hanson's resignation, Jim Burton was hired as CalPERS sixth CEO. Formerly a Board representative and Assistant Executive Officer for Investment Operations, Burton was more than qualified to lead the Retirement System into the coming decade.

conglomerate, acquired Hachette, a publishing firm, but CalPERS claimed that Matra had not disclosed to interested shareholders a large order of military equipment sold to Taiwan one week prior to the merger. If this transaction had been disclosed, the claimants stated, the exchange ratio of Hachette to Matra stock would have been at least 20 to 5 rather than the agreed upon ratio of 13 to 5.[98] The claim was ultimately unsuccessful, but the move sent a signal that "activist U.S. shareholders are becoming more vocal and watchful of the way their foreign corporate holdings are governed and how they perform," *Pensions & Investments* reported in April 1993. [99]

CalPERS also flexed its financial muscle in Japan. During the summer of 1994, CalPERS cast its proxy votes at several shareholder meetings of Japanese corporations. With nearly $4 billion worth of stock in 280 Japanese companies, CalPERS was a significant player in Japan's capital markets. The system supported several proposals to raise dividends and one proposal to allow more open debate at shareholder meetings. It also voted against various proposals at other firms due to either excessive or inadequate dividend payout rates.[100]

After the California Legislature lifted the ban on South African investment in 1991, CalPERS also considered reinvesting in South Africa. CalPERS consultant, Wilshire Associates Inc., reported after the lifting of the ban that South Africa had a well-developed infrastructure and financial system. The political situation remained a major concern, though many financial consultants felt South Africa badly needed foreign investment to stimulate its economy.[101]

Indeed, the mood toward South Africa had changed considerably with the dismantling of apartheid. Some even questioned the financial wisdom of divestment in the first place. Wilshire Associates Inc., estimated that divestment resulted in $529 million in "net investment-opportunity losses" to CalPERS.[102] The System began investing in South Africa once again.

CalPERS also considered investing in foreign nations that the United States had once regarded as virtual enemies. In September 1995, the CalPERS investment committee upgraded investment opportunities in China from a "not recommended" to a

Celebration in Soweto, South Africa, over the release of civil rights leader Nelson Mandela from jail, February 1990. California's Legislature lifted its ban on South African investments in 1991. By then, there were signs of improvement in the country and many financial consultants believed investment would help its situation. Apartheid formally ended in 1994.

"recommended" rating. The committee ranked nations on several factors including: political risk, future growth prospects, liquidity, market openness, market regulation, and taxation. Although China had limited investment opportunities, the potential for growth in its economy appeared quite substantial.[103]

Affordable Housing

On the homefront, Labor Secretary Robert Reich was urging CalPERS and other pension funds in the mid-1990s to invest in "socially useful" programs such as affordable housing. Reich had said that pension funds were "positioned like no other force in the American economy to raise incomes and spark new jobs."[104] Reich subsequently differentiated between social investments and economically targeted investments (ETIs) that are designed to produce competitive financial returns. Then-Board President Bill Crist noted in 1994 that CalPERS had about $1.6 billion in ETIs, primarily in housing. Political pressure to utilize pension fund assets for economic development was evident in Senator Barbara Boxer's (D-CA) statement that "ETIs could mean jobs and affordable housing and better, stronger communities."[105]

California Controller and CalPERS Board Member Gray Davis wrote an article in which he discussed how CalPERS investment in affordable housing was a good move for the pension fund. By taking over where savings and loans left off after the bank scandals of the late 1980s, CalPERS real estate investment not only helped construct homes for first-time buyers, it put construction workers back to work. And its preliminary returns were 20 percent. "As proud as we are of the social returns of this investment," Davis wrote, "we can crow about its economic value as well."[106]

With unprecedented growth in size and influence and sweeping changes in almost every area of its existence—from leadership to investment policies to fund autonomy to street address—it was difficult to imagine CalPERS could have another era as eventful and transformative as the 1980s to mid-1990s. But then again, CalPERS had developed a habit of exceeding expectations.

Bill Crist, date unknown. In 1994, then-Board President Bill Crist recognized that CalPERS $1.6 billion in economically targeted investments held the potential to stimulate California's economy.

6: Building a Secure Tomorrow

The turn of the 21st century brought unprecedented change around the world and at CalPERS. The Retirement System was tested by world events, challenged by ups and downs of the financial markets—and empowered by technological advances and opportunities for extraordinary innovation.

When the System emerged from these challenges, it ascended to new heights. CalPERS redoubled its corporate governance efforts with stunning success. Growth in membership and assets soared. The workplace thrived, with state-of-the-art technologies complementing the System's open, diverse, and progressive culture. Throughout this time of change, CalPERS kept its focus on its members and employers—building new and better ways to provide health benefits, retirement benefits, and other services.

In 1994, CEO Dale Hanson retired, handing the CalPERS helm to James E. Burton. Burton entered State service as an analyst for the California Highway Patrol in 1976, became Governor Jerry Brown's Deputy Chief of Staff in 1982, and later headed the State's Commission on State Finance. In that role, he worked closely with State Treasurer Jesse Unruh and often sat in for him on the CalPERS Board. He then served as Gray Davis' Deputy when Davis was State Controller, and often represented him on the Board as well. In 1992, Burton joined CalPERS as Assistant Executive Officer for Investment Operations.

Under his tenure as CEO, CalPERS excelled further in the public pension community in terms of quality customer service, member confidence, fiscal security, and management effectiveness.

From the outset, Burton was interested in developing all areas of the System's operations. Well aware of the State's ailing economy, Burton wanted to pursue creative investment opportunities within California and build upon the State-focused programs CalPERS already had in place, such as the Member Home Loan Program. He wanted to make better use of the Internet and other technology in CalPERS customer service operations and its internal communications. And he wanted to strengthen the System's strategic planning process.

Former CEO Jim Burton (*left*) and former Board President William Crist, date unknown. Burton served as CalPERS CEO from 1994 to 2002.

The nature of the CalPERS mission—providing financial security for public employees in their retirement—hinges upon careful, long-term thinking. Though there had been efforts to do so, CalPERS engaged in developing its most formal, enterprise-wide strategic plan. Under Burton's recommendation, the CalPERS Board adopted its first Strategic Plan in 1996. The plan documented the System's goals, articulated its commitment to fostering a first-rate work environment and culture, and reinforced its business philosophy for the next decade. CalPERS also enacted Annual Plans to work incrementally toward the goals of the Strategic Plan. "We were trying to build the infrastructure here, both in our business technology and human infrastructure, to improve how we provide service to our members," Burton explained in a 2000 interview. "It was hard work, but [it] worked."[1]

Another prominent figure notable for advances and growth of the CalPERS Fund and in the security of members' retirement and health benefits was Dr. William D. Crist. He was elected to the Board in 1987 and became Board President in 1992. During his tenure,

CalPERS prominently advocated strong corporate governance principles requiring the attention and dedication of company officers, directors, and shareowners. As a Professor of Economics and scholar, he wrote scores of articles about collective bargaining in higher education, public retirement systems, and corporate governance.

In 2002, Burton retired from public service, moving to a career in the private sector financial world. The Board of Administration appointed Fred Buenrostro to lead the System in the new millennium. Buenrostro brought many years of public service experience and a network of relationships. Prior to becoming CalPERS CEO, he was the Chief Deputy Director of the Department of Personnel Administration, where he was responsible for the overall administration of the Department. He also served as the Director's top advisor on a wide range of policies and programs affecting State employees. In that role, he also sat on the CalPERS Board for many years. He also served as the representative to the CalPERS and CalSTRS Boards for two State Controllers, three State Treasurers, and the Director of the Department of Personnel Administration.

Buenrostro led the System's efforts to ensure retention and recruitment of senior investment officials. His leadership emphasized the pursuit of innovative health care initiatives that ensured quality health care at reasonable costs, while also protecting the insurance pool. And he further emphasized a workplace environment that resulted in CalPERS being a destination employer.

Protecting Retirement Benefits

The nature of the CalPERS mission—providing financial security for public employees in their retirement—hinges upon careful, long-term thinking. Front and center in this philosophy, of course, is ensuring quality service to its membership, which grew from more than 1 million in 1996 to more than 1.5 million in 2006. And key to protecting the financial security of members is protecting its Fund. Once CalPERS gained the unfettered ability to invest in common stock in the 1980s, the Board was able to build the Fund dramatically—bringing its assets from $100 billion in 1996 to more than $200 billion a decade later.

In 1992, Proposition 162 was passed by the voters to protect CalPERS and other public pension plans from raids by legislative or executive bodies. The effort, led by organized labor, was to prevent the Governor from tampering with the assets of the Fund. At the root of the matter were several moves by the Wilson Administration to

CEO Fred Buenrostro, 2003. In 2002, Buenrostro became CalPERS seventh CEO. He previously served as the Chief Deputy Director of the Department of Personnel Administration.

Return on Investment Rises 20% for Calpers

SACRAMENTO, June 18 (AP) — The California Public Employees' Retirement System reported today that it had a 20.1 percent return on investments in the year that ended on March 31, up from an 8 percent return a year earlier.

Calpers is one of the largest institutional investors in the world. It manages assets of $99.6 billion, providing retirement and health benefits to one million current and retired public employees and their families.

In a report delivered to the Calpers investment committee, the pension consultant Wilshire Associates said the strong performance was helped by an asset allocation policy adopted in December 1994.

The policy calls for a three-year shift of fund assets into the higher-returning equity markets. The one-year Calpers return on total equity investments yielded 26.8 percent.

"The Calpers fund has more than doubled over the last 10 years due to continued top performance," said Charles Valdes, the Calpers investment committee chairman.

The report indicated several other factors that helped performance, including active international equity and bond managers and private equity investments, Calpers said.

Excerpt of an article in the *New York Times*, 1996. Thanks to savvy investing decisions, CalPERS fund skyrocketed from an impressive $100 billion in 1996 to more than $200 billion in 2006.

CalPERS Public Agency Employers:
An Overview

Though CalPERS was created to provide benefits for State employees only, today more than 1.2 million of its members work for cities, counties, schools, and other local public agencies. The 2,600-plus public agency employers that contract with CalPERS are a vital and valued part of the System. They hail from every corner of California, representing an extraordinary range in size and function and reflecting the diversity and uniqueness of California itself.

The Golden Gate Bridge Highway & Transportation District

Los Angeles County Office of Education

CalTrans

Los Angeles County Office of Education employees, 2007. With more than 78,000 members receiving benefits, the Los Angeles County Office of Education is one of CalPERS largest contracting employers. The agency, which has contracted with CalPERS since 1971, manages benefits for more than 70 school districts and serves more than 1.7 million school-age children.

A Golden Gate Bridge Highway and Transportation District employee, 1994. The Golden Gate Bridge Highway and Transportation District was formed in 1928 to finance, design, and construct the Golden Gate Bridge, which links San Francisco to Marin County. Sixteen years later, it joined the Retirement System. Today, the district oversees the bridge, Golden Gate Transit, and the Golden Gate Ferry, and more than 600 of its employees are CalPERS members.

CalTrans employees, 2002. More than 300,000 CalPERS members today are State employees, working for agencies such as CalTrans. Founded as the Bureau of Highways in 1895, CalTrans today has more than 23,000 employees. Its workforce includes attorneys, cooks, engineers, ferryboat deck hands, toll collectors, highway workers, and numerous others. As with all State agencies, CalTrans employees have been CalPERS members from the System's inception.

Russian River Fire Protection District

Russian River Fire Protection District employees evacuating a woman and her cats after a flood, 2006. Employees of the Russian River Fire Protection District provide fire, rescue, and emergency medical services to about 10,000 residents of Sonoma County. The 17-square-mile district—which has contracted with CalPERS since 1985—encompasses vineyards and redwood forests, as well as commercial and residential areas.

Santa Cruz Consolidated Emergency Communications Center

A Santa Cruz Consolidated Emergency Communications Center employee, 2006. The Santa Cruz Consolidated Emergency Communications Center provides 911 dispatch and other public safety services to the County of Santa Cruz as well as the Cities of Santa Cruz, Capitola, and Watsonville. Its employees have been in CalPERS since the center was established in 1995. Currently, more than 80 center employees belong to the Retirement System.

Murrieta Valley Cemetery District

Murrieta Cemetery District employee doing landscaping work at the district's cemetery, 2007. The Murrieta Valley Cemetery District is one of CalPERS recent additions, having joined as a contracting agency in December 2006. The property it oversees, Riverside County's Laurel Cemetery, is more than a century old, and was maintained by volunteers for decades. In 1938, members of a local historical society formed the district after learning the property needed to be part of an association to receive certain funding. As of 2007, the district's two employees were both in CalPERS.

Nevada City

Nevada City, late 1800s. One of California's historic gold rush towns, Nevada City was incorporated in 1851, making it one of the State's oldest cities. It began contracting with CalPERS more than a century later, in 1965. A booming town of 10,000 in 1850, Nevada City is much smaller today, with about 2,800 residents. More than 30 city employees are covered by CalPERS.

withhold its employer contributions to the Fund in order to use the money to balance the State's General Budget. These efforts included legislation designed to have the Governor control who was appointed actuary to the System, and thus control the actuary's setting of the annual employer contribution. The Administration gained budgetary relief when it changed the method of payment of contributions. These actions so enraged a group of retirees that they held a symbolic protest on the sidewalks of the CalPERS building—locked hand in hand around the four-block headquarters to protest what they believed was political interference. This was, in part, the start of a grassroots effort that resulted in the passage of Proposition 162, ensuring against future political interference. And, as for the money lost by the actions of the Wilson Administration, CalPERS sued to restore the funds. Ultimately the case, *Board of Administration vs. Wilson*, ended with the Governor required to restore $1.36 billion to the Fund. General Counsel Peter Mixon identified it as one of the most significant court cases for CalPERS.[2]

Meanwhile, CalPERS was experiencing excellent investment returns. In 1999, proposals were passed by the CalPERS Board of Administration for retirement benefit equity and to improve retirement benefits for State and classified school employees and retirees. The changes were signed into law.

Soon thereafter in 2003, in the wake of a crippling electricity crisis, Californians took the drastic step of recalling Governor Gray Davis, a former CalPERS Board member and a supporter of the System, in a historic special election. In his place, voters elected movie star, body builder, and longtime Republican activist Arnold Schwarzenegger.

By this time, the downturn in the financial markets had reduced the market value of assets for CalPERS, and employers—who enjoyed a holiday from making contributions to the System during the previous four to five years—were suddenly being required to resume contributions. For many employers, this created a hardship since the economic downturn was also affecting their revenue sources.

Critics of defined benefit plans were said to use this time as an opportunity to try to completely change the benefit design of CalPERS and other pension funds.

Governor Gray Davis (*left*) and Governor-Elect Arnold Schwarzenegger, 2003. Following a defeat in California's historic gubernatorial recall vote, Davis, a former CalPERS Board Member, sat down with Governor-Elect Arnold Schwarzenegger.

Against a backdrop of a budget deficit, in 2004 Schwarzenegger proposed eliminating the CalPERS defined benefit pension plan and replacing it with a defined contribution program. Labor groups recognized this as a serious new threat to California's public workers and retirees.

Under a defined benefit pension plan—the kind of plan CalPERS has administered and funded from its inception—participants are guaranteed a specified sum each month for the rest of their lives when they retire. The amount is based on their age, years of service, and highest average salary, regardless of the stock market's rise and fall. Under defined contribution plans, which are closely akin to 401(k) plans, the employer and employee both contribute a fixed amount. When employees retire, their account balances depend on how much was contributed to their fund and the success of its investments. Assuming the stock market performed well and the Fund's investments were solid, employees would receive a lump sum that would support them for the rest of their lives upon retirement. Labor groups maintained that retirees would be left penniless if they outlived their 401(k) asset plan.

CEO Fred Buenrostro had seen similar attempts to switch retirement plans before in California, which he described as the "poster child" for the defined benefit/defined contribution debate. "To those who are proposing it, replacing a defined benefit plan with a defined contribution plan always seems like a new concept," Buenrostro said in a 2005 speech. "Actually, the idea comes out about every 10 years or so. It is trotted out during economic downturns as a way to fix government costs, and trotted out during upswings as an 'empowerment' tool—a way for individuals to take personal charge of building their future," he said. "In truth, it is neither." [3]

A voter initiative campaign was gearing up by a group sympathetic to Assemblyman Keith Richman, who lobbied for the switch to a defined contribution plan. But the plan to take the initiative forward began to unravel when it was asserted by the Attorney General's office that it would, by its nature, have eliminated death and disability retirement for police and firefighters' widows. Opponents of the move to defined contribution plans also pointed out that the change would not have resulted in any first-year budget savings, and the cost of setting up the plan would have made the State's financial situation worse that year, not better. CSEA strongly opposed changing the plan, as did numerous labor groups, who mounted a media campaign

Cartoon published in *Pensions & Investments*, 1996. Efforts to overhaul CalPERS and other State pension funds from defined benefit to defined contribution plans periodically surfaced in California. In 2004, Governor Arnold Schwarzenegger again proposed a switch to defined contribution plans, which are similar to 401(k) plans.

blasting the proposal. Two of Schwarzenegger's appointees to the State Teachers' Retirement System voted against the initiative. They were later recalled from their posts by the Governor.

Early in 2005, after the nonpartisan Survey and Policy Research Institute found Schwarzenegger's public approval rating had dropped from 59 percent in January 2004 to 43 percent in April 2005, he abandoned the defined contribution initiative and established the Post-Retirement Benefits Commission. The Commission, comprised of six members appointed by him and six appointed by the Legislature, is expected to come up with recommendations for funding of post-retirement benefits. Their report was due in January 2008.

While this debate garnered many headlines, the System was also working on a variety of programs to serve its members and employers. In 1999, it supported S.B. 400, a bill passed by the California Legislature that revised the benefit formulas for most State and school system members for the first time in decades to ensure benefit equity.

Innovative Investments

In the late 1990s and 2000s, CalPERS investment portfolio has remained relatively consistent in terms of the proportions of each of its asset categories. As of December 31, 2006, public equities made up 63.2 percent of CalPERS portfolio—40 percent of which were U.S.-based and 23.2 percent international. Fixed income instruments, or bonds, made up 23.1 percent. Real estate investments comprised 7.5 percent, and private equities, 5.6 percent.[4] "Throughout the 11 years I've been here, there have been ups and downs in the market, but our assets have continued to grow and outperform the market," Patricia Macht, CalPERS Assistant Executive Officer of Public Affairs, noted in a 2006 interview. "During the economic downturns, our investment staff maximizes its purchases; often they are able to buy stocks at bargain-basement prices. When the market's really high, we ride that, because we're invested across the board in all of the stocks. We're also well diversified in all of the asset categories."[5]

At the same time, the CalPERS Board expanded the reach of its portfolio, investing in promising new ventures, including emerging markets and environmental technologies, and launching new investment initiatives. In 1990, CalPERS established a new

Protestors outside of a fundraiser for Governor Arnold Schwarzenegger, 2005. Dissatisfaction with Governor Schwarzenegger surged in 2005, bolstered by growing disenchantment with his proposal to change State pension funds to defined contribution plans. Schwarzenegger later abandoned his proposal.

program specializing in private equity investments called the Alternative Investment Management (AIM) program. With more than $35 billion committed to investments in this asset class by the mid-2000s, CalPERS became one of the largest private equity investors in the world. By September 30, 2006, the AIM Program had generated profits of $9.4 billion for CalPERS.

During this era, CalPERS also found great success with corporate governance funds. In 1996, the System hired California-based Relational Investors (RI), a fund that earned a 25.4 percent annual return on average over the next decade. RI worked— and continues to work today—by targeting underperforming public companies that it believed could benefit from improved corporate governance. Once it makes its investment, RI discusses investment objectives and the company's performance with its managers. With the company's board, RI talks about strategic corporate governance and management issues. And, since the Fund typically acquires equity positions of less than 10 percent, RI also communicates with other shareowners to gain their support. If the company continues to underperform or where other factors are warranted, RI sponsors shareowner proposals or seeks representation on the board.[6]

The CalPERS Board adopted an Economically Targeted Investments policy in 1993. Through this initiative, CalPERS committed itself to making investments designed to produce a competitive rate of return, while also creating economic benefits for areas and populations within California. Almost all of these investments were in two asset classes, private equity and real estate. They have remained so in recent years, while growing to encompass the gamut of California's diverse economy. One example was San Diego-based Delimex—a supplier of frozen Mexican foods to two California wholesale food chains. Delimex approached CalPERS about a possible partnership to expand in California. The company had $27 million in revenues, $15 million in cash flow, a proven track record, and a promising future in its market. CalPERS invested $25 million—$5 million as a co-investment and $20 million with Fenway Partners, a New York-based private investment firm. Delimex built a 122,000-square-foot production plant and two subsequent additions. It doubled sales to more than $160 million and tripled profitability. In all, CalPERS investments in California exceeded $12 billion by 2006.

Earvin "Magic" Johnson (*left*) and CalPERS then-Board President William Crist at a press conference for CalPERS joint venture with the basketball legend, 1996. CalPERS and Johnson together invested $51.5 million in retail real estate, focusing on minority neighborhoods in Los Angeles, Oakland, San Francisco, and other California cities.

Supporting the Home Team:
CalPERS Investments in California

Home to the most diverse population in the nation, California boasts the eighth largest economy in the world, with strengths in agriculture, manufacturing, foreign trade, and professional services.

In recent decades, the Golden State has become a leader in advanced telecommunications, multimedia, biotechnology, and—of course—the Internet. California also leads the nation's entertainment and tourism industries. It is therefore no surprise that the State is well represented in CalPERS investment portfolio. Beginning with real estate investments in the early 1980s, CalPERS California investments extend across all of its asset areas.

In the private equity sector, CalPERS launched the California Initiative Program to invest in companies in underserved urban and rural markets—primarily in California—that historically have had limited access to institutional equity capital. The program has generated healthy returns and economic expansion, with its assets showing a 16.3 percent annual return on investment. Companies in the program have created almost 2,500 jobs, including nearly 600 in California. They employ more than 5,000 Californians, about 2,000 of whom live in economically disadvantaged areas.

In March 2007, the CalPERS Alternative Investment Management Program announced a $500 million investment vehicle for the second phase of the California Initiative Program. CalPERS will earmark half of the allocation for California-based private equity funds and the other half for direct co-investments in California-based companies that are compatible with the program's goals.

"These new ventures, and especially those in California, will help us achieve investment diversification and solid returns while fostering greater economic vitality across the State," said Russell Read, CalPERS Chief Investment Officer.

State seal of California, date unknown. Devoted to the betterment of its home State, CalPERS seeks out investments that will expand its assets while strengthening California's economy.

CalPERS also launched into hedge fund investments in 2002 with the goal of diversifying its investment portfolio, managing risk, and adding value to the Fund. It took great care in structuring its program following the collapse of Long-Term Capital Management. CalPERS program explicitly limits the Fund to having no more risk than half that of the U.S. equity market—that is, risk no greater than 50 percent of the risk of the Standard & Poor's 500. In addition, a committee of highly skilled investment professionals reviews every hedge fund investment before it is added to its investment portfolio. At the end of 2006, the System had $4.6 billion invested in the hedge fund market.

CalPERS has always been among the first to identify the next "big thing" for investing. It was among the first to invest in the biotechnology sector, to invest in senior housing, and among the first to invest in farmland set for vineyard development.

Gap's Crown Vineyard in Sonoma County, California, date unknown. CalPERS joined with Premier Pacific Vineyards in 2000 to invest in farmland for high-end vineyard production. In 2003, the venture began developing Gap's Crown, a property cultivating Chardonnays and Pinot Noirs.

But one innovative investment area that gained considerable attention is its investments related to the environment. In 2004, after a yearlong study, the CalPERS passed an environmental investing program. The Board then held an in-depth workshop about environmental investing, and pledged to invest up to $500 million in environmental public equity funds. The growing global demand for diminishing natural resources (whose prices are high and volatile), the increasing demand for cleaner energy and fuel production capacity, and the increasing restraints on fossil fuel supplies all factored into this decision.

"Capital market opportunities are shifting toward the natural resources sector, including renewable technologies," Board President Rob Feckner noted in 2006. "And that shift is across virtually all equity, fixed income, and real estate markets. We believe the profits will be there."[7] Indeed, in 2000, energy and other natural-resource stocks accounted for less than eight percent of the S&P 500. By 2006, they made up 12.5 percent.

In 2004, in keeping with other environmentally related investments, CalPERS approved a $200 million special private equity fund to invest in environmental equity funds, or "cleantech." It was the first public fund to do so. CalPERS hired six private equity managers to target investments in solutions that were more efficient and less polluting than existing products, services, or technologies.

CalPERS Board President Rob Feckner at a Board meeting in Sacramento, 2005. Under Feckner's leadership, CalPERS expanded its Cleantech program, which involves investing in technologies that hold promise for the environment.

Cleantech encompasses not only clean energy—geothermal, hydro, wind, solar biomass, clean coal, wave and tidal energies, and landfill gas—but also clean fuels such as biodiesel, ethanol, and hydrogen. Finally, Cleantech looks to new technologies—emissions controls, air filtration, water purification, pollution control, fuel cells, waste management, recycling, transportation, battery storage, energy efficiency, and sensors—for investment possibilities. With market conditions and societal trends pointing to a sustained growth in these areas, CalPERS expanded its cleantech program in 2007, adding $400 million and naming Pacific Corporate Group to manage the fund.

Pulitzer Prize-winning author Thomas Friedman wrote the book *The World Is Flat: A Brief History of the Twenty-First Century*. To Friedman, "flat" means connected, and in the 1990s and 2000s technology innovations gave people more ways than ever before to communicate, collaborate, and conduct business. "A new global platform is flattening our world, and only by accepting and embracing that fact can we as investors and regulators in the world achieve success," senior Board Member Bob Carlson said in 2006.[8]

For CalPERS, this meant bringing its corporate governance principles to the international arena. In 1999, it created its Global Corporate Governance Principles, adopting specific standards for France, Germany, the United Kingdom, and Japan. These principles have been adapted by the Organization for Economic Cooperation and Development. They have also become part of the road map for good governance created by the International Corporate Governance Network, a London-based institution CalPERS helped create in the mid-1990s.

日米株価水準比較（過去6ヶ月） 2003/11/4

日経平均 10825.75 +266.16

NYダウ 9858.46 +57.34

NASDAQ 1967.70 +35.49

Money trader on the phone in front of a monitor showing a surge in Tokyo stock value, 2003. CalPERS successfully expanded its corporate governance program to investments in Japan and Europe in 2001.

CalPERS also expanded its corporate governance investments into Europe and Japan in 2001, when it increased its corporate governance investments to $3 billion. Less than three years later, its $200 million investment in a fund to revive underperforming publicly traded companies in Japan produced an annual return of 61 percent.[9] The same year, CalPERS expanded its private equity investment portfolio to include $200 million in Central and Eastern Europe investments along with those in developed countries. Emerging markets generally include all countries in Latin America, Eastern Europe, Russia, and Asia; except Japan, Australia, and New Zealand.

Two years later, CalPERS revised its investment evaluation policy in the emerging market area, adding market transparency, freedom of the press, accounting standards, political stability, and acceptable labor and civil liberties practices to the traditional financial factors such as liquidity and volatility.

Internationalism became increasingly prominent in CalPERS real estate investments in the 2000s as well. At the peak of the real estate market in 2004, CalPERS owned more than $13 billion in real estate assets. However, it correctly anticipated the 2006-07 downturn in the real estate market and sold more than $3 billion in its core real estate assets in 2005 and 2006. This perceptive move led to a 57 percent profit, its highest-ever return on real estate investments.

At the same time, CalPERS recognized that real estate was still undervalued in many booming economies throughout the world, and began developing new international investment programs to take advantage of this trend. "We expect international real estate will be a key growth area for our portfolio," explained Carlson in 2006, "and we anticipate that over the next five years approximately half of our real estate portfolio will be invested there."[10]

In 2001, the System's international investments totaled $36 billion. By 2007, more than 30 percent of CalPERS $225 billion portfolio was invested outside the United States, not including the domestic companies in CalPERS portfolio with ties to Europe, Asia, and Latin America. And, CalPERS announced in 2007 that it would commit $400 million for new private equity partnership investments in emerging markets in Eastern Europe, Latin America, and Asia.

CalPERS continues to explore new investments and new strategies. In 2006, it launched a $500 million commodities pilot program for investments directly linked to prices of energy, metals, and agricultural products, and in companies that produce and distribute such natural resource commodities. Its goal is to capture both the investment benefits of commodities while improving the risk and return characteristics of its related stock, bond, and real estate investments. And in 2007, CalPERS decided to begin investing in infrastructure.

The Business of Health Care

As the third-largest purchaser of health benefits in the United States, CalPERS was firmly established as a national leader in efforts to contain rising health care premiums by the late 1990s. But affordable health care remained a national problem. "If the U.S.

Cartoon published in the *Calgary Sun*, 2006. Correctly anticipating a decline in the North American housing market, CalPERS sold off more than $3 billion in real estate holdings between 2005 and 2006.

health care system were a patient, it would be on a gurney bound for the emergency room," CalPERS Board Member Priya Mathur said in a 2006 speech. "It's badly fractured and inefficient and it's fast becoming unaffordable."[11]

Ten years earlier, CalPERS sat in the driver's seat when it came to negotiating affordable premiums for its members. For a long time, CalPERS had received bids for health plans from as many as 25 different health care organizations—each with their own offering. As prices began to rise, CalPERS adopted the "competitive" model of negotiating—standardizing benefits for all members and asking HMOs to bid on the business each year. Using this model, premiums declined from double-digit yearly increases to low, single-digit increases from 1989 to 1998, bucking a national trend. Occasionally the premiums even fell. But in 1998, medical and prescription drug costs began to rise, the industry consolidated, and fewer players bid on the business. The march for higher premiums began again in 1999, and increased each year, peaking at a premium increase of nearly 26 percent in 2003. In fact, between 2002 and 2007, premiums for the Basic HMO plans rose 101 percent. "Every health plan out there was charging the same amount, and they were all going up at the same, very rapid, rate," said Jarvio Grevious, CalPERS Deputy Executive Officer of Benefits Administration.[12]

But unlike the vast majority of companies and organizations that were similarly battered, CalPERS, with its large risk pool, began tackling the drivers of heath care.

Excerpt of an article in the *New York Times*, 2002. Employers nationwide felt the strain of skyrocketing health care costs in the late 1990s and early 2000s.

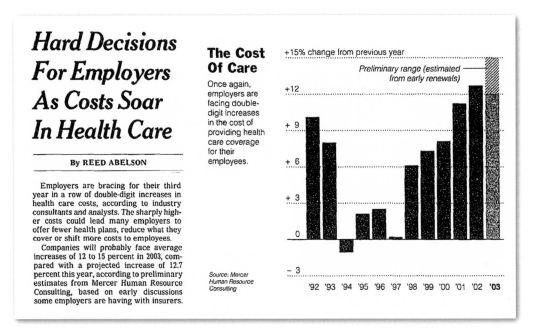

"Trying to mitigate the cost impact by shifting it off to employee and employer members was not what we were about. That's not where we wanted to be. And it really wouldn't have helped restrain health care costs anyway, because other factors caused the increases," said Grevious.[13]

Instead, CalPERS adopted a host of strategies to control health premium costs. Faced with rate increases that were simply unacceptable, the Board acted, reducing its HMO offerings from seven plans to three and consolidating its State network HMO membership with Blue Shield of California. Blue Shield became an official strategic partner with CalPERS for health care. This saved employers and enrollees $77 million in premiums in 2003 alone.

In 2003, CalPERS and Blue Shield revealed the extent to which hospital charges were one of the primary drivers of increased costs. One hospital system, for example, was 60 percent more expensive than comparable Northern California hospitals, and 80 percent higher than Blue Shield's Statewide average—with no indication of higher quality. In one large urban county hospital, open heart surgery cost just over $14,000; the same surgery in the same county—but it a different hospital—cost nearly $31,000.[14]

In 2005, CalPERS dropped 24 hospitals it considered higher in cost than necessary, saving more than $31 million that year and an estimated $46 million more each year after that. "Hospitals all across the country are going to take notice. They probably recall in the past how much of a leader CalPERS has been," said Paul Ginsberg, president of System for Studying Health Care Change, a Washington research group.[15]

CalPERS instituted regional pricing for public agency members in 2005, both to encourage employers in lower-cost Southern California to remain in the System and to stabilize its risk pool. It split the State into five regions, better aligning employers in each region with actual health care premium market prices. This not only persuaded employers to remain in the program, but also attracted new employers, increasing the risk pool. Regional pricing kept 2005 premiums from increasing by $40 million. As a result of these and other strategic initiatives, in 2006 the California Legislative Analyst's Office credited CalPERS with saving the State of California more than $168 million since 2002.

Cartoon published in the *Salt Lake Tribune*, 2007. CalPERS tackled obstacles to affordable health care head-on in the early 2000s, dropping hospitals with costs it considered higher than necessary and instituting regional pricing, among other measures.

Another part of the health care arena where CalPERS was able to create savings was prescription drugs. In the 2000s, prescription drugs accounted for 20 percent—or $860 million annually—of CalPERS total program costs. By providing its members with incentives to shift from brand name to generic drugs and from retail to mail-order purchases, CalPERS saved $27 million in 2005.

CalPERS also devoted much attention to ensuring the best possible quality of health care for its members. With nearly a third of its membership aged 50 or older, chronic diseases like diabetes, heart disease, and asthma became an issue of special concern to CalPERS. The System created a chronic disease care management program, which works with members to ensure they get regular checkups, use medications as prescribed, and call for advice and help whenever it's needed. For members who require high-end specialty care, such as coronary artery bypass grafts or organ transplants, CalPERS identified hospitals it considered "Centers of Expertise," selected because of their record of successfully performing a large number of these procedures. And, for its nearly 90,000 members who live in remote rural areas as of 2006, CalPERS was the first employer health care purchaser in California to include telemedicine as a specific benefit, linking rural members with health care specialists when they need them.

Hospital care costs have remained the most problematic issue for health benefit purchasers and CalPERS is no exception. In 2005, CalPERS launched the Partnership for Change to promote hospital performance transparency, manage hospital costs, and ensure a high-value hospital network. There are two key components of the Partnership for Change—the California Hospital Assessment and Reporting Taskforce (CHART) and the Hospital Value Initiative.

CalPERS Partnership for Change is endorsed by the Purchasers' Coalition, a group of employers and labor unions that purchases health care for more than 4.5 million Californians.

Because of its experience and expertise, CalPERS emerged as a key participant in the ongoing debate over health care costs and coverage in the United States. In late 2001, it joined the National Coalition on Health Care, the nation's largest health care alliance, made up of some 100 organizations employing or representing more than 150 million Americans.

A man having his blood pressure tested at a telemedicine kiosk. CalPERS in 2006 became the first employer health care purchaser in California to provide telemedicine as a benefit to its members. With more than 50 telemedicine sites throughout California, the CalPERS program links members in remote rural areas with health care specialists.

However, while public and private sector employers in the United States faced many similar health care challenges by the 2000s, solutions that worked for corporate America did not necessarily help governmental health care purchasers. Public sector health care purchasers were spending more than $12 billion annually by the mid-2000s on health benefits for active and retired public employees and their families—but they often found themselves without a voice when federal and state lawmakers were considering critical policy decisions. In 2005, under the leadership of Jarvio Grevious, CalPERS and six other public health care purchasers formed the Public Sector Health Care Roundtable.

By its second annual conference in November 2006, the Public Sector Health Care Roundtable had won some meaningful victories, including successfully lobbying Congress to adopt health information technology legislation and advancing legislative proposals to make the market friendlier to generic drugs by lowering barriers to their availability. The same month, U.S. voters sent a new Democratic majority to Congress, which boded well for future accomplishments for the organization. "We believe there will be more willingness to talk about innovative health initiatives and federal health policy," Grevious said after the election, "and we expect there will be more Congressional hearings on issues we care about and would like to be a part of."[16]

By 2006, the national landscape for health care financing and quality of care was, as Fred Buenrostro remarked, "more challenging … than it ever has been." Its strides and successes notwithstanding, CalPERS struggled with health care challenges like every other provider. "Sometimes I feel like we're going two to three steps forward, and other times it takes great effort just to keep standing still," Buenrostro said. Far from resigning itself to standing still, however, CalPERS remained committed to finding new ways to provide reasonably priced health care coverage to its members. "We can't afford to take our eye off the ball; we can't afford to stop trying every single approach that might get us where we need to be," Buenrostro said. "And hard as that may be sometimes, it is all worth it, because it is our duty to protect our beneficiaries."[17]

Deputy Executive Officer of Benefits Administration Jarvio Grevious, 2006. Grevious, who leads CalPERS efforts to provide affordable health care to members, is a strong voice for health care reform nationwide.

The CalPERS Long-Term Care Program

In the early 1990s, the fact that people were living longer and medical costs were continuing to escalate prompted CalPERS to take a bold step to help ensure the

Cartoon published in *Pensions & Investments*, 2006. A series of corporate scandals in the 2000s tested the strength of the corporate governance movement in the United States. CalPERS rose to the occasion, leading efforts to fight corruption and hold businesses accountable for their actions.

financial future of its members. In 1995, when the marketplace for long-term care insurance was relatively new, CalPERS launched its Long-Term Care Program. As the nation's only voluntary, self-funded, not-for-profit program it offered a way to protect personal assets against the catastrophic costs of long-term care.

Available not only to CalPERS members but to any California public employee, their parents, parents-in law, and adult siblings, enrollees receive protection from the costs of extended care, including nursing home care. CalPERS offers a selection of plan options, including a comprehensive plan with coverage for both in-home and care facility services, a facilities-only plan, varying daily benefit and total coverage amounts, and an inflation protection feature.

Now moving into its second decade of operation, the CalPERS Long-Term Care Program covers more than 174,000 subscribers and is paying out more than $78 million in annual benefits.

Corporate Governance

In the 21st century, CalPERS actions to protect and enhance its members financial security were more visible—and produced more dramatic results—in the area of

An Expanding Board

An important metric for evaluating corporate governance is the size of an organization's board of administrators. If there are fewer than five members or more than 15, adding or deleting members can make a big difference in how the organization is run.

CalPERS began with seven Board Members but soon added an eighth (chosen by the University of California Regents), when nonacademic University of California employees were admitted to the System in 1937. By the early 1960s, it became clear to supporters of a health care program for State employees that SERS provided a ready-made organizational structure for administering such a program. The 1962 legislation charging SERS with this responsibility also included a provision to add three Board Members (who would vote only on health care), bringing the Board total to 11. In 1982, a change in legislation removed the State Director of Finance from the Board, while adding the State Treasurer and the State Controller.

Today, the CalPERS Board consists of 13 Members who are elected, appointed, or hold office ex officio. The Board composition, which is mandated by law and cannot be changed unless approved by a majority of the registered voters in the State, breaks down as follows:

CalPERS Board, 2006. Standing (*from left*): David Gilb, Marjorie Berte, Charles P. Valdes, Philip Angelides, Debbie Endsley (DPA Representative), Mike Quevedo, Jr., Robert F. Carlson, Steve Westly, Karen Green Ross (State Controller Representative), Kurato Shimada. Seated (*from left*): Maeley L. Tom, Tony Oliveira, Priya Mathur, Rob Feckner, and George Diehr.

Six elected Members:

- Two elected by CalPERS members
- One elected by active State members
- One elected by active CalPERS school members
- One elected by active CalPERS public agency members (employed by contracting public agencies)
- One elected by retired members of CalPERS

Three appointed Members:

- Two appointed by the Governor—an elected official of a local government and an official of a life insurer
- One public representative appointed jointly by the Speaker of the Assembly and the Senate Rules Committee

Four Ex Officio Members:

- The State Treasurer
- The State Controller
- The Director of the Department of Personnel Administration
- A designee of the State Personnel Board

corporate governance than anywhere else. "Over the past two decades, we have learned that shareowners can achieve impressive results by holding companies accountable for their own self-regulation," Board Vice President Bob Carlson said in 2006. "By being actively involved, we can push corporations to think responsibly, act ethically, and manage prudently—to do the right thing to enhance our investment returns."[18]

"We vote our proxies—and then post many of them on our Web site for other investors to see," Carlson continued. "We challenge companies and the status quo in an effort to prevent the dysfunction and greed that has become so prevalent in the world economy. We publish an annual list of underperforming companies, our Focus List. And we put our money where our mouth is, and invest with partners that use corporate governance investment strategies to earn value for our Fund by turning around ailing companies."[19]

Launched in 1987, the CalPERS annual Focus List was its first corporate governance strategy, and the only one to have spawned a common saying among investors. Outside experts found that once companies are added to the list, they usually improve their performance. The list has become so influential that Wall Street money managers call its release the "CalPERS Effect," alluding to the tendency for brokers to signal a "buy" for that year's listed companies.

One of the most comprehensive studies of the CalPERS Effect was done by Wilshire Associates, who examined the performance of 122 companies placed on the Focus List from 1987 through Fall 2004. The before-and-after analysis found that in the five years before they were added to the Focus List, the companies, returns averaged 91.7 percent below their respective benchmarks, while for the five years after they were put on the list, the companies' returns averaged 16.4 percent above their benchmarks.[20]

In assessing the success of CalPERS Focus List, Board member George Diehr remarked in 2005 that the Retirement System had "made some monumental achievements with a number of companies behind their boardroom doors. Companies have agreed to change the way they elect directors and to move to annual elections. They have altered their boards and added new independent directors. We have worked behind the scenes to instill greater independence on the boards. They have removed

Traders on the New York Stock Exchange floor, 2006. The influence of CalPERS annual Focus List in turning around the performance of corporations listed is so striking that the phenomenon has become known on Wall Street as the "CalPERS Effect."

the supermajority requirements embedded in their bylaws and they have changed their compensation plans so that executives and senior management are paid for performance. Our work speaks for itself."[21]

But developments coming out of corporate boardrooms in the 2000s were not all good—far from it. In 2001 and 2002, investors lost more than $100 billion when two of the largest and seemingly most successful corporations in the United States collapsed. The surprise bankruptcies of Enron and WorldCom were the two largest corporate bankruptcies in U.S. history. They shook the foundations of the stock market and cost tens of thousands employees their life savings. If such a tremendous financial cloud could be said to have had any silver lining, it was that their corporate fraud and accounting misdeeds ultimately led to the most significant change to federal securities law since the New Deal: the Sarbanes-Oxley Act.

CalPERS was closely involved in the creation of this act. Unfortunately, its name was also linked to that of Enron—although CalPERS was not involved in any of the misdeeds of its officers. CalPERS did several years previously invest alongside of Enron in an energy investment, an investment that resulted in a good rate of return. After CalPERS was bought out of the investment, it was learned that Enron's chief financial officer, Andrew Fastow, led a series of other (non-CalPERS) investments that failed.

By late October 2001, Enron's earnings "overstatements" and its hundreds of million of dollars in losses had become public knowledge. In November, Enron said it might merge or sell itself to Dynergy, a rival energy company. CalPERS, which also owned shares in Dynergy, said it would oppose the appointment of anyone on the Enron board to the board of any company with which it might merge. Dynergy withdrew from further discussion with Enron and on December 2, Enron filed for bankruptcy.

Almost before investors had time to calculate their Enron losses, WorldCom took center stage. On March 11, 2002, the SEC asked WorldCom for information about its accounting procedures and loans to its officers. Things quickly went downhill for the giant telecommunications company. On July 21, less than a year after Enron's collapse, WorldCom filed for bankruptcy protection, later announcing it had uncovered $11 billion in fraudulent accounting entries.

Former Enron employees moving out of their Houston offices after the energy company's collapse, 2001. CalPERS name was unfortunately linked with the Enron scandal because of an investment partnership the System had formed with Enron years earlier, though CalPERS was not involved in the company's financial transgressions.

WorldCom executives being sworn in before testifying in front of the House Committee on Financial Services, 2002. CalPERS lost $268 million because of WorldCom's collapse, though it eventually recovered more than $200 million after filing suit with other California pension funds against the telecommunications firm.

Following WorldCom's collapse, CalPERS, CalSTRS, and the Los Angeles County Employee Retirement Association filed a joint lawsuit against the bankrupt company. In it, the three pension funds asked for full recovery of a combined $318.5 million loss from a May 2001 WorldCom bond issue—CalPERS alone had lost $268 million. Along with former CEO Bernard Ebbers and 14 other WorldCom executives, the lawsuit included the banks that had underwritten the bond issue. Among other allegations, it accused the investment bankers of failing to do adequate due diligence before underwriting the bonds, sending a clear message to the investment banking community that the funds would not tolerate this breach of ethical conduct.

Justice was served in 2005, when the three funds recovered more than $257.4 million; CalPERS received more than $200 million of that sum. Federal prosecutors charged Ebbers with conspiracy, securities fraud, and false regulatory filings for his role in the massive accounting fraud, and a jury found him guilty of all counts in March 2005.

Meanwhile, at CalPERS much work was going on to advocate for reform. "When we recognized the depth and magnitude of the financial crisis, we became one of the first investors to embark on a financial reform initiative," Buenrostro said in 2005.[22] CalPERS urged Congress, the New York Stock Exchange, the SEC, and others to raise the quality of company audit committee members, to create clear and effective laws and regulations ensuring that company audits were truly independent, and to develop accounting standards to end unintelligible or manipulative financial statements that confused or even deceived investors.

Working closely with U.S. Senator Paul Sarbanes and federal regulators, CalPERS provided technical assistance to those crafting the Sarbanes-Oxley Act. Signed into law on July 30, 2002, Sarbanes-Oxley's reforms were significant: auditor independence, accounting industry oversight through a new Public Accounting Oversight Board (PAOB), and a set of badly needed enforcement tools for the SEC, which increased its ability to regulate securities markets and compensate injured investors. CalPERS former General Counsel Kayla Gillan was appointed to the PAOB as a member.

Then CalPERS sued AOL Time Warner, for fraud and sought to recover more than $250 million in losses due to accounting irregularities both before and after the two companies merged in January 2001. In March 2007, the lawsuit was settled, and CalPERS recovered $117.7 million of its investment.

Hardly a year had passed after the Sarbanes-Oxley success before CalPERS tackled the New York Stock Exchange (NYSE), the world's largest equity marketplace. That June, CalPERS had decided to crack down on executive compensation plans in corporate America. In late August, the NYSE announced that its chairman, Richard A. Grasso, had signed a new employment contract and negotiated a new pay package with its board of directors. As part of that package, Grasso's deferred compensation, savings, and retirement plan benefits had been "restructured" and distributed to him in a lump sum. This came to $139.5 million before taxes, and Grasso wasn't even retiring.[23]

When the news broke, CalPERS officials reacted, saying Grasso's enormous pay package was unconscionable for the chairman of the public stock exchange. On September 17, CalPERS, State Treasurer Phil Angelides (then a member of CalPERS Board), and California State Teachers' Retirement System held a joint news conference and called for Grasso to resign immediately. Less than 24 hours later, NYSE's board convened an emergency meeting and Grasso resigned.

President George W. Bush signing the Corporate Responsibility Act, otherwise known as the Sarbanes-Oxley Act, July 30, 2002. Suffering heavy losses from the Enron and WorldCom scandals, CalPERS embarked on a number of financial regulatory initiatives and aided in the act's creation.

New York Stock Exchange Chairman Richard Grasso speaking to reporters about his pay package, 2003. CalPERS publicly condemned Grasso's exorbitant pay package in September 2003, calling for his resignation at a press conference. Less than 24 hours later, Grasso's departure was announced.

Excerpt from an article in the *New York Times*, December 17, 2003. CalPERS took the lead on a class-action lawsuit against the New York Stock Exchange and its seven specialist trading firms in 2003, alleging that illegal trading practices had shortchanged investors.

Six months later, CalPERS challenged NYSE again, this time suing the stock exchange and its seven specialist trading firms for jointly conspiring to shortchange investors in a widespread trading fraud scheme that had generated "untold shareowner losses." CalPERS financial interest was considerable, since most of the companies within its portfolio— then worth $60 billion— were traded on the NYSE. The suit alleged that the specialist firms participated in trade manipulations and the NYSE purposefully allowed the activity, enhancing profits to both the Exchange and the firms while cheating investors out of the best prices for stock trades.

CalPERS filed its lawsuit after reported allegations from the SEC that the specialists engaged in practices known as front-running and interpositioning, in which they failed to fill outstanding buy and sell orders at the best prices, intervening when it benefited the NYSE and the firms themselves. The lawsuit charged that the specialist firms violated federal law by routinely stepping into completed trades.

The CalPERS lawsuit also asked the court to consolidate other class-action lawsuits regarding the specialist firms and to designate it the lead plaintiff. In June, U.S. District Court Judge Robert Sweet named CalPERS and Empire Programs Inc. co-lead plaintiffs in the suit (Empire Programs later withdrew as a lead plaintiff). As of mid-2007, the lawsuit's outcome was pending before the courts.

CalPERS traditional approach to improving the performance of corporations in which it invests has been to hold on to its shares and work for change from within. But in three significant cases—involving South Africa, tobacco companies, and the Sudan—CalPERS walked away from problematic investments.

In the first instance, the California Legislature in 1988 required that CalPERS and other public pensions in the State sell their shares in companies that did business in South Africa because of its racist apartheid policy. When South Africa lifted apartheid in 1991, CalPERS resumed its investments.

It was the CalPERS Board, not the Legislature that decided in 2000 that the System would sell its primary tobacco holdings, then worth more than $525 million. The health hazards of tobacco had been well documented by that time, but the risks themselves were not the basis for CalPERS decision. Rather, it was the specter of costly lawsuits and other blows to the tobacco industry because of those risks that persuaded CalPERS. "The unusual and unique challenges that the tobacco industry faced, including the threat of extensive litigation … threatened to substantially reduce our shareowner value in tobacco," Board Member George Diehr explained, "so we divested to protect our members' assets in the long term."[24]

Actor George Clooney (*left*) with Governor Arnold Schwarzenegger speaking about California legislation requiring the divestment of State pension money from Sudan, 2006.

CalPERS faced divestiture a third time as it was called on to protest the mass killings in the Darfur region of Sudan, where by 2007 more than 450,000 people had died and 2.5 million remained in refugee camps. In May 2006, the System announced it would ban future investment in nine companies with business operations in Sudan. The pension fund also adopted a position statement that urged the federal government to publish a definitive list of companies with Sudan ties, asked already identified companies to work with such international human rights groups as the United Nations Global Compact to fully declare their business operations in Sudan, and encouraged engagement with companies to effect change.

Four months later, Governor Schwarzenegger signed a law prohibiting such investments.

CalPERS continued to remain focused on an area that had long been part of its corporate governance agenda—the rules and practices of corporate boardrooms. During the 2004 proxy season, CalPERS found that 16 directors at nine publicly held companies were not elected by a majority vote of the shareowners. In March 2005—in time for that year's proxy seasons—CalPERS began advocating a majority voting standard for corporate America.

The standard required that a director candidate in an uncontested election receive a majority of the votes cast by shareowners to be elected to the board. Otherwise, an unchallenged candidate could be elected to the board by a single vote—even if all others voted to withhold support. By October 2006, more than 140 companies had adopted a majority voting standard. CalPERS also agreed to adopt the new Public Company Accounting Board (PCAB) proposals on auditor independence as a guideline for its own proxy votes. In 2005, CalPERS had decided to vote against all audit committee members where the audit committee also did consulting work and audits. After much feedback on the "shotgun" approach, CalPERS resumed voting its proxy based on a focused approach.

CalPERS experience in 2004 with the Walt Disney Company provided an apt example for the majority voting standard at work, as well as a good many other corporate governance principles. At the time, CalPERS was Disney's 29th largest single shareholder, owning 9.9 million shares worth more than $235 million. Disney's share prices had declined more than 23 percent since 1999, almost five times more than the losses incurred by the S&P 500 index. On February 25, CalPERS announced it would withhold voting for Michael D. Eisner for Board Chairman and CEO of the company, calling the company's performance "dismal."

In the election, 43 percent of Disney's shareowners withheld their votes from Eisner, and CalPERS urged him to step down as Chairman and CEO by the end of the year, saying that splitting the positions would be the best way for Disney to promote true independence and accountability. CalPERS also remained concerned about the independence of Disney's auditor, PricewaterhouseCoopers, and recommended that the board ban it from performing any non-auditing functions for the company. In June, CalPERS named Disney to its 2004 Focus List of poorly performing companies. Disney's board stripped Eisner of his chairmanship, but he remained CEO and a board member. That September, Eisner announced he would retire in two years when his contract ended, but he left a year early.

Disney Chairman and CEO Michael Eisner at the company's annual shareholder meeting, 2005. Eisner lost his chairmanship in 2004 at the urging of CalPERS and other Disney shareowners. A year later, Eisner retired as CEO.

Protest outside of a Home Depot shareowners meeting, 2006. CalPERS championed a shareowner resolution in 2006 urging Home Depot to reform its executive pay plan. The company had paid its chief executive more than $190 million over five years, despite declining stock value.

In October, CalPERS and three other large public pension funds submitted a shareowner resolution to the SEC to give shareowners the right to nominate directors at the Walt Disney Company. Together the funds owned more than 18 million shares in Disney, but were largely shut out of its director nominations system. After meeting and discussing the issue with CalPERS and others, Disney's board agreed to allow shareowners to suggest independent directors to its board, and the pension funds withdrew their SEC resolution.

Grossly overpaid executives remained a CalPERS target, and a widespread investor concern, throughout the early and mid-2000s. In 2006, Mercer Human Resource Consulting surveyed 350 large U.S. companies in 2006 and found that median CEO salary and bonus in 2005 hit $2.4 million, an increase of 7.1 percent from 2004 and 13.7 percent from 2003.[25] During its decades of corporate governance reform, CalPERS has held the overarching requirement that pay be linked to performance.

Home Depot, for instance, gave its chief executive more than $190 million over a five-year period during the 2000s, while its stock value fell by 12 percent. CalPERS reacted by urging other shareowners to support a resolution requiring Home Depot to adopt a non-binding vote on its executive pay plan. CalPERS also filed a shareowners'

**Corporate spying.
Questionable
compensation practices.
Criminal investigations.
Had enough?**

**At HP, you can make
a change for the better.**

Sadly, we believe shareowners have no meaningful way to hold accountable dysfunctional, entrenched boards that harm a company's ability to generate long-term value. At Hewlett Packard, shareowners have an historic opportunity to exercise democracy by approving a shareowner right to nominate directors in a way that is cost effective and efficient, using company proxy materials.

If you own HP stock, it is time to cast your vote in favor of shareowners. Join the California Public Employees' Retirement System and the California State Teachers' Retirement System in supporting Proposal 3. Glass Lewis, a proxy advisor service, recommends a vote in favor of Proposal 3.

A vote for Proposal 3 is a landmark vote for good corporate governance, director accountability and long-term value creation. For more information, contact The Altman Group at 800-314-9816.

Vote Yes on Proposal 3. CalPERS CalSTRS

Ad placed by CalPERS and the California State Teachers' Retirement System in the *Wall Street Journal*, February 28, 2007. The two retirement systems campaigned vigorously for a greater voice for Hewlett-Packard shareowners after the company's chief executive resigned for poor performance but still received a severance package of more than $21 million.

suit against Hewlett-Packard (HP) contesting the $21 million-plus severance package it handed its chief executive—after she resigned for poor performance. In early 2007, CalPERS and CalSTRS sent other HP shareowners a flier headlined "Corporate spying. Questionable compensation practices. Criminal investigations. Had enough?" along with a letter urging them to support their proposal allowing shareowners to nominate candidates to the HP board.[26]

In March 2007, 39 percent of HP shareowners voted for the CalSTRS/CalPERS proposal. "This landmark vote will have a material impact well beyond HP, and will likely establish a new core principle in American business—that shareowners need the basic right to nominate directors particularly in extreme circumstances such as those we sadly experienced at HP," CalPERS Chief Investment Officer, Russell Read, said in a press statement. "Two out of every five shareowners took a stand in favor of democracy. We urge HP to not ignore the guidance of those thousands who voted and who own over $32 billion worth of HP stock."[27]

In June 2006, after media allegations about companies that allowed their top executives to backdate their stock options so they paid the lowest price—a practice Pat Macht likened to "betting on a race after you know the outcome"[28]—CalPERS asked 24 companies to respond to the allegations. Among other things, it urged them not to use company resources to cover any tax or legal liability for executives implicated for wrongdoing in options backdating. At the same time, the SEC was also investigating possible criminal activity involved in both stock-option backdating and "spring loading," which involves executives using inside information to buy the stock when the share falls, thereby maximizing their profits when they sell it later.

Things heated up quickly. On October 17, 2006, Rachel Beck, business correspondent for the Associated Press, wrote, "More than 135 companies have disclosed in SEC filings that they are under government investigation or conducting internal reviews of their option programs, leading to the ouster or resignations of 34 top executives at 17 companies so far."[29] Beck cited one particularly egregious example: William McGuire, former chief executive officer of UnitedHealth Group, who had allegedly received $1.6 billion in stock options on the days the company's stock price hit yearly lows in 1997, 1999, and 2000. In September 2006, CalPERS was named the lead plaintiff in a lawsuit filed against UnitedHealth over its stock-option grant practices.

Moreover, while UnitedHealth Group's employees made do under a 401(k) plan, McGuire was covered by a defined benefit health care and retirement policy. In an April 2006 letter to UnitedHealth, CalPERS President Rob Feckner minced no words: "These stock option grants are an insult and add injury in a market of sky-rocketing health care costs in America, and as the third largest health care purchaser we find this intolerable and unsustainable. In addition, how can you and the Board promote a program that requires your own employees to accept a risky 401(k) plan as their retirement and a health savings account plan, when you grant an egregious package of defined benefits to your CEO?"[30]

Environmental Investing

At the CalPERS of the 21st century, equity investments and corporate governance have often gone hand-in-hand, and that has certainly been true of its environmental strategies. Its 2005 corporate governance environmental strategy calling on companies to provide better reporting and transparency of their environmental liabilities and risks is a textbook example of the System's tradition of actively working from within boardrooms to promote change. With the world growing increasingly aware of environmental issues, and environmental regulation on the rise, this information was crucial for shareowners. Specifically, Board President Feckner said shareowners needed to know whether companies in which they invest are "going down the path of adopting practices that let them survive in a world of increasing environmental concern and regulation? Or, are they taking the path of denial, risk, liability, and cost?"[31]

In 2005, CalPERS joined 139 other investors and leaders in the Global Carbon Disclosure program, an initiative seeking to improve the transparency of business risks associated with climate change. At the same time, CalPERS sought improved emissions data transparency in the auto industry by supporting shareowner proposals at Ford and General Motors calling for this action. In December 2005, Ford responded by releasing the "Ford Report on the Business Impact of Climate Change," pledging to improve the company's environmental data transparency and timely disclosure.

Specialist Jeff Reymann (*second from right*) leads trading of UnitedHealth shares at the New York Stock Exchange, 2006. CalPERS spearheaded a lawsuit against UnitedHealth Group in 2006 following a damning report on the health insurance provider's stock-option grant practices.

Leon Shahinian, CalPERS Senior Investment Officer for the Alternate Investment Management Program, speaking at the CalPERS Environmental Investing Conference, 2005. CalPERS has taken an active shareowner role on corporate environmental practices, encouraging companies to adopt ecologically sound policies to remain profitable in a changing world.

Advocates of environmental investment reform at a ceremony at the New York Stock Exchange launching the UN Principles for Responsible Investment, 2006. CalPERS Board Member Priya Mathur (*far right*) and other CalPERS officials contributed to the drafting of the principles, which established global best practices for environmental investment.

CalPERS employees assist guests at a Los Angeles Retirement Planning Month event, 2002. CalPERS expanded its customer service efforts significantly in the 1990s and 2000s, reaching out to members through retirement planning fairs and other initiatives.

The same year, CalPERS, along with leading investors and other organizations worldwide, launched the Climate Risk Disclosure Initiative, a new effort to improve corporate disclosure of the risks and opportunities posed by global climate change. The initiative provided investors with tools for analyzing how climate change could affect a given company's business potential, as well as the efforts the company had made to address those climate change-related risks and opportunities. CalPERS was also among a group of investors that asked the 30 largest U.S.-based insurance companies to report on business implications from climate change.

In 2005, CalPERS, CalSTRS, and the Carbon Disclosure Project, a coalition of institutional investors with more than $21 trillion in assets, joined together to develop the Greenhouse Gas Reporting Project. The organizations designed the project to improve the reporting of accurate and timely data on greenhouse gas emissions by the electric utilities industry. CalPERS contacted every company in its utilities portfolio to express its strong support for the project.

Early in 2006, CalPERS said it would begin to identify companies in the transportation, utilities, oil, and natural gas sectors that fail to meet minimum standards of environmental data disclosure on greenhouse gas production and other environmental threats. Board President Rob Feckner and Interim Chief Investment Officer Anne Stausboll were among an international group of investing officials who helped write voluntary guidelines for a new United Nations environmental investment initiative in 2006: the United Nations Principles for Responsible Investment.

Making Customers Count

While the headlines about CalPERS often revolved around the investment and health benefits arena, a great deal of energy and care was being given to the bread and butter of meeting customers' needs.

During the last decade and a half, CalPERS reengineered many of the ways members accessed retirement applications, applied for service credit, or received education and counseling for retirement. A state-of-the-art Call Center was developed, Regional Offices took on more counseling responsibilities and held Retirement Fairs, and Web-based information and education programs proliferated.

CalPERS Board meeting, 2007. While the Board has launched numerous investment programs in recent years, it has also continued to focus on providing responsive service to the more than 1.5 million CalPERS members.

Member Spotlight: Margie Cate Greene

When Margie Cate Greene celebrated her 109th birthday in 2005, CalPERS celebrated with her, interviewing their oldest member and marveling at her continued zest for life.

A Texas native, Margie moved to California with her husband just after World War I, settling in sleepy Long Beach. Upon arrival in California, Margie immediately went back to school—to study acting. She'd taken music and voice lessons since she was a child and wanted to perform on stage. She did so, quite successfully, appearing with Robert Mitchum in *Stage Door* at the Long Beach Playhouse in 1938.

Margie retired from the theater upon the birth of her daughter, who died in the 1950s of leukemia at age 17. As Margie recalled, "Once I was over the worst part of losing her, I knew I needed to do more than just play bridge all day, so I started looking around for a job." She found one as a juvenile officer (one of only three women officers) with the Long Beach Police Department. "I loved that job—I just really loved helping all those people," Margie said. Her dedication led to her election as president of the California Women's Peace Officers Association. In that role she traveled throughout the United States. "It was a fabulous time of my life," said Margie.

Margie Cate Greene, 2005. A strong and vibrant woman who lived to 109, Margie Cate Greene was celebrated as CalPERS oldest member.

After 18 years, Margie retired from the Long Beach Police Department and began receiving her CalPERS pension. During the CalPERS interview some 43 years later, she laughingly shared how she still looked forward to receiving that check each month.

When asked her secret to reaching age 109 and looking decades younger, Margie responded: "The things I've done have catered to a healthy and long life." Although Margie passed away in 2006, she left words of wisdom for any age: "If we can develop a tendency towards loving every day and giving our all, it all comes back double."

Personal care to members who need it the most are legendary. Late in the afternoon on November 27, 2006, CalPERS information technology staff member Anita Lee received an urgent call. Michael Lauffer, Chief Counsel of the State Water Resources Control Board, was on the other end of the line. One of his employees had been battling cancer, he told Anita, but his doctors believed it was in remission. Unfortunately, his health had suddenly deteriorated over the Thanksgiving weekend and he was hospitalized. His doctors told the employee's wife the prognosis was extremely dire and he could die any minute. Because the man was fading in and out of consciousness, he needed to go through the process of retirement immediately.

Lee, whose work in IT normally doesn't give her the opportunity to help members directly, knew just what to do. She relayed the urgency of the situation to Denise Hilson at the CalPERS Regional Office in Glendale and helped Lauffer's staff contact her directly. By this time, Denise's official workday was done. Nevertheless, she immediately called the employee's family and volunteered to come to the hospital to help him and his family with the retirement paperwork. That evening she spent more than two hours with the CalPERS member and his family, explaining retirement options and enabling him to retire.

"This amazing service gave the employee and his family great comfort during a very difficult time," Lauffer wrote. "Your staff, particularly Ms. Lee and Ms. Hilson, should be commended for their dedication and service to CalPERS members. Please convey our heartfelt thanks and appreciation."[32]

Though the circumstances were extraordinary, the actions Lee and Hilson took that day illustrate the kind of service CalPERS staff gives its 1.5 million members and 2,600 employers every day. Member communication and support are an integral part of CalPERS core values, and the System has developed many programs to inform and educate members about their benefits and the investments CalPERS makes on their behalf.

CalPERS has also made sweeping improvements and changes in its systems and processes for dealing with employers. Much of the change began in 1991, when Ron Seeling became Chief Actuary of CalPERS.[33] When he was hired, eight people reported to him. By 2007, he had 200 people under his direction—and fully half of those were charged with serving CalPERS employers. Seeling identified employer

Ron Seeling, 2004. Seeling became CalPERS Chief Actuary in 1991 and implemented sweeping changes that enhanced CalPERS service to employers that contract with the System for benefits.

services as the area that had changed most dramatically since he'd been at CalPERS.[34] Robert Walton, a veteran CalPERS executive, said in 2000 that because of advancements in employer services over previous decade, "We actually act as a consultant to the employers, to help them in their retirement planning and policies and changes in the retirement structure for their members."[35]

Another innovation made by Seeling and his growing staff was the Employer Forum, an annual three-day educational event each October for CalPERS employers. Ken Marzion, Assistant Executive Officer for the Actuarial and Employers Services, described how they made it happen: "From 1994, 1995, 1996, up to about 1999, we were pushing for additional employer education efforts. Finally, in 2000, we had our first Employer Forum, a conference of about 700 employers getting together, where we educate them as much as we can on all the facets of CalPERS."

"The first time we did it, everyone was a little concerned. 'Are we really doing the right thing?'" he continued. "The first year was a major success and it has been in place ever since. The education touches on health benefits, retirement benefits, investment returns, and whatever else we have any involvement in. The Forum has been a huge success, and some who attend for the first time say, 'I can't believe I haven't been to this before. There's so much information here!'" The numbers rose each year, and by 2006, one-third or more of CalPERS employers were attending these fairs.

Employers were having a tough time meeting their pension contribution obligations in the early 2000s. CalPERS had to take steps to alleviate the unpredictability of these contribution rates for their employers and, in 2003, began creating two programs— risk pooling and rate smoothing—to help. Rate smoothing, which was initiated in 2005, helped employer assets by applying gains and losses over seven years instead of the previous three. "It is working," Seeling said in 2007. "Some 2,000 local government plans had their contributions changed by less than 1 percent. The plans are getting healthier and the employers aren't whipsawed by changes in the economy like they were earlier."[36] In 2006, rate smoothing saved the State of California millions of dollars in pension contributions to CalPERS. Employers paid $186 million less for State workers and $77 million less for school employees.

Twin Cities Police Authority employees, 2006. The Twin Cities Police Authority is among the CalPERS contracting agencies that benefit from risk pooling—a practice that keeps the contribution costs of employers with fewer than 100 members stable.

More than 1,500 CalPERS employers had fewer than 100 employees by 2007, and between 300 and 400 had fewer than 10. CalPERS Actuarial Services developed risk pooling for employers with fewer than 100 members. Before risk pooling, if an employer with fewer than 10 employees unexpectedly lost an employee due to death or disability, the financial results could be devastating, causing the employer's contributions to skyrocket. Risk pooling brought employers with fewer than 100 members into a single plan. "It's like an insurance concept," Marzion said. "If you were among a group of 10 homeowners paying for fire insurance on your house, and one of these 10 houses burned down, your rate would get pretty high."[37]

The concept of risk pooling may sound simple, but its execution was anything but easy. "Risk pooling was a very hard thing to do, and it required a lot of tact and political skills," Seeling said. "After all, you're taking these employers and trying to get them to trust each other, and they've always been big on self-determination. Whenever I talk about risk pooling, I say, 'This was like taking scrambled eggs, having to uncook them, and then putting them back in their shell.'"[38]

On March 1, 2007, CalPERS took a major step forward, opening up a fund that lets employers invest so they can cover retiree medical benefits in the future. Called the

CalPERS by the Numbers

Longtime CalPERS employee Jack Din recalls the mood in the office several decades ago, when the System's assets first reached $1 billion.

"We said, 'Wow.' I mean, it was just unheard of to have that kind of money," said Din, who served as Chief of CalPERS Membership Division.

Today, CalPERS has passed that highlight more than 200 times over and has reached numerous other important milestones during the past several years in terms of members and employers as well as investments. To name just a few:

- 1996: CalPERS assets reach $100 billion

- 2002: 1.4 million member files converted to electronic images (about 48 million pages)

- 2006: CalPERS has made more than 128,000 home loans during the first 25 years of its Member Home Loan Program

- 2006: CalPERS surpasses 1.5 million member mark

- 2006: CalPERS surpasses the 2,600 contracting employer mark

- 2006: CalPERS tops $200 billion in assets

Average CalPERS Employer Contribution Rate (As a Percentage of Payroll)

The cost for employers contracting for benefits with CalPERS, though it has had fluctuations, is close today to what it was 20 years ago.

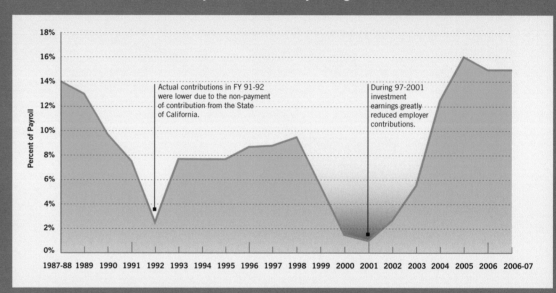

Growth in CalPERS Investment Assets

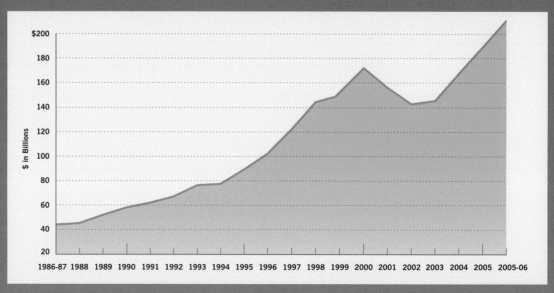

How CalPERS Pays for Benefits

Over the years, CalPERS investments have covered an increasingly large portion of the cost of benefits in relation to member and employer contributions.

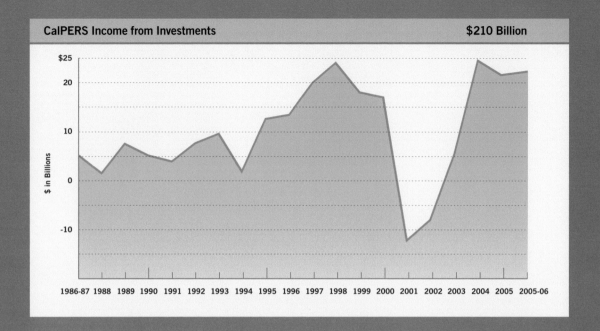

CalPERS Income from Investments **$210 Billion**

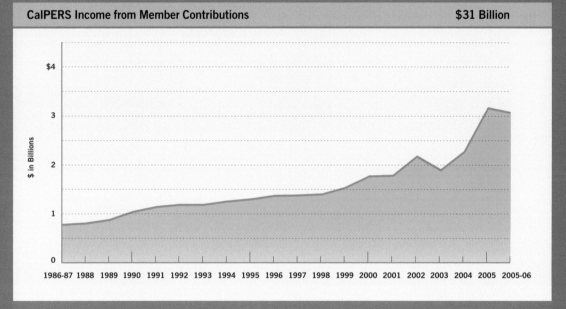

CalPERS Income from Member Contributions **$31 Billion**

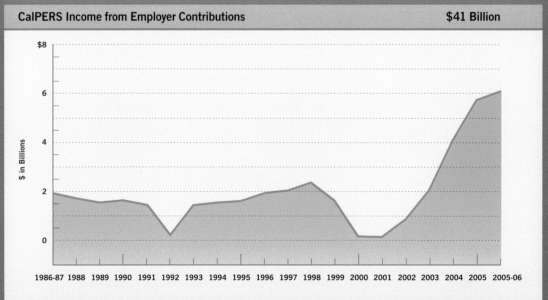

CalPERS Income from Employer Contributions **$41 Billion**

A City of Thousand Oaks librarian helping patrons at one of the city's libraries, 2006. In 2007, Thousand Oaks became the first member of the California Employers' Retiree Benefit Trust Fund, which enables public employers to invest toward future retiree medical benefits.

California Employers' Retiree Benefit Trust Fund, it also helps employers comply with the new Governmental Accounting Standards Board Statement 45 (GASB 45), which require public employers to begin reporting future retiree health and other benefits liabilities in their financial statements. The City of Thousand Oaks, California, became the first public agency to be a member of the trust.

As the number of CalPERS members soared past 1.5 million, the System took advantage of new communications technology to ensure each member continued to receive the individual service and attention the System has provided for 75 years—and then some. It combined its benefits services and post-retirement services sections to help smooth its members' transitions from "employees" to "retirees" and provide them with a seamless flow of services.

Like every other member and shareowner organization in the United States, CalPERS traditionally used the U.S. Postal Service to keep its members informed about the investments made on their behalf. In the 1990s and 2000s, however, CalPERS increasingly took advantage of the astonishing advances in technology to make communication with members more efficient and accessible. The CalPERS Web site provides in-depth information on every aspect of the organization, easily searchable and available 24 hours a day. Employers benefited too, because the System was able to create ACES, the Automated Communications Exchange System, which allowed them to send in payroll and contribution data via the Internet rather than through the mail.

Depending on their interests, CalPERS members today can subscribe to a host of e-mail updates. CalPERS eNews and eAlerts tell them about significant CalPERS activities, major developments, and upcoming events. CalPERS ePress delivers the System's news releases instantaneously. For members who like to know what their Board is doing, CalPERS eAgenda delivers each Board meeting's agenda in advance. If the Board is covering a topic of particular interest to a member, in-depth information about each agenda item is just a click or two away on the CalPERS Web site.

Getting access to information about the background and training of medical doctors frustrates patients throughout the United States. This is not so for CalPERS members, however. All they have to do is search CalPERS Web site's online physician directory, which has extensive background information on thousands of physicians affiliated with its HMOs and PPOs, making it much easier for members to compare doctors locally and locate those who participate in their particular health plan.

Communication improvements were not confined to the Internet. In 2002, CalPERS set up a centralized Customer Contact Center for members and employers, providing benefit services, and health benefit services information support. A year later, the System launched a consolidated toll-free telephone number—888-CalPERS—for both members and employers.

Presently, CalPERS also offers its members programs to improve their financial health. Many school and public agency employees can defer a portion of their salaries from taxes and increase their retirement nest eggs by investing in CalPERS 457 Plan. Established in 1995, the 457 Plan is a deferred compensation program whereby members may invest in CalPERS-managed funds of their choice. As of 2007, more than 23,500 members from 24,000 agencies participate in the plan. CalPERS invests $662 million on their behalf. In 2004, CalPERS instituted an additional retirement service credit option that members can purchase and apply toward their retirement benefits.

Pamphlet introducing CalPERS eAgenda Alerts, 2005. CalPERS has advanced its communications systems to give members convenient electronic access to CalPERS news, benefits information, Board activities, and other information.

Members have long been able to take part in the CalPERS Member Home Loan Program, which was started after the lack of affordable home loans for members became evident. Investment Committee Chair Charles Valdes was having lunch with his assistant at his office, CalTrans. The assistant was facing eviction from her apartment because she couldn't afford the increase in rent. Ironically, the monthly payments would be less if she instead purchased a town house, but she didn't have the money for a down payment. That problem led to the notion that perhaps CalPERS could help members attain the dream of home ownership by allowing members to use a portion of their retirement balance as collateral . Ultimately, it generated a home loan program that since inception has provided home loans to more than 128,000 CalPERS members, providing capital exceeding $20.6 billion.

Proving that neither technology nor the System ever stop improving, in October 2006, CalPERS announced its pension program information system was undergoing a significant makeover. It entered into a five-year contract with Accenture to develop an ambitious, consolidated pension information system that will provide a faster, more reliable and more cost-effective web-based service.

CalPERS—A Diversified & Leading-Edge Workplace

California is the nation's most diverse state. Roughly 41 percent of its 37 million residents are non-Hispanic white, 37 percent are Latino, 12 percent are Asians, and 6 percent are African-Americans. About 27 percent of its residents are immigrants, mostly from Latin America or Asia. About a quarter of its schoolchildren come from homes where English is not the first spoken language. Always a bellwether for the rest of the United States, the U.S. Census predicts that by 2050 the overall U.S. population as a whole will very much resemble California's current populace.[39]

From its Board of Administration to top executives on down, CalPERS mirrors the diversity of California. Fred Buenrostro, who became the System's seventh Chief Executive Officer in 2002, is also its first Latino CEO. His two deputies, Jarvio Grevious, Deputy Executive Officer for Benefits Administration, and Gloria Moore Andrews, Deputy Executive Officer for Operations, are both African-Americans. And, while all three are passionately committed to improving diversity, they are equally celebrated for their influence and experience in the pension industry.[40]

CEO Fred Buenrostro at CalPERS Educational Forum, 2003. CalPERS staff is led by a team of executives representing the diversity of its members, its employees, and the State as a whole. Buenrostro, CEO since 2002, is CalPERS first Latino chief executive.

Participants in CalPERS International Day, 2005. CalPERS takes pride in its diversity, holding regular cultural awareness programs for employees.

In 2001, CalPERS adopted a diversity policy that guides its work, culture, and investment operations. Diversity awareness cultivates a positive work environment, promotes a climate equally advantageous to all its employers, and ensures all team members treat each other with dignity and respect. At CalPERS, all differences are recognized and valued. The System held its first-ever diversity investment conference bringing together more than 700 investment professionals to learn about the investment programs at CalPERS.

In April 2007, CalPERS received Sacramento's prestigious Workplace Excellence Award. Without the efforts of each and every CalPERS employee, said Buenrostro, this accolade wouldn't have been possible. "CalPERS is known as a leader in investment strategies, and we apply that same philosophy by investing in our employees," he said. "CalPERS employees are 'our' greatest assets."[41]

More than a third of CalPERS employees have been with the System for longer than 10 years.[42] In an era where job-hopping can be considered the norm rather than the exception, this is a notable achievement. What makes employees stay is a progressive, caring workplace that offers its employees top-notch programs. The CalPERS Training Unit, for example, offers more than 80 courses—from career development and leadership to on-site college courses—so employees have the opportunity to grow and advance in their careers.

Diverse Rewards

The roots of CalPERS commitment to diversity began in 1985 when Board Member Bob Carlson, chair of the Proposition 21 Committee, signed off on giving unused money from the proposition campaign to help a number of causes, including diversity in investments.

A portion of the unused money went to form CALAPERS—the Statewide group of pension funds, which remains a strong public pension industry group today. Another portion went to fund a new foundation set up by the Institute for Fiduciary Education, whose purpose was to bring diversity to the ranks of investment professionals. It ultimately became known as the Robert Toigo Foundation, named for its founder.

Robert Toigo and his wife, Sue, saw something that the financial markets were either too busy or too insular to see: the need to identify and match quality businesses with quality minority graduates from quality business schools. The program started with seven students from Columbia University Business School. It has grown to sponsor more than 500 topflight students at all of the most prestigious business schools in the country.

CalPERS Diversity Committee, date unknown. The value CalPERS places on workplace diversity shows in System-wide events like International Days, Black History Month celebrations, Asian Festivals, and other educational and cultural programs.

In 2000, the CalPERS Board adopted a diversity policy that guides both its work culture and its investment operations. The policy recognizes that a positive work environment is cultivated through diversity awareness, ensuring that team members treat each other with dignity and respect and that differences are recognized and valued.

Further expanding on its commitment to diversity, CalPERS launched a Diversity Outreach Program in 2004, infusing diversity into staff training and hiring, contracting, and investing. Coordinated by a CalPERS Diversity Office, the program offers International Days, Black History Month celebrations, Asian Festivals, and other educational events and cultural fairs. Through these and other diversity awareness and outreach events, the program aims to maintain the CalPERS workplace as one characterized by tolerance, understanding, respect, and appreciation of diversity.

CalPERS dedication to diversity extends beyond employees to its vendors as well as its investments. In 1998, the Board created the Manager Development Program, providing not only opportunities for minority- and women-owned firms to manage its assets but also venture capital to help the firms grow and prosper.

"There are compelling fiduciary reasons for pursuing our diversity investment strategy," said CalPERS Board Member Charles P. Valdes. He explained that "doing business with emerging managers and markets is smart from an investment standpoint," asserting that "these investments are the right thing to do for California."

In its real estate investments, the CalPERS diversity initiatives have stimulated local economies, created jobs, generated new and expanded business opportunities, produced more affordable housing, and improved communities. Its California Urban Real Estate program was designed to create portfolio value by developing real estate projects in urban neighborhoods. Since its launch in 1995, the program has generated more than $107 million in overall profits and a rate of return averaging more than 20 percent each year.

To further support diversity investment opportunities, CalPERS co-sponsored a Diversity Investment Conference. With more than 500 corporate and public institutional investors in attendance, the conference included a networking forum and workshops on investment diversity strategies for real estate, private equity, public markets, and more.

"Diversity is an important business strategy that can give us a competitive advantage in the financial marketplace," CalPERS CEO Fred Buenrostro explained. "And that's what it is all about for us—being able to get the best returns possible for our members."

CalPERS Wellness Works program is another. Its mission is to create an environment that educates and motivates employees toward living a balanced and healthy life by promoting physical, spiritual, and emotional well-being. From Weight Watchers at Work to a recently opened on-site fitness center to health screenings and flu shots, CalPERS helps its employees achieve and maintain their physical peak.

CalPERS employees rank its award-winning Recognition Program as their favorite. They may be recognized day-to-day with a Rock Award, a timely message from other employees for a job well done. The ACE Award salutes employees for their excellence in communications, customer service, and core values; and more than 400 people won it in 2006. And, the APEX (Achieving Performance Excellence) Award is the highest honor employees can receive, showing them that their peers, supervisors, and managers consider them CalPERS role models of excellence.

Or perhaps the reason CalPERS employees like working for the System is that they are kept in the know, and their feedback and input is sought. CalPERS hosts quarterly All Staff Forums and Executive Brown Bag lunches to make sure employees know about, understand, and—most important—contribute to the System's strategic direction.

CalPERS Bike to Work Day, 2003. CalPERS promotes healthy practices and balanced lifestyles for its employees through numerous events and services.

"CalPERS is a great place to work because there is diversity in the tasks, the responsibilities, the challenges, and, yes, in the people we serve as well as work with," Retirement Program Specialist and 35-year CalPERS veteran Kathy Anderson said in 2007. "When I first sought State employment, I was given position availability cards for three different departments. I decided to apply first for the position in the Public Employees' Retirement System because that card indicated the lowest percentage of time spent typing. I never got to the other two departments.

"Thirty-five years later, and with my hands now more often on a keyboard than holding pen and paper, I have never regretted that decision," she continued. "My duties have changed many times over those years; opportunities have been available for self-improvement and promotion. But the feeling of satisfaction in helping others and the friendliness, the 'family' feeling, with those I work with has remained constant. And, as CalPERS has grown, so has the department's commitment to providing a desirable working environment for staff and quality service for our internal and external customers … CalPERS is a great place to work!"[43]

CalPERS Greatest Asset

CalPERS provides more than 1.5 million public employees with sound, reliable retirement and health benefits. For the 2,000 who work for the Retirement System itself, the retirement benefits they will receive at the end of their careers are just the beginning.

CalPERS leadership understands the System's employees are the source of its strength and the foundation for its success. The return investment in employees is evident in everything from office policy to recognition efforts to the headquarters building itself.

For many years, the CalPERS workplace was small. Employees all knew each other, and many became close friends—lunching together regularly long after they retired. Today, CalPERS main offices in Lincoln Plaza are large, but the intimate workplace feeling remains. While staff may not know the names of every one of their 2,000 coworkers, they still consider them their "CalPERS family." Everyone is greeted on a first-name basis— up to and including the CEO.

Over its existence, CalPERS CEOs have greatly influenced the creation of an open, progressive atmosphere. Jim Burton, CEO from 1994 to 2002, underscored the System's commitment to employees when he instituted the first CalPERS Strategic Plan in 1996. Today, the second goal of the current 12-point Plan is still to "Foster a work environment that values quality, respect, diversity, integrity, openness, communication, and accountability."

Burton also introduced numerous programs, policies, and events to make this goal a reality. The employee recognition program he initiated—which includes the ACE (Achieving Communications Excellence) and APEX (Achieving Performance Excellence) Awards— has itself been recognized for excellence. In 2002, CalPERS won top honors from the nonprofit National Association of Employee Recognition for its approach to recognizing employee achievement.

Board Members and Executives roll up their sleeves to collectively reward the System's employees as well, serving them sundaes at the annual CalPERS ice cream social. Executive Brown Bag lunches provide employees a venue to talk with Executives about issues or concerns. At yearly All Staff Forums, the CalPERS leadership team shares information on strategy, major events, achievements, and other business developments.

Every two years, CalPERS conducts an extensive Employee Survey to solicit feedback directly from employees about what is running smoothly in the workplace and what areas could be improved. Then, it gets to work on implementing changes.

Through the 2005 Employee Survey, for example, CalPERS identified four areas to work on: Accountability for Performance, Growth and Development, Managing Workload, and Open Communication and Employee Engagement. Employee teams enacted a host of initiatives in response, and will look to the 2007 Employee Survey results to gauge the effectiveness of these measures and overall improvement.

CEO Fred Buenrostro at a reception for the Achieving Performance Excellence (APEX) Awards, 2007. Buenrostro and other CalPERS leaders have made a priority of rewarding employees for outstanding work.

When asked about workplace strengths, employees invariably mention the All Staff Training and Wellness Programs. CalPERS offers employees more than 80 courses on a variety of work-related topics, as well as on-site college courses, a state-of-the-art computer training facility, and a full-service library. The Wellness Program encompasses a vast array of health-related programs and perks, including an on-site Fitness Center with extended hours, a Weight Watchers program, on-site flu shots, and health screenings and counseling.

The System has instituted numerous other offerings to ensure workers are happy as well as healthy. Flexible work schedules, an on-site Montessori child care facility, family and social events, performance groups, and a celebrated cafeteria are among the benefits of working at CalPERS. The thinking behind all of these features, of course, is that happy, healthy employees are productive employees—and employees that stay. And CalPERS employees *do* stay. CalPERS has long strived to be a "destination employer," with evident success: a third of the staff have been with the organization for a decade or longer.

CalPERS employees are a high-performing team—and not just in the office. Many give their time, money, or both to charities and community causes, and CalPERS affords them time to do so. Since 1956, CalPERS employees have participated in the California State Employees Charitable Campaign, where in addition to their personal monthly donation pledges, they sponsor events such as Chili Cook Offs, Cake Auctions, and Golf Tournaments, all of which benefit the United Way. CalPERS has participated in the Susan G. Komen Race for the Cure since 1998 and the March of Dimes WalkAmerica since 1995. For more than 20 years, CalPERS has also held blood drives in conjunction with BloodSource, a California blood bank.

In 2007, CalPERS was awarded the Sacramento Area Workplace Excellence Leader Award—selected above 85 other nominated companies. This award recognizes extraordinary employers that provide exceptional benefits, programs, and training and promote diversity, health, safety, advancement, and security.

But perhaps Associate Personnel Analyst Sheri McMann's sentiments say it best for many CalPERS employees: "I have worked for several State agencies and I have to say CalPERS is THE BEST all the way around," she wrote. "The people are happy and friendly—and most that I have met have either been here their whole career or have transferred (like myself) and have finally found HOME."

Retirement System employee Heather Huerta with her daughter on CalPERS Bring Your Kids to Work Day, 2005. CalPERS family-friendly, close-knit atmosphere helps make it a destination employer.

Deputy Executive Officers Gloria Moore-Andrews (*at right*) and Jarvio Grevious presenting awards at United Way thank-you celebration, 2006. CalPERS gives employees time to give back to the community. Among the numerous events and fundraisers employees participate in are the Chili Cook Offs, Cake Auctions, and Golf Tournaments, which they hold to benefit the United Way.

Opposite page
Children enjoying sundaes at the Retirement System's annual ice cream social at Lincoln Plaza, 2006. CalPERS continues to build on its success, ensuring a secure future for the members of tomorrow.

Despite its warm feel, CalPERS workplace is big—and growing. It took 20 years for the System to outgrow its Lincoln Plaza headquarters, but in 2001, builders began construction on its second building, a double-winged expansion called "Lincoln Plaza East and West." In 2005, CalPERS cut the ribbon on the new structure at a special Family Day celebration for all its employees. The building launched a major revitalization of the R Street corridor—a historic thoroughfare that, decades ago, provided the route for the first passenger rail service in the Western United States, from Sacramento to Folsom. As the 75th anniversary of CalPERS approached, the System was embarking on a major residential development alongside its new headquarters complex. Its vision includes an urban, residential, and retail neighborhood that at its peak will create a 1,000-family neighborhood and a new gateway to the City of Sacramento.

Both of the Lincoln Plaza buildings were built with the most energy-efficient technology available at the time. Green building elements abound throughout. CalPERS installed photovoltaic panels, which produce enough energy to light all underground parking, and it raised floors throughout so heat, air, and all power, data, and communications lines come in from below. CalPERS landscaped the outside with drought-tolerant landscaping and automated drip irrigation systems to minimize water use. It used renewable and recycled materials throughout, and installed special shades to help reduce energy demands. Lincoln Plaza East and West not only demonstrate CalPERS commitment to the environment and Cleantech, but show the beautiful results green building standards can bring. It recently received the nation's highest "green building" certification offered, known as the LEED (Leadership in Energy and Environmental Design) plaque.

Attendees of CalPERS Lincoln Plaza headquarters Family Day celebration, 2005. With its workplace expansion complete, CalPERS began planning the development of a neighboring residential and commercial area to serve more than 1,000 Sacramento families.

Over its 75-year history, CalPERS has evolved from a small

Retirement System for State employees to the nation's largest public pension fund, a major provider of health benefits, and a deliverer of first-class customer service. It is a world leader in corporate governance and an innovative investor. Through dedication to its members, employers, and employees; vision of its 13-member Board of Administration; and the "heart" with which each employee delivers its service (directly or indirectly) to participants of the System, CalPERS core mission remains unchanged and stronger than ever.

CalPERS Leaders

Board of Administration Members 1932-Present

Former and current Members of the Board of Administration are listed to the right. If a Member has served as President or Vice President during their tenure, it is so noted, although the inclusive dates of such service are not indicated.

Sidney L. Abrams
2001-2005

Ronald Alvarado
1996-1999, 2005-2007

Philip Angelides
1999-2006

Malvern W. Aust
Vice President
1973-1979

Roy M. Bell
1975-1978

Henry H. Benedict
President &
Vice President
1938-1951

Marjorie Berte
Currently on Board,
since 2005

Marilyn M. Bowles
1981-1982

Lester Breslow, M.D.
1961-1969

Arthur J. Brown
1942-1943

Kathleen Brown
1991-1994

Willie L. Brown, Jr.
2000-2005

Patrick Bryne
1962-1967

Harry Bubb
1995-1997

Edward J. Callan
1932-1941

Robert F. Carlson
President &
Vice President
Currently on Board,
since 1971

Richard "Bud"
Carpenter
1995

John E. Carr
1959-1961

John Chiang
Currently on Board,
since 2007

Hale Champion
1961-1966

Roger Chandler
1987-1992

Ford A. Chatters
1944-1946 & 1953

Richard Chavez
Vice President
1985-1989

Thomas J. Clark
1990-1999

Kathleen Connell
1995-2002

John R. Cornwell
President &
Vice President
1932-1955

Kenneth Cory
1983-1987

Ralph H. Cowing
1949-1952

Jerry P. Cremins
1992-1997

William Dale Crist
President
1986-2003

Gray Davis
1986-1994

W. James Dawson,
D.D.S.
1969-1976

James S. Dean
1944-1953

George Diehr
Currently on Board,
since 2003

Bill D. Ellis
President &
Vice President
1976-1994

Rob Feckner
President &
Vice President
Currently on Board,
since 1999

Michael Flaherman
1995-2003

Matt Fong
1995-1998

Stanley Fowler
President &
Vice President
1954-1976

Richard P. Fradd
1985-1989

Michael Franchetti
1982-1983

Michael Frost
1983-1984

Donald Gallagher
President &
Vice President
1942-1957, 1961-1970

William R. Gianelli
1978-1980

Phil S. Gibson
1939

David Gilb
Currently on Board,
since 2006

Jesse E. Goodwin
1971-1975

Mary Ann Graves
1979-1982

Robert D. Gray
1955-1963

Bartlett T. Grimes
1969-1981

Marilyn M. Hallisey
1980-1981

John J. Hamlyn
1943-1944

William J. Hammond
1972-1976

Sean Harrigan
President
1999-2005

John F. Hassler
1943-1944

Thomas Hayes
1989-1990

Robert R. Headley
Vice President
1968-1973

A. W. "Joe" Hislop
1963-1971

Theodore H. Jenner
1950-1954

Walter C. Kennedy
President &
Vice President
1943-1961

George L. Killion
1940-1943

Anna Kolz
1959-1960

S. Jon Kreedman
1979-1983

Bert W. Levit
1959

Richard A. Liebes
1961-1968

Bill Lockyer
Currently on Board,
since 2007

William G. Maas
1967-1972

Lloyd McAdams
1982-1983

John K. "Ken"
MacDonald
1977-1979

Hugh K. McKevitt
1932-1934

T. K. Marshall
1982-1987

Priya Sara Mathur
Currently on Board,
since 2003

Marty Morgenstern
1999-2003

James D. Mosman
1985-1989

T. H. Mugford
1958

Michael Navarro
2004-2007

Tony Oliveira
Currently on Board,
since 2006

Emery Olson
1946-1949, 1953-1955

Verne Orr
1970-1974

Paul E. Owen
1958-1959

Otto Palombo
Vice President
1960-1971

John M. Peirce
1953-1958

Jake Petrosino
President
1979-1995

Roy C. Ploss
1951-1959

John D. Porter
1965-1968

Michael Quevedo, Jr.
Currently on Board,
since 1998

Prescott "Scotty"
R. Reed
1976-1984

John R. Richards
1939-1940

Wilson C. Riles, Jr.
1979-1983

Harry B. Riley
1939-1941

Lucy E. Ritter
1961-1969

Harold H. Robinson
Vice President
1946-1962

William B. Rosenberg
1993-2002

Mel Rubin
1980-1985

Robert L. Sanders
1984-1988

Kurato Shimada
1987-1999
Currently on Board,
since 2002

Brenda Y. Shockley
1982-1984

Richard "Sid" T.
Silberman
1978-1980

Gordon P. Smith
1967-1968

Ivan C. Sperbeck
1941-1942

Thomas E. Stanton
President
1932-1950

Thomas A. Stead
Vice President
1955-1963

Joseph H. Stephens
1932-1946

Arlin E. Stockburger
Vice President
1934-1939

James A. Taylor
1968-1972

Joseph Thomas
1997-2001

David Tirapelle
1988-1998

Maeley L. Tom
Currently on Board,
since 2005

Susan Tohbe
1980-1984

Samuel R. Trozzo
1972-1973

Neville W. Turner, M.D.
1970-1975

D. Gordon Tyndall
1960-1964

Jesse Unruh
1983-1987

Charles "Chuck" P.
Valdes
Vice President
Currently on Board,
since 1984

Rolland A. Vandegrift
President
1932-1934

Karl E. Verhoye
1974-1978

Alfred "Al" Villalobos
1993-1995

Lorrie I. Ward
1989-1992

Madale Watson
1984-1992

Caspar W. Weinberger
1967-1969

Steve Westly
2003-2006

Elizabeth M. Whitney
1983-1988

Jack D. Wickware
1989-1993

Arthur J. Wiedel
1975-1979

Jack G. Willard
1979-1987

Fred B. Wood
1935-1939

Frank M. Woods
1971-1978

Joseph L. Wyatt, Jr.
1963-1971

Linda Tsao Yang
Vice President
1977-1980

Executive Officers 1932-Present

Earl W. Chapman
1932-1956

Edward K. Coombs*
1956

William E. Payne
1956-1974

Carl J. Blechinger
1975-1983

Sidney C. McCausland
1984-1986

Kenneth G. Thomason*
1987

Dale M. Hanson
1987-1994

Richard H. Koppes*
1994

James E. Burton
1994-2002

Robert D. Walton*
2002

Fred Buenrostro, Jr.
2002-Present

*Interim or Acting
Executive Officer*

The History of CalPERS: A Timeline

1921

- Discussion among California State government employees on the possibility of establishing retirement provisions for State employees.

1923

- California Governor Friend W. Richardson supports a feasibility study for a State government retirement system. The Legislature does not appropriate the required $5,000 funding for the study.

1927

- California Governor C. C. Young supports a feasibility study for a State government retirement system, and the Legislature appropriates $6,000 for the study (Chapter 431, Statutes of 1927). The Commission on Pensions of State Employees (Pension Commission) is thereby created. This Commission was chaired by W. A. Johnstone, chairman of the State Civil Service Commission. Other members were: J. C. Whitman, Ralph T. Fisher, and John F. Dalton.

1929

- The Pension Commission report is submitted to the Legislature. It calls for $1,368,200 in funding for the first 18 months of operation. Actuarial advice is obtained by the Commission from Professor H. H. Mowbray of the University of California and Barrett N. Coates of Coates and Herfurth, San Francisco. Governor Young calls for a popular vote for approval; vote scheduled for November 1930.

- Wall Street stock market crash (October).

1930

- Four informally organized groups of State employees from Sacramento, San Francisco, and Los Angeles raise $41,000 to fund a letter-writing campaign in support of a State retirement system. The group mails more than 1 million letters.

- The voters of California approve the Amendment to the California Constitution—Section 22A, Article IV, which authorizes the State Legislature to provide for the payment of retirement salaries to State employees.

1931

- The Legislature (including Governor James Rolph, Jr.) considers funding for the approved Retirement System.

- The California State Employees Association is formed.

- The California Senate approves the retirement plan (Senate Bill No. 683) by a vote of 29 to 5 and the Assembly approves it by a vote of 56 to 2 (Chapter 700, Statutes of 1931).

- Governor Rolph signs the retirement plan into law (June 9, 1931).

1932

- State Employees' Retirement System (SERS) begins operation (January 1, 1932) with the following basic provisions:
  - Full-time State employees automatically become members. New employees become members after six months' service.
  - Retirement allowances are financed jointly by monthly contributions from employees and the State.
  - Employee contributions and retirement allowances are based on salaries up to $416.66 per month.
  - Members who leave State employment prior to 20 years of service will receive their contributions, plus interest.

- Retirement allowances are based on the "$1/70$ at 65" formula.

- The service retirement for miscellaneous members require 20 years of service, and the minimum retirement age is 60; 65 is considered the normal retirement age.

- The accumulated contributions, plus interest, and one month's salary for each year of service up to six years is paid to a members' beneficiary if the member dies before retirement.

- Retirement is compulsory at age 75 (effective January 1, 1933) and scheduled to be reduced to 70 in 1937.

- A "prior service" provision is allowed to members who worked for the State prior to enactment of the Retirement System.

- Disability retirement requires 10 years of service.

- Optional retirement plans are offered that provide for a reduced member allowance in return for an increased survivor allowance.

- The death benefit consists of a return of contributions with interest plus up to six months' salary.

1933

- The first service retirements begin on January 1, 1933.
- The compulsory retirement is at age 75.

1935

- U.S. Congress enacts the Old Age & Survivors' Insurance (OASI) program—Social Security Act.
- California Highway Patrol Retirement Act passes, which includes:
  - Highway Patrol members can retire at age 60 with 20 years of service and receive a service retirement allowance of approximately half pay (see 1941).
  - Compulsory retirement age is reduced from 75 to 65 (see 1937).
  - Industrial disability retirement, with no minimum service requirement.
  - Industrial death benefit.

1937

- Legislature passes Senate Bill No. 32, which contains numerous changes to the Retirement System:
  - Legislation grants the SERS Board of Administration authority to set the rate of member contributions to ensure the Fund's adequacy.
  - The SERS Board receives authority to adjust the interest rates it pays on member contributions.
  - The SERS Board receives authority to adjust mortality tables as needed.
- Compulsory age for retirement is reduced to 70 (65 for Highway Patrol members).

- County Employees' Retirement Law is created.
- Judges' Retirement System is created and administered by the State Controller (see 1979).
- University of California nonacademic employees become members of SERS.

1939

- Legislation sponsored by the California League of Municipalities permits political subdivisions (any "municipal corporation" such as cities, counties, school districts, and special districts of California) to contract with the System (Chapter 927, Statutes of 1939).
- Agencies can contract to permit their safety members to retire at age 55.
- Widows and children of State prison employees killed in the line of duty are eligible for allowances comparable to those for widows and children of State Highway Patrolmen killed in the line of duty.

1941

- For Highway Patrol members, minimum retirement age is reduced from 60 to 50 years old, with 20 years of service.

1943

- Any public agency in California can choose to contract with SERS for coverage (Chapter 640, Statutes of 1943).

1945

- Minimum retirement age for State miscellaneous members is lowered to age 55 from 60. Local public agencies are allowed to amend contracts to provide the same benefit.

- Governor Earl Warren signs a set of 10 retirement bills creating the "1/60 at 60" formula, effective October 1, 1945.
- Lump sum death benefit is added: $300 in 1945 (see 1953).
- Members with $500 in contributions can leave their money on deposit and later apply to retire (see 1971).

1947

- SERS begins administration of the Legislators' Retirement System, which provides benefits to legislators, constitutional officers, and certain legislative employees (see 1990).
- All County Superintendents of Schools must contract with SERS to include non-certificated employees as members of the System by July 1, 1949.
- The SERS Board modifies investment policy on October 24, 1947. Previously, SERS invested only in U.S. government bonds and municipal bonds. After the change, SERS began investing in telephone, electric, and gas utilities.

1949

- Highway Patrol Class: ½ continuance (Survivor Continuance) is created (see 1953).

1951

- Proposal (not passed by the Legislature) to change the formula for retirement allowances from "1/60 at age 60" to "1/50 at age 60."
- Federal Social Security Act is amended to extend Social Security coverage to public employees not already covered by a retirement system.

1953

- A. Alan Post, Legislative Auditor, conducts a survey of retirement systems including: SERS; the Legislators' Retirement System, the Judges' Retirement System, State Teachers' Retirement System, and the University of California Retirement System. The complete report, issued in 1954, also addressed considerations of integrating SERS with OASI.

- Lump sum death benefit is increased from $300 to $400.

- Local agencies can amend their contracts to provide ½ continuance.

1954

- Average monthly compensation used in benefit calculations will be based on a three-year average, instead of a five-year average.

1955

- SERS takes over administration of the federal Social Security program for California public employees. SERS members vote to turn down integration of OASI coverage with SERS.

- Local agencies can amend their contracts to provide a monthly pre-retirement death benefit for police officers and firefighters.

- California Legislature authorizes SERS investment in building certificates. Subsequently, the Board purchased building certificates for seven State office buildings, one in which SERS located its offices along with other State agencies.

1957

- Temporary Annuity benefit is created, payable until age 65 (see 1963).

- Reciprocity is established between SERS and the county systems created in 1937.

- Survivor benefits are created (optional for contracting agencies).

1959

- Survivor benefits are added (optional to contracting agencies).

- Miscellaneous members are allowed to take a service retirement at age 55, if they have $500 on deposit or 20 years of service.

1961

- Industrial death benefit allowance is increased from 50 percent of final compensation to 75 percent, if certain conditions apply.

- The Legislature passes the Meyers-Geddes Hospital and Medical Care Act (Chapter 1236, Statutes of 1961) (see 1962).

1962

- SERS begins administering new Meyers-Geddes Hospital and Medical Care Act for State employees; this program was renamed in 1978 as the Public Employees' Hospital and Medical Care Act (PEMHCA). It was initially open only to State employees, then numbering 77,405 (see 1967 and 1978).

1963

- Temporary Annuity is payable at age 62 (lowered from age 65; see 1957).

1964

- SERS creates a mortgage loan department.

1966

- SERS first commercial real estate loan is for a San Francisco Bay Area shopping center.

1967

- The name of SERS is changed to the Public Employees' Retirement System (PERS).

- PEMHCA (see 1962) is amended to extend health benefits to any public agency electing to contract with SERS for coverage (Chapter 1455, Statutes of 1967).

- Stocks are added to the PERS investment portfolio due to their historic performance compared to fixed income investments.

1968

- The retired member lump sum death benefit is increased to $500.

- The annual cost-of-living adjustment (COLA) is made applicable to retirement and death allowances. The maximum increase is 1½ percent.

1971

- Members with five years of service credit (instead of the $500 minimum established in 1945) can leave their money on deposit and later apply to retire.

- The 1957 Survivor Benefit is extended (mandatory) to all local members.

- The mandatory retirement age for miscellaneous members is reduced from 70 to 67 over three years (see 1979).

1972

- University of California system leaves SERS to start its own retirement system.

1973

- Credit is allowed for unused sick leave at retirement, subject to certain conditions.

- Local employers will determine the eligibility of their safety members for disability retirement.

1974

- The Employee Retirement Income Security Act (ERISA) requires that funds for retirement plans be placed in a separate trust fund.

- State law passes allowing members to convert unused sick leave to service credit.

1975

- Minimum retirement age for miscellaneous members is reduced from age 55 to 50.

1977

- Separate male and female benefit factor rates are abolished in favor of a single table.

1978

- Employers may, upon certification of competency, retain employees beyond compulsory retirement age (optional to contracting agencies).

- The Meyers-Gedes Act of 1961 is renamed as the Public Employees' Medical and Hospital Care Act (PEMHCA).

1979

- The mandatory retirement age for miscellaneous members is increased from 67 to 70 (see 1971).

- PERS assumes administration of the Judges' Retirement System from the State Controller (see 1937).

- Retirement Fund is designated as a trust created solely for the benefit of the membership.

1980

- PERS administers new Volunteer Firefighters' Length of Service Award System, which provides a monthly award to firefighters who have served for at least 10 years. The program is subsidized by the fire departments that contract with PERS for the program.

1981

- CalPERS Member Home Loan Program is launched.

- Contracting agencies can pay all, or a portion, of a member's contributions creditable to the member's account.

- Retired member lump sum death benefit is increased to $600 (optional to contracting agencies).

- Implementation of the Accounting and Resource Management System (ARMS) and the Member System. The ARMS eliminated manual posting of ledgers for both support and retirement funding accounting. Automation of the Member System replaced the manual file system used since SERS creation.

1982

- CalPERS celebrates 50th anniversary.

1983

- Unisex mortality tables are implemented for those hired after July 1, 1982.

- Carl Blechinger retires as Executive Officer on December 31, 1983.

- Legislation changes CalPERS Board to 13 members.

1984

- Voters pass Proposition 21.

- PERS initiates corporate governance program.

- Individual Dividend Disbursement Account (IDDA) benefit is created by legislation to restore purchasing power of retirees to 75 percent (funded from investment earnings).

1985

- Legislation provides a Second Tier retirement plan for State industrial and State miscellaneous members. First Tier members can elect to move to Second Tier and receive a refund of their contributions.

1986

- CalPERS moves to Lincoln Plaza headquarters building.

1987

- Implemented Electronic Fund Transfer service— early direct deposit service.

- CalPERS develops automated PC-based program for employer payroll reporting.

1988

- CalPERS selects a Washington, D.C. representative to monitor national issues and federal legislation.

- Extraordinary Performance Dividend Account (EPDA) is created, which could increase retirement benefits above the 75 percent level.

1989

- PERS Care self-funded health plan launches, consolidating four fee-for-service health plans.

1990

- Long-Term Care Act allows PERS to offer long-term care insurance to PERS, STRS, and County Employees' Retirement Law of 1937 members.

- Legislators' Retirement System becomes a closed retirement system for Legislators (still covers Constitutional Officers and some legislative employees) after voters approve Proposition 140, prohibiting Legislators first elected after November 1990 from receiving retirement benefits.

- Legislation establishes the CalPERS Public Agency 457 Deferred Compensation Program.

1991

- A.B. 702 (Chapter 83) transfers significant control over actuarial functions from the PERS Board to an actuary appointed by the Governor. This law also required that funds from various special accounts be used to offset employer contributions. The law also closed entry to the First Tier retirement plan by requiring new State employees to be placed in the Second Tier plan that provides a lower level of benefits and a lesser liability to the State.

- Retirement and financial planning seminars are introduced for members.

1992

- California voters approve Proposition 162 (amended Article XVI, Section 17 of the California Constitution) and establish the CalPERS Board absolute and exclusive (plenary) authority over the administration and investment of retirement funds.

- The term CalPERS is used hereafter to refer to the California Public Employees' Retirement System.

- Introduces standardized benefits across health plans in the health program.

- Establishes new compensation review unit, internal estimate audits, and proposes new legislation to better define compensation in response to pension spiking issues.

- Legislation adds Purchasing Power Protection Allowance, replacing IDDA and EPDA benefits.

1993

- CalPERS adds a customer toll-free phone number.

1994

- Adds PERS Choice PPO self-funded health plan.

- The Judges' Retirement System II is created in response to the high cost and growing unfunded liability of JRS.

1995

- CalPERS investment portfolio grows 16.4 percent to $87.8 billion.

- CalPERS has largest single quarterly returns to date of 7.2 percent.

- Expanded Annual Member Statements to include retirement estimates (for members age 45).

- Issues first Health Plan Quality Report.

- Launches an employer Bulletin Board System, which includes online education calendars, circular letters, benefit options, contract info, payroll info, and more.

1996

- CalPERS investment portfolio reaches $100 billion mark on May 14, 1996.

- Long-Term Care Program expands to include all California public employees and retirees.

- CalPERS launches international corporate governance program.

1997

- CalPERS On-Line Web site premieres.

1998

- Actuarial Valuation System (AVS, a computerized calculation tool to complete annual valuations) launches.

- Co-sponsors legislation that allows spouses of peace officers and firefighters killed in line of duty to keep benefits at remarriage.

1999

- The CalPERS Board passes a resolution that calls for retirement benefit equity. S.B. 400 (authored by Senator Deborah Ortiz) improves retirement benefits for State and classified school employees and retirees.

2000

- Consolidates two member telephone information centers to one in efforts to provide more centralized customer assistance.

- May 2000 marks the first annual Retirement Planning Month. Events are held for members to learn more about financial and retirement planning.

- Groundbreaking takes place for the Lincoln Plaza Headquarters Expansion Project. The site is located directly across the street from the existing CalPERS location and will house two six-story buildings.

- First Employer Conference is held (name later changed to CalPERS Educational Forum).

- A new electronic reporting system for employers is launched—Automated Communication Exchange System (ACES). This product allows employers to report and complete health and retirement administration transactions.

2002

- 1.4 million member files (about 48 million pages) are converted to electronic images.

- CalPERS introduces the new Customer Contact Center to improve telephone services for members and employers. Includes a self-service interactive voice response system.

2004

- Legislation passes that allows for a new Additional Retirement Service Credit benefit.

- To help control costs of health care and monthly member premiums, CalPERS introduces the first narrow network of health providers. This was in response to unwillingness of provider group to reduce costs to purchasers (Blue Shield/ Sutter network).

- Redesigned CalPERS On-Line Web site is launched, which provides customized member and employer information and online services.

- Initiated risk pooling and initiatives to address employer contribution rate fluctuation.

- Legislation institutes the State Alternate Retirement Program, requiring new State employees to contribute to a Department of Personnel Administration defined contribution plan rather than CalPERS for their first two years of employment.

2005

- The new Lincoln Plaza East and West buildings open.

- Debate begins on the advantages of a defined benefit (DB) plan versus a defined contribution (DC) plan. Governor Arnold Schwarzenegger introduces proposals to replace the CalPERS DB plan as a way to counter the State's ongoing fiscal crisis.

- CalPERS begins work on a new electronic pension information system that will replace all existing computer systems, enabling faster, more cost-efficient benefits administration and customer services.

2006

- CalPERS crosses several significant milestones:
  - Surpassed $200 billion in assets.
  - Surpassed 1.5 million members.
  - Surpassed 2,600 contracting public employers.

- Starts Health Purchasers Coalition, which includes some major U.S. corporations, such as General Motors.

- Institutes ban on investment in companies with business operations in Sudan.

- CalPERS agrees not to make future investments with businesses operating in the Sudan.

CalPERS Membership & Investment Fund Growth

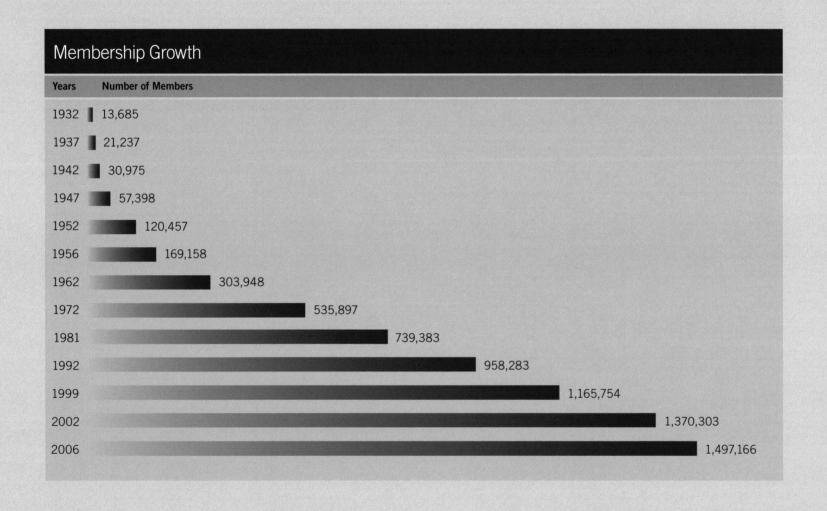

Membership Growth

Years	Number of Members
1932	13,685
1937	21,237
1942	30,975
1947	57,398
1952	120,457
1956	169,158
1962	303,948
1972	535,897
1981	739,383
1992	958,283
1999	1,165,754
2002	1,370,303
2006	1,497,166

Investment Fund Growth

Years	Dollars
1932	$877,368
1939	17,696,107
1944	41,338,962
1948	112,107,143
1956	615,114,678
1964	1,950,721,710
1972	4,846,190,894
1981	14,893,224,673
1985	26,171,923,819
1996	100,711,644,000
1999	159,396,341,242
2002	141,825,348,179
2006	209,871,688,027

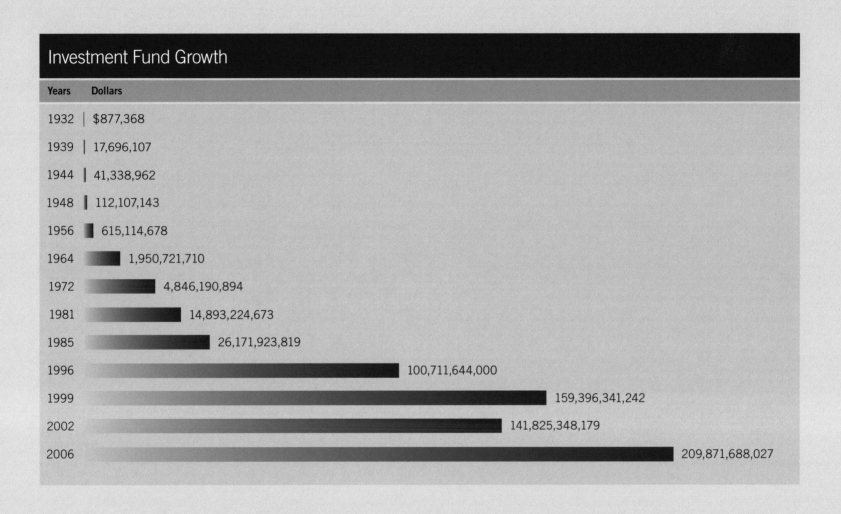

CalPERS
75 Years

Afterword

More than seven decades after the inception of CalPERS, the organization's leaders and staff continue to broaden the company's reach and services. The pension fund is on a path to becoming an integrated full-service provider for financial- and health-related products and services for its members and employers.

By capitalizing on the strengths and expertise of its world-class investment team, CalPERS has been able to expand its products and services, creating a suite of investment fund options for local public agencies. The System has launched the California Employers' Retiree Benefit Trust Fund, a program that helps public employers finance the future costs of retiree health care—in large part from CalPERS investment earnings. In an effort to generate superior portfolio returns and improve quality and efficiency in the nation's health care market, CalPERS investment advisers continue to explore opportunities in health care-focused private equity funds. And, as part of its overarching belief of providing ongoing, accessible support to members, the System premiered my|CalPERS (as part of CalPERS On-Line), a personalized Web portal that offers a "snapshot" of all the benefits they receive.

The CalPERS brand remains strong. Surveys show that members of the System continue to be satisfied with the level of service they receive, and they trust CalPERS. And, the Retirement System itself has become a "destination" employer, receiving industry accolades for fostering an exceptional workplace.

It is evident that CalPERS is still on the steady, successful course its founders established 75 years ago. The System continues to navigate its course using the same values to achieve excellence—dedication, vision, and heart. By remaining true to its guiding principles, CalPERS future is certain to be as rich as its past.

Acknowledgments

Historian & Writer
Christopher J. Castaneda

Project Manager
Nancy Quinlan

*Research,
Writing & Production
Services*
The History Factory

Contributing Writers
Patricia K. Macht

Brad Pacheco

Nancy Quinlan

Research & Archives
Ava Goldman

Esther Marcroft

Jennifer Milre

Norma Norwood

Natalie Searl

Graphic Design
Pivot Design

Manuela Hieronimus
(*cover*)

Interview Participants
Gloria Moore-Andrews

Mark Anson

Peter Araldi

Ellen Baltezore

Carl Blechinger

James E. Burton

Robert F. Carlson

Bud Carpenter

Roberta Cournoyer

David Cox

Jack Din

Mary Egersdorff

David Felderstein

Jarvio Grevious

Dale Hanson

Anna E. (Ethel) Johnson

Gary Jones

Teruko (Terry) Kagiyama

Marion Keith

Jack Lyall

Bill McGrew

Sid McCausland

Sandra McEvilly

Patricia K. Macht

Ken Marzion

Alan Milligan

Peter Mixon

N. Deane Moore

Gene Reich

Natalie Searl

Ron Seeling

Jim Smith

Dorothy Taylor

Annajean Turkalay

Charles Valdes

Robert D. Walton

Marcella Weldon

Carl C. Wilberg

Robert W. Wilson

Notes

1: A Progressive Proposition

[1] Leon Anthony Negri, "The Formation and Early Development of the California State Employees Association, 1931-1938" (M.A. thesis, California State University, Sacramento, 1969), p. 18.

[2] Jackson K. Putnam, *Old-Age Politics in California: From Richardson to Reagan* (Stanford: Stanford University Press, 1970), p. 15. Also see Lewis A. Hilban and Clio Lloyn, *California's Legislature Thirty-Seventh Session, Final Calendar of Legislative Business, 1907* (Sacramento: California State Printing Office, 1907).

[3] Putnam, *Old-Age Politics in California*, p. 16.

[4] National Education Association, *Teacher Retirement Systems: A Summary of the 1971 Legal Provisions for Retirement Systems to Which Teachers Belong* (National Education Association, Office of Teacher Retirement, 1972), p. 18. Also see "Funding and Benefits History," www.calstrs.org/aboutstrs/funding.html (accessed on July 22, 2001), p. 1.

[5] Abraham Epstein, "The American State Old Age Pension System in Operation," *Annals of the American Academy of Political and Social Science* Vol. 170 (November 1933), pp. 107-111.

[6] Putnam, *Old-Age Politics in California*, pp. 18, 20.

[7] Quoted in Putnam, *Old-Age Politics in California*, p. 19.

[8] Putnam, *Old-Age Politics in California*, p. 22. Also see Daniel J.B. Mitchell, *Pension Politics and the Elderly: Historic Social Movements and Their Lessons for Our Aging Society* (Armonk, NY: M.E. Sharpe, 2000), p. 19.

[9] See Negri, "The Formation and Early Development of the California State Employees Association, 1931-1938," p. 24. These employees included: Fred A. Taylor, John T. Stafford, William McElvaine, Daniel Sullivan, John M. Welsh, Ernest Escher, Lodema Shurtleff, Mabel Geller, Sadie Ames, E. J. Callen, and William Chamberlain, as well as six others.

[10] Negri, "The Formation and Early Development of the California State Employees Association, 1931-1938," p. 24. A different version of Governor Richardson's reaction is in California State Employees' Retirement System, *The First 25 Years* (Sacramento, 1957), pp. 6-7.

[11] *Seventh Biennial Report of the California State Civil Service Commission to the Governor* (Sacramento: California State Printing Office, December 1930), p. 18.

[12] See *Report of the Commission on Pensions of State Employees* (Sacramento: California State Printing Office, 1929), p. 11. This report is hereinafter cited as: Pension Commission Report.

[13] Assembly Bill No. 38, Chapter 431 (signed May 10, 1927), p. 1.

[14] Ibid. Also see *The First 25 Years*, p. 7; and Negri, "The Formation and Early Development of the California State Employees Association, 1931-1938," p. 24.

[15] Pension Commission Report, p. 17.

[16] Minutes of the Meeting of the State Pension Commission, December 19, 1927. (Pension Commission folder, Box 42, Library Files, CalPERS).

[17] Pension Commission Report, p. 6.

[18] Ibid., p. 8.

[19] Ibid., p. 9.

[20] Ibid.

[21] Ibid.

[22] Ibid.

[23] Ibid., p. 10.

[24] Under the Pension Commission's plan, the absolute maximum age limit for State workers would be 75.

[25] Pension Commission Report, p. 13.

[26] Ibid., p. 14.

[27] Ibid., pp. 11-12.

[28] Ibid., pp. 15-16.

[29] Ibid., p. 17.

[30] *The First 25 Years*, p. 7.

[31] Assembly Constitutional Amendment No. 37 (filed with the Secretary of State, May 15, 1929).

[32] George Shaw, "State Employees Organize for Retirement System," *The Civil Service Employee* (September 1930), p. 7.

[33] Ibid. Also see *Through the Years with CSEA, 1931-1999* (CSEA, nd), p. 1.

[34] See Negri, "The Formation and Early Development of the California State Employees Association, 1931-1938," p. 26. Also, "Whitaker, Top Publicist, Dies," *San Francisco Examiner*, November 4, 1961, p. 36.

[35] Letter from State Employees' Retirement Campaign Committee to Fellow State Employee, July 25, 1930.

[36] Negri, "The Formation and Early Development of the California State Employees Association, 1931-1938," p. 27.

[37] Ibid., p. 29.

38"Letter, unsigned, from State Employees' Retirement Campaign Committee to Fellow State Employee, September 9, 1930."

39Memorandum from State Employees' Retirement Campaign Committee, October 1, 1930.

40Form letter from Clem Whitaker, October 16, 1930.

41Campaign advertisement, *Sacramento Union*, November 3, 1930, Part II, p. 6:8.

42*Los Angeles Times*, November 4, 1930, Part II, p. 4:2. Also, *Sacramento Bee*, November 3, 1930, p. 5:6.

43"Latest Returns on Statewide Propositions," *San Francisco Chronicle*, November 7, 1930.

44*The First 25 Years*, p. 8.

45Thomas E. Stanton, Jr., "The State Employees Retirement Act," *California State Employees Association*, Bulletin No. 1 (July 1, 1931).

46Ibid.

47*The First 25 Years*, p. 9. Also see Pension Commission Report, p. 45.

48Senate Bill No. 683, Chapter 700, p. 1.

49Ibid., pp. 12-13.

50Ibid., p. 13.

51Ibid.

52SERS Minutes, October 23, 1931; November 4, 1931; January 4, 1932.

53SERS Minutes, November 4, 1931.

54Pension Commission Report, p. 11.

2: The Defining Years

1SERS Minutes, January 4, 1932.

2Ibid.

3California State Employees' Retirement System, *The First 25 Years* (Sacramento, 1957), p. 15.

4Ibid.

5State of California, *State Employees' Retirement Act* (Sacramento: California State Printing Office, 1935), p. 21.

6Earl W. Chapman, "New Retirement Rates," *State Employees' Magazine* (May 1941), p. 5 in folder: Employees' Retirement System–Articles on June 1934-Sept. 1945, Box 1, B01344, California State Archives.

7*The First 25 Years*, p. 15.

8Ibid.

9Gerald D. Nash, et. al., *Social Security: The First Half-Century* (Albuquerque: University of New Mexico Press, 1988), pp. 5-6.

10Ibid., p. 7.

11Ibid., p. 6.

12Abraham Holtzman, *The Townsend Movement: A Political Study* (New York: Bookman Associates, Inc., 1963), pp. 32-33.

13Ibid., p. 33.

14Nash, et. al., *Social Security*, p. 6.

15Ibid., p. 7.

16Ibid., pp. 7-8. OAI was originally called Old Age Benefits.

17Ibid., p. 9.

18Ibid., p. 10.

19Earl W. Chapman, "Retirement Act: Amendments Improve, Administration of Law, Assure Continuance of System …" *Midstate Review* (September 1937), p. 7, in folder: Employees' Retirement System–Articles on June 1934-Sept. 1945, Box 1, B01344, California State Archives.

20Earl W. Chapman, "Retirement: A System Appreciated By Employees–Young and Old …," *Midstate Review* (June 1937), p. 5, in folder: Employees' Retirement System–Articles on June 1934-Sept. 1945, Box 1, B01344, California State Archives.

21*The First 25 Years*, p. 16.

22Ibid.

23Ibid., p. 17.

24Ibid.

25California State Employees' Retirement System, *Report of the Board of Administration* (June 30, 1939), pp. 5, 6, 17-18.

26*The First 25 Years*, p. 19.

27Ibid., pp. 10-12.

28"Seven Cities Now Under State Retirement System," *Western City* (December 1942), p. 20.

29*The First 25 Years*, p. 19.

30Ibid.

31Ibid.

32Ibid., p. 20.

33Ibid., pp. 20-21.

34Ibid., p. 23.

35Ibid., pp. 23-24.

36SERS Board Meeting Minutes, January 27, 1939.

37Ibid.

38SERS Board Meeting Minutes, April 27, 1939.

39Ibid.

40Ibid.

41SERS Board Meeting Minutes, January 26, 1940.

42SERS Board Meeting Minutes, October 18, 1940.

43SERS Board Meeting Minutes, March 21, 1941; October 10, 1941; April 17, 1942; July 10, 1942.

44SERS Board Meeting Minutes, October 23, 1942. Also see SERS, *Annual Report* (June 30, 1949), p. 1.

45SERS, *Annual Report* (June 30, 1942), p. 22; and SERS, *Annual Report* (June 30, 1947), pp. 10-11. Also see Marcella Weldon, Oral history interview by Christopher J. Castaneda, November 21, 2000. CalPERS History Collection, Sacramento, California.

46*The First 25 Years*, p. 23.

47Weldon, Oral history Interview by Christopher J. Castaneda, November 21, 2000.

3: Investing for Life

1California State Employees' Retirement System, *The First 25 Years* (Sacramento, 1957), pp. 20-21.

2Ibid., p. 21.

3Ibid.

4Ibid.

5Ibid.

6Ibid., p. 24.

7Ibid.

8SERS Board Meeting Minutes, July 26, 1946.

9SERS Board Meeting Minutes, July 10, 1947.

10SERS Board Meeting Minutes, October 24, 1947.

11*The First 25 Years*, pp. 25-26.

12Ibid., p. 26.

13Memo by Ralph R. Nelson, Actuary, January 12, 1950, in folder: State Employees' Retirement System and Teachers Retirement System, Consolidation of, in Box B01344, Box 1, California State Archives.

14Ibid.

15Memo by Ralph R. Nelson, Actuary, January 20, 1950, in folder: State Employees' Retirement System and Teachers Retirement System, Consolidation of, in Box B01344, Box 1, California State Archives.

[16]Memo by Ralph R. Nelson, Actuary, January 12, 1950.

[17]Report to Joint Legislative Budget Committee prepared by Legislative Auditor, "Integration with Old Age and Survivors' Insurance," *Survey of Retirement Systems State of California*, Parts I-IV.

[18]Senate Bill No. 474, June 13, 1954 (Amended June 1, 1953).

[19]Ibid.

[20]Memorandum by Edward K. Coombs, "Legislative Action on Senate Bill 474, June 2, 1953," in Box B01344, Box 1, California State Archives.

[21]See Assembly Bill 2373. Also see Earl W. Chapman to Fred W. Links, Department of Finance, May 9, 1955.

[22]Dedication Ceremony brochure. Located in Box B01344, Box 1, California State Archives.

[23]Report to Joint Legislative Budget Committee prepared by Legislative Auditor, "Integration with Old Age and Survivors' Insurance," *Survey of Retirement Systems State of California*, Part II (December, 1954), pp. 2-3, 33. This report is hereafter referred to as: *Survey of Retirement Systems State of California*, Part II.

[24]Survey of Retirement Systems State of California, Part II, p. 2.

[25]Sarah Juni, "A Most Unusual Law," Oasis (May 1961), p. 8.

[26]Ibid. Also see *Survey of Retirement Systems. State of California*, Part II, p. 3; and *The First 25 Years*, p. 27.

[27]*Survey of Retirement Systems State of California*, Part II, pp. 4-6, 30, 34.

[28]Ibid., pp. 10, 12.

[29]Ibid., pp. 4-6.

[30]Ibid., pp. 23.

[31]Ibid., p. 35.

[32]*Survey of Retirement Systems State of California*, Part II, pp. 36-7.

[33]"Retirement System Answers Typical Employee Questions," *The California State Employee*, September 1959 (CSEA: Sacramento), p. 6. Also see *The First 25 Years*, p. 27.

[34]*The First 25 Years*, p. 28.

[35]Carl Blechinger, Oral history interview by Christopher J. Castaneda, September 27, 2000, p. 3.

[36]*The First 25 Years*, p. 28.

[37]*The First 25 Years*, pp. 13, 29.

[38]Ibid., p. 29.

[39]Blechinger, Oral history interview by Christopher J. Castaneda, September 27, 2000, p. 4.

[40]*The First 25 Years*, p. 29.

[41]Ibid., pp. 13, 29.

[42]Juni, "A Most Unusual Law," p. 8.

[43]See chart attached to front cover of the folder titled, "Social Security Administration 1957." Located in Box B01344, Box 1, California State Archives.

[44]Social Security Administration, "Narrative essay on the history of Social Security," http://www.ssa.gov/history/briefhistory3.html (accessed on April 4, 2007).

[45]"General Council Set CSEA's Position on Coordination," *The California State Employee*, August 1959 (Sacramento: CSEA), p. 14.

[46]"CSEA Survivors' Plan Adopted; Election on OASDI Set for Sept. 30," *The California State Employee*, August 1959 (Sacramento: CSEA), pp. 1 and 14.

[47]Ibid., p. 1.

[48]Ibid.

[49]"Employees to Decide This Month on Survivors' Plan; OASDI Coordination Loses," *The California State Employee*, Nov. 1959 (Sacramento: CSEA), p. 1.

[50]Ibid.

[51]Memo by H. A. Allmendinger to All Members of Sacramento Chapter No. 2, CSEA, in folder: Social Security State Employees, in Box B01344, Box 1, California State Archives.

[52]"To Coordinate, or Not? Your Decision is Due." *The California State Employee*, November 1961 (Sacramento: CSEA), pp. 1, 8. Also see "Notice of Right to Transfer," Pamphlet from State Employees' Retirement System (September 1, 1961), signed by William E. Payne. Located in Box B01344, Box 1, California State Archives.

[53]Richard Rodda, "US-State Pension Tie Is Argued," *Sacramento Bee*, July 13, 1961. A copy of this article is located in folder: Social Security State Employees, in Box B01344, Box 1, California State Archives.

[54]Ibid.

[55]Ibid.

[56]Ibid.

[57]"Coordination Bill Signed, November 6 Election Set," *The California State Employee*, August 1961 (Sacramento: CSEA), p. 1.

[58]Ibid.

4: New Benefits. New Leadership. New Name.

[1]"State Finds 20 Return," *Sacramento Union* (January 8, 1962).

[2]Richard Rodda, "State Employees Retire For 2nd Time With Higher Pensions," *Sacramento Bee*, January 7, 1962, in folder: Social Security–State Employees, Box B01344, Box 1, California State Archives.

[3]"OASDI, Finance To Be Studied," *The California State Employee*, Vol. 37, No. 22 (November 25, 1966), pp. 1 and 4.

[4]Ibid.

[5]See *The California State Employee*, Vol. 38, No. 12 (June 30, 1967), pp. A-D.

[6]"Social Security Poll Cards Ask: Should OASDI Stay with SERS?" *The California State Employee*, Vol. 38, No. 13 (July 14, 1967), p. 5.

[7]*The California State Employee*, Vol. 38, No. 13 (July 14, 1967), p. 9.

[8]Ibid., p. 8.

[9]"CSEA Board of Directors Refers OASDI Poll Results Back to G.C.," *The California State Employee*, Vol. 38, No. 17 (September 15, 1967), p. 11.

[10]"Top Stories of 1967-September: Social Security Poll Results," *The California State Employee*, Vol. 38, No. 24 (December 29, 1967), p. 11.

[11]R.W. Wilson, untitled manuscript on the SERS health and medical benefits program, 1982, Prologue.

[12]Ibid., pp. 1 and 2a.

[13]Ibid., p. 2a

[14]Ibid.

[15]Ibid., Prologue.

[16]Ibid., see Footnote 1 for the Prologue.

[17]Ibid., see "Footnotes," No. 2.

[18]Ibid., "Legislative Profile: Foreword."

[19]"Brown Asks Health Plan Aid, P.T. Pay Boost; Other Salary Decisions Delayed," *The California State Employee*, Vol. 33, No. 1 (January, 1961), p. 1.

[20]R. W. Wilson, untitled manuscript on the SERS health and medical benefits program, 1982, "Legislative Profile: Forward," p. 2.

[21]Ibid.

[22]"SERS Sets Health Plan Programs," *The California State Employee*, Vol. 32, No. 11 (November, 1961), p. 1.

23"Presenting: Ten Health Plans," *The California State Employee*, Vol. 32, No. 11 (November, 1961), p. 14.

24"CSEA, SERS to Merge Cal-West Health Plans," *The California State Employee*, Vol. 37, No. 19 (October 14, 1966), p. 12.

25Press Release, Assemblyman E. Richard Barnes, August 1, 1968, Box #, B01344, California State Archives.

26Ibid.

27Meeting of 8-11-61, Investment Policy Discussions, Board of Administration (April, 1954, through 11-28-62), Box#1, B01344, California State Archives.

28Meeting of 2-7-64, Investment Policy Discussions, Board of Administration (April, 1954, through 11-28-62), Box#1, B01344, California State Archives.

29Jim Smith, Oral History Interview by Christopher J. Castaneda, December 4, 2000, p. 3.

30Ibid., p. 7.

31Ibid., p. 4.

32Carl C. Wilberg, Oral History Interview by Christopher J. Castaneda, November 10, 2000.

33Meeting of 2-10-61, *Investment Policy Discussions, Board of Administration* (April, 1954, through 11-28-62), Box #1, B01344, California State Archives.

34Ibid.

35"California Press Lining Up for Proposition #1," *The California State Employee* Vol. 37, No. 17 (September 16, 1966), p. 1.

36"Proposition 1–a yes vote helps," *The California State Employee*, Vol. 37, No. 20 (October 28, 1966), p. 12.

37"California Press Lining Up for Proposition #1," *The California State Employee* Vol. 37, No. 17 (September 16, 1966), p. 8.

38"Investments by SERS," *The California State Employee* Vol. 37, No. 18 (September 30, 1966), p. 13.

39Ibid.

40"Proposition 1–a yes vote helps," *The California State Employee*, Vol. 37, No. 20 (October 28, 1966), p. 12.

41Press Release, Assemblyman E. Richard Barnes, August 1, 1968. Box #1, B01344, California State Archives.

42"Governor Signs 14 CSEA Bills, But Vetoes 5," *The California State Employee*, Vol. 38, No. 17 (September 15, 1967), p. 9.

43"SERS Names Investment Counsel To Give Advice on Stock Market," *The California State Employee*, Vol. 38, No. 20 (October 27, 1967), p. 11.

44Ibid.

45"Governor Vetoes Retired Pay Bill," *The California State Employee*, Vol. 38, No. 17 (September 15, 1967), p. 9.

46Meeting of 10-11-62, *Investment Policy Discussions, Board of Administration* (April, 1954, through 11-28-62), Box #1, B01344, California State Archives.

47"SERS Division Chief Class Established by Personnel Board," *The California State Employee*, Vol. 38, No. 20 (October 27, 1967), p. 7.

48"SERS Names Investment Counsel To Give Advice on Stock Market," *The California State Employee*, Vol. 38, No. 20 (October 27, 1967), p. 12.

49Congressional Budget Office, *Tax Policy for Pensions and Other Retirement Savings* (Congress of the United States, U.S. GPO, April 1987), pp. 134-136. Also see "Statement of President Ford on Signing Pension Legislation," *Pension & Welfare News* (November 1974), p. 2. (Note, statistics in this paragraph are drawn from both articles.)

50Congressional Budget Office, *Tax Policy for Pensions and Other Retirement Savings* (Congress of the United States, U.S. GPO, April 1987), p. 135.

51William Graebner, *A History of Retirement: The Meaning and Function of An American Institution, 1885-1978* (Yale University Press: New Haven, 1980), p. 242.

52Peter F. Drucker, *The Unseen Revolution: How Pension Fund Socialism Came to America* (New York: Harper & Row Publishers, 1976), pp. 20-21.

53Ibid., p. 21.

54See "ERISA Remembered," *Employee Benefit Plan Review* (June 1984), p. 7.

55"The Employee Retirement Security Act," *Pension & Welfare News* (November 1974), p. 4.

56"Statement of President Ford on Signing Pension Legislation," *Pension & Welfare News* (November 1974), pp. 2 and 159.

57"The Innovators: Jacob Javits," *Global Custodian* (Fall 1999), p. 62. Also see "Main Features of the Legislation," *Pension & Welfare News* (November 1974), p. 30.

58Interim Report of Activities of the Pension Task Force of the Subcommittee on Labor Standards, Committee on Education and Labor, House of Representatives, March 31, 1976, p. v. (Quoted in Bill Horne Associates, "California's Public Retirement Plans," Vol. 1 (September, 1978), p. 1.)

59Testimony by Dan M. McGill on the Retirement Income Security for Employees Act, 1972, Hearings, June 20-21, 1972, Subcommittee on Labor, Committee on Public Employment and Retirement, March 16, 1977. (Quoted in Bill Horne Associates, "California's Public Retirement Plans," Vol. 1 (September, 1978), p. 103.)

60Quoted in Bill Horne Associates, "California's Public Retirement Plans," Vol. 1 (September, 1978), pp. 106-7 and 199-20.

61Brochure for Employee Benefit Research Institute, no date.

62Carl Blechinger, Oral History Interview by Christopher J. Castaneda, May 24, 2000.

63Ibid.

64Ibid.

65R.W. Wilson, untitled manuscript on the SERS health and medical benefits program, 1982, Introduction, p. 1.

66Robert Wilson, Oral History Interview by Christopher J. Castaneda, October 27, 2000, p. 44.

67Public Employees' Retirement System, *Fiftieth Annual Report* (June 30, 1981), p. 26.

68Ibid., p. 89.

69Wilberg, Oral History Interview by Christopher J. Castaneda, November 10, 2000, p. 9.

5: Influence & Integrity

1Fred R. Bleakley, "A Trustee Takes on the Greenmailers," *New York Times*, February 10, 1985, p. 6F.

2Ibid.

3Ibid.

4Fran Hawthorne, "Gold stakes," *Institutional Investor* (August 1988), 158. Also see *Institutional Investor* (May 1987).

5"A move to make institutions start using their stockholder clout," *Businessweek* (August 6, 1984), p. 70.

6 "Council of Institutional Investors Formed to Take Stand on Corporate Takeover Issues," *BNA Pension Reporter* (January 28, 1985), Investments section.

7 Bleakley, "A Trustee Takes on the Greenmailers," *New York Times* (February 10, 1985), p. 6F.

8 See Chuck Paustian, "Insider Deals May Hurt Shareholders," *Pensions and Investment Age*, Vol. 13, Issue 26 (December 1985), p. 41.

9 "A move to make institutions start using their stockholder clout," *Businessweek* (August 6, 1984), p. 70. Jim Lewis, "Pension Power: Unruh leads quiet drive for corporate influence," *Sacramento Bee* (October or November, 1985-exact date unknown), Section A. "Takeover Tangles," Fortune (March 4, 1985).

10 Joel Chernoff, "Council debates future: Corporate recruiter or corporate watchdog?" *Pensions & Investment Age* (November 11, 1985), p. 86.

11 Council of Institutional Investors, *Annual Report 1986/7*, pp. 5-6. Lewis, "Pension Power: Unruh leads quiet drive for corporate influence," *Sacramento Bee* (October or November, 1985-exact date unknown), Section A.

12 Patricia Sullivan, "A Paper Loss on Unocal," *California Journal* (August 1985), p. 307.

13 "Council heading for the crossroads," *Pensions & Investment Age* (November 25, 1985). Also see "In defense of the Council of Institutional Investors," *Institutional Investor* (September 1988), p. 27.

14 Marilyn Geewax, "Funds' council is praised: SEC chairman invites comments from group," *Atlanta Journal* (October 30, 1985). Charles Pluckhahn, "Pension-Fund Group Offers 'Shareholder Bill of Rights,'" *Investor's Daily* (December 11, 1985), p. 36.

15 Bleakley, "A Trustee Takes on the Greenmailers," *New York Times*, February 10, 1985, p. 6F.

16 William Glaberson, "Head of G.M. Sees End To Perot Controversy," *New York Times*, January 29, 1987.

17 Hilary Rosenberg, "The revolt of the institutional shareholds," *Institutional Investor*, (May, 1987).

18 Ibid.; Albert Lee, "Call Me Roger," Regardie's (May 1988), p. 148.

19 Kenneth Klee, "Dale Hanson pulls in his horns," *Institutional Investor* (no date), p. 11.

20 See Michael P. Smith, "Shareholder Activism by Institutional Investors: Evidence from CalPERS," *Journal of Finance*, Vol. LI, No. 1, (March 1996), pp. 227-252.

21 "Letter to the Editor," *PERS Update* (December 1983), p. 6.

22 Ed Mendel, "Purring and Stirring $45 billion in pension funds," *Golden State Report* (March 1986), pp. 30-31.

23 Ibid., p. 28.

24 Ibid.

25 Ibid., pp. 28-29.

26 Ibid., p. 28. Janice Fillip, "Lincoln Plaza is at peace with its neighbors," *Sacramento Union*, (November 2, 1988), p. 26.

27 Mendel, "Purring and Stirring $45 billion in pension funds," *Golden State Report*, (March 1986), p. 28.

28 Fillip, "Lincoln Plaza is at peace with its neighbors," *Sacramento Union*, (November 2, 1986), p. 26.

29 Mendel, "Purring and Stirring $45 billion in pension funds," *Golden State Report* (March 1986), p. 28. Also see "PERS Funds: Who Should Determine the Investments?" *Sacramento Bee* (March 20, 1985), p. B12.

30 Ted Reed, "State pension funds grapple with divestiture," *Sacramento Bee* (no date), p. D6.

31 For background on the divestiture issue prior to divestiture, see Stuart A. Baldwin, et. al., *Pension Funds & Ethical Investment: A Study of Investment Practices and Opportunities State of California Retirement Systems* (New York City: Council on Economic Priorities, 1986).

32 Douglas Shuit, "State Pension Fund Board Fires Director," [Unknown Paper], June 19, 1986, p. 3. Also see "Raid On The Pensions," *Sacramento Bee*, April 29, 1982.

33 See PERS Retirement Betterment Committee Inc., "Progress Report," (February 16, 1987), pp. 1-2.

34 Douglas Shuit, "State Pension Fund Board Fires Director," [Unknown Paper], June 19, 1986, p. 3. Also see "Raid On The Pensions," *Sacramento Bee*, April 29, 1982.

35 Charles Valdes, Oral History Interview by Christopher J. Castaneda, December 5, 2000, p. 16.

36 Ibid.

37 Ed Salzman, "Jesse's bouncing baby," *Golden State Report*, (March 1989), p. 31. Also see Kathleen N. Crighton, "The Council of Institutional Investors at the Crossroads," *Pension World*, (June 1987), p. 26.

38 Fran Hawthorne, "Gold stakes," *Institutional Investor*, (August 1988), 158.

39 Ibid., p. 160.

40 Ibid.

41 Not long after Hanson took over, Wall Street experienced a major stock drop. On October 19, 1987, the Dow Jones Average fell by 508 points, and the market remained unsettled afterwards. Hanson reminded members that PERS was a defined benefit program meaning that benefits were fixed by contract regardless of the level of contribution or investment return. See "PERS remains sound despite stock crash," *The California State Retiree*, (November, 1987), p. 1.

42 James E. Burton, and Dale Hanson, Oral History Interview by Christopher J. Castaneda, November 21, 2000, p. 15.

43 Harvard Business School, "California PERS," Harvard Business School case, N9-291-045 (July 10, 1991), p. 2.

44 Ibid., p. 3.

45 Robert B. Gunnison and Greg Lucas, "Rough Hearing for Wilson Pension Fund Plan," *San Francisco Chronicle*, (no date, 1990s folder), p. A-13. Also see Dan Walters, "Wilson's budget hits a new snag," *San Jose Mercury News*, (June 20, 1991).

46 Joyce Terhaar, "Wilson seeks sway over PERS," *Sacramento Bee*, June 14, 1991, (Business section,), p. 1.

47 Thorne Gray, "Wilson-Senate budget unravels," *Sacramento Bee*, June 25, 1991; Harry Bernstein, "Forays Into Finance Benefit Workers," *Los Angeles Times*, June 25, 1991, p. D3.

48 Paul Jacobs, "Layoff Threat Issued in Budget Fight," *Los Angeles Times*, June 25, 1991.

49 "New cutback threat in pension-fund struggle," *Sacramento Union*, June 16, 1991.

50 Thom Calandra, "Money Talks," *San Francisco Examiner*, June 23, 1991.

51 Robert B. Gunnison and Vlae Kershner, "U.S. Probe of Wilson's Pension Fight," *San Francisco Chronicle*, June 20, 1991.

52 Ibid.

53 U.S. Probe Of Wilson's Pension Fight," *San Francisco Chronicle*, June 20, 1991, p. 1.

54 John Howard, "Wilson's use of pensions fires debate," *Sacramento Union*, June 19, 1991, p. 1.

55 Ibid., p. A4.

56 Joyce Terhaar, "Wilson's plans for PERS funds battered at hearing," *Sacramento Bee*, June 25, 1991, E1.

57 June Gibbs Brown, "Audit of State of California's Pension Fund," Department of Health and Human Services: Office of Inspector General, A-09-92-00116 (August, 1994), p. 2-3.

58 *BNA Pension Reporter*, Vol. 20 (February 8, 1993), p. 358.

59 "California fund to up in-house management," *Pensions & Investments*, (September 20, 1993).

60 David Felderstein, Oral history interview conducted by Christopher J. Castaneda, September 13, 2000, p. 35.

61 Robert D. Walton, Oral history inteview conducted by Christopher J. Castaneda, May 24, 2000, pp. 18-19.

62 Robert F. Carlson, Oral history interview conducted by Christopher J. Castaneda, May 24, 2000, p. 21.

63 "California to Pay $1.36 Billion To CalPERS After State Court Ruling," *Pension & Benefits*, Vol. 24, No. 22, p. 1303.

64 "California Senate Panel Rejects Bill on Moving Public-Pension Funds," *Wall Street Journal* (July 5, 1996), p. C24.

65 "Pension: Public funds influencing corporations," *Sacramento Bee*, June 23, 1991, p. D8.

66 Ibid.

67 Floyd Norris, "A Debate Grows Over Proxy Rules," *New York Times*, December 18, 1990, p. D8.

68 Dale Hanson, "Much, much more than investors," *Financial Executive*, March 1993, p. 48.

69 Floyd Norris, "A Debate Grows Over Proxy Rules," *New York Times*, December 18, 1990, p. D8.

70 Ibid.

71 Dale Hanson, "Much, much more than investors," *Financial Executive* (March 1993), p. 48.

72 Ricki Fulman, "Pension Funds Led Corporate Governance Revolution: Not Just for Gadflys Anymore, Investor Activism Gets Results," *Pensions & Investments*, (February 9, 1998), p. 19.

73 Ibid.

74 Victor F. Zonana, "Pension Funds Flex Muscles," *Los Angeles Times*, June 21, 1991.

75 "Pension: Public funds influencing corporations," *Sacramento Bee*, June 23, 1991, p. D8.

76 Victor F. Zonana, "Pension Funds Flex Muscles," *Los Angeles Times*, June 21, 1991.

77 Susan Pulliam, "Calpers Goes Over CEO's Heads In Its Quest for Higher Returns," *Wall Street Journal* (January 22, 1993), p. C1.

78 Ibid.

79 Lawrence M. Fisher, "Big Pension Fund Prodding 12 Companies," *New York Times*, January 23, 1993, p. 36.

80 James Kim, "Strategy shift weighed," *USA Today*, February 23, 1993, p. 2B.

81 Ibid.

82 James Kim, "CEO of CalPERS wields clout," *USA Today*, February 23, 1993, p. 1B.

83 Terry Williams, "California fund officials at odds over realty targets," *Pensions & Investments*, February 8, 1993, p. 3.

84 George Anders, "While Head of Calpers Lectures Other Firms, His Own Board Frets," *Wall Street Journal* (January 29, 1993).

85 Steve Hemmerick, "Housing to return 20.3%," *Pensions & Investments* (August 23, 1993)

86 Jessica Sommar, "Calpers: $ 2 billion to spend and not a decent deal in sight," *Investment Dealers' Digest* (May 4, 1992).

87 "Fund makes energy bet," *Pensions & Investments*, (July 12, 1993), p. 6; Hilary Rosenberg, "CalPERS goes direct," *Institutional Investor*, (September, 1993), p. 191.

88 William Power, "Calpers Becomes A Direct Partner With Enron Unit," *Wall Street Journal* (July 1, 1993), p. 11.

89 "CalPERS Investments," *BNA Pension & Benefits Reporter*, (Dec. 12, 1994), p. 2330.

90 George Anders, "While Head of Calpers Lectures Other Firms, His Own Board Frets," *Wall Street Journal*, (January 29, 1993), p. A1.

91 Leslie Scism, "Calpers to Link Chief's Pay To Bottom Line," *Wall Street Journal*, (November 22, 1993), p. C1.

92 Andrew LePage, "Chief Investment Manager Resigns from California Public-Pension Fund," *Sacramento Bee*, January 15, 2000.

93 Ibid.

94 Ibid.

95 Andrea Adelson, "Calpers Chooses a Less Adversarial Voice," *New York Times*, September 17, 1994, p. 36.

96 "CalPERS Says Its Target Firms Are Behaving More Responsibly," *Investors Business Daily* (June 9, 1995), p. A2. Also, "CalPERS Releases Top Replies on Requests for Self-Analysis," *BNA Pension & Benefits Reporter*, Vol. 22 (June 5, 1995), p. 1328.

97 "CALPERS, other funds takes the corporate governance crusade overseas," *Plan Sponsor*, (February 1995), p. 43.

98 Mariene Givant Star, "California to sue over French merger," *Pensions & Investments* (September 19, 1993), p. 4.

99 Ibid.

100 "CalPERS votes proxies at meetings of shareholders of Japanese firms," *BNA Pension & Benefits Reporter*, (July 18, 1994), p. 1415.

101 "CalPERS Investments," *BNA Pension & Benefits Reporter*, (Dec. 12, 1994), p. 2330.

102 "South Africa Divestment Cost California Millions," *BNA Pension & Benefits Reporter*, Vol. 22, (February 27, 1995), p. 555.

103 "CalPERS lists China as 'prudent' country," *BNA Pension & Benefits Reporter*, Vol. 22, (May 1, 1995), p. 1113.

104 David A. Vise, "Labor Dept. Offers Guidelines to Spur Pension Fund's 'Targeted' Investments," *Washington Post*, June 23, 1994, p. A6.

105 Ibid. Also see H. Jane Lehman, "Use of Pension Fund Investing," *Washington Post*, June 25, 1994, p. F5.

106 Gray Davis and James Z. Pugash, "CalPERS is putting its money down on the state's economy," *Sacramento Bee*, January 15, 1994, p. B7.

6: Building a Secure Tomorrow

[1] James E. Burton and Dale Hanson, Oral History Interview by Christopher J. Castaneda, November 21, 2000, pp. 30-31.

[2] Peter Mixon, Interview by The History Factory, January 5, 2007.

[3] Fred Buenrostro, "The California Experience," speech to the National Association of State Retirement Administrators, August 7, 2005.

[4] CalPERS Facts at a Glance, Investment Portfolio, December 31, 2006.

[5] Patricia K. Macht, Interview by The History Factory, Dec. 13, 2006.

[6] George Diehr, "Doing Well by Doing Good: The CalPERS Experience," speech to the Public Sector Pension Conference, November 3, 2005.

[7] Fred Buenrostro, "The CalPERS Venture into Clean Tech Investing," speech to the SACRS Fall Conference, November 16, 2006.

[8] Robert Carlson, "Investment Flows, Increasingly Democratic, Increasingly Global," speech, May 2, 2006.

[9] Priya Mather, "Corporate Governance in the New Japan–Revisited," speech to The Japan Society of Northern California, June 28, 2006.

[10] Carlson, "Investment Flows, Increasingly Democratic, Increasingly Global," May 2, 2006.

[11] Priya Mather, "CalPERS Health Care: Making Every Dollar Count," speech to CalPERS Employer HR Manager Forum, August 2, 2005.

[12] Jarvio Grevious, Interview by The History Factory, January 4, 2007.

[13] Ibid.

[14] Jarvio Grevious, "What is the Current Status and Future of Retirement Health Benefits?," speech to Harvard Law School Capital Matters, Managing Labor's Capital IV, April 26-28, 2006.

[15] Dale Kasler, "CalPERS again at the forefront, but whether its dumping of higher-cost hospitals is a trend remains unclear," *Sacramento Bee*, May 23, 2004.

[16] Jarvio Grevious, Welcome speech at the Public Sector Health Care Roundtable Second Annual Conference and Business Meeting, November 27, 2006.

[17] Buenrostro, "The CalPERS Venture into Clean Tech Investing," March 3, 2006.

[18] Robert Carlson, "Institutional Investors–A New World Order," speech at the Madinat Jumeirah Conference Center, Dubai, May 3, 2006.

[19] Ibid.

[20] Andrew Junkin, "The 'CalPERS Effect' on Targeted Company Share Price," *Wilshire Associates*, July 27, 2006.

[21] Diehr, "Doing Well by Doing Good: The CalPERS Experience," November 3, 2005.

[22] Fred Buenrostro, "Integrating Capital Markets – Ultimate Challenge of the Present," speech to the IOSCO Technical Committee Conference, Oct. 5, 2005.

[23] NYSE Group, Inc., "NYSE Announces New Contract For Dick Grasso Through May 2007," press release, August 27, 2003.

[24] Diehr, "Doing Well by Doing Good: The CalPERS Experience," Nov. 3, 2005.

[25] Erin White and Aaron O. Patrick, "Shareowners Push for Vote on Executive Pay," *Wall Street Journal*, Feb. 26, 2007.

[26] CalPERS sent the letter on February 20, 2007.

[27] "CalPERS Issues Statement on HP Vote," press release, March 14, 2007.

[28] Patricia K. Macht, "CalPERS: A Force for Good Corporate Governance," speech to The Parhad Programs, September 20, 2006.

[29] Rachel Beck, "UnitedHealth Controls Lax," *Wichita Times*, October 17, 2006.

[30] Excerpted from a letter from Rob Feckner to James A. Johnson, Chair, Compensation Committee, UnitedHealth Group, April 25, 2006.

[31] Rob Feckner, speech to Ceres Conference Panel, March 30, 2005.

[32] Excerpt from letter from Michael A.M. Lauffer, Chief Counsel, State Water Resources Control Board to Fred Buenrostro, Dec. 28, 2006.

[33] Ron Seeling, Interview by The History Factory, February 27, 2007.

[34] Ibid.

[35] Ibid.

[36] Seeling, Interview, February 27, 2007.

[37] Ken Marzion, Interview by The History Factory, January 5, 2007.

[38] Seeling, Interview, February 27, 2007.

[39] Peter Schrag, "As California Goes," *The Nation*, March 30, 2007.

[40] Rob Feckner, Welcome remarks, speech to NAACP Sacramento Branch Installation Reception, February 1, 2007.

[41] CalPERS video script, SWEL Award, April 4, 2007.

[42] Application for 2007 SWEL WorkPlace Excellence Leadership Award, submitted by CalPERS staff Gilda Carpenter, Kristen Claudy, Micki Gibbs, and Thea Myers.

[43] Ibid.

Index

Page numbers in *italic* indicate photographs or illustrations; those in **bold** indicate charts or tables.

C

Cake Auctions, 225

Calgary Sun, 193, *193*

California Division of Highways, 105, *105*

California Employers' Retiree Benefit Trust Fund, 215, 218, *218*

California HealthCare Foundation, 196

California Highway Patrol Retirement Act, *46-47*, 46-48, 53

California Hospital Assessment and Reporting Taskforce (CHART), 196

California Physicians' Service (CPS), 103, 109

California's Public Employees' Retirement System. *See* CalPERS

California State Employee, The, 83, *83*, 114

California State Employees (occupations, gender, salaries), 1927, **9**

California State Employees Association. *See* CSEA

California State Employees Charitable Campaign, 225

California State Fairgrounds (Sacramento), 116, *117*

California State Office Building No. 1, 153, *153*

California State seal, 189, *189*

California State Teachers' Retirement System (CalSTRS), 3, 5, 51, 71, 73, 148, 201, 208, 210, 222

California State University, 159

California Taxpayers Association (Cal-Tax), 161

California Urban Real Estate program, 222

California Western States Life and Occidental Life Insurance Companies of California (CWO), *104*, 104-105, 109

California Women's Peace Officers Association, 212

Callan, Edward J., 27, 30, **31**, 228

Call Center, 210

CalPERS (California Public Employees' Retirement System), vi-vii, 239. *See also* investments
average employer contribution rates, 216, **216**
Board Members (1932 to present), 199, *199*, 228-229
building a secure tomorrow (late 1990s to present), 179-226
defining years of SERS (1930s), 35-63

diversity of, 220-221, *220-222*, 222
expansion of SERS (1960s to 1970s), 97-133
founding principle and mission, 101, 181, 226, 229
influence and integrity (1980s to mid-1990s), 133, 135-177
investing for life (1940s to 1950s), 65-95
membership growth (1932 to 2006), **236**
milestones, 216
name changed to, 154, *154*
one-on-one connection with members, *76*, 76-77, *100*, 101, 213
origins of SERS (1910s to 1920s), 1-33
technology upgrades, 119, *119*, 154, 155, 180, 218-219, *219*
timeline, 230-235
voter-approved propositions central to, 29, *29*
Web site, 77, 219

"CalPERS Effect," 200, *200*

CalSTRS (California State Teachers' Retirement System), 3, 5, 51, 71, 73, 148, 201, 208, 210, 222

Cal-Tax (California Taxpayers Association), 161

CalTrans, 36, *37*, 159, 182, *182*

campaigning for SERS, 16-28, *17-18*, *20-21*, **22**, *23-25*, **26**, 27

Campaigns, Inc., 19

canning method, WV 4-H Fair, 2, *2*

Carlson, Robert F., 29, 126, 128, 135, *135*, 150, *150*, 160, *160*, 164, 165, 191, 198, 199, *199*, 200, 222, 229

Carpenter, Richard ("Bud"), 229

Carr, John E., 110, 229

cartoons, CalPERS, 156, *156*

Cayelli, Sharon, 160

CCC (Civilian Conservation Corps), 39, *39*, 42

Centers of Expertise (hospitals), 196

Centinela Capital Partners, 222

Central Emergency Hospital (San Francisco), 104, *104*

Chaindex, 119, *119*

Champion, Hale, 229

Champion International Corporation, 167, 169

Chandler, Roger, 229

Chapman, Earl W., vii, 27, 31, *31*, 35, *35*, 44, 46, 62, *64*, 65, *65*, 79, 82, 85, 86, 87, 88, 126, 127, 229

CHART (California Hospital Assessment and Reporting Taskforce), 196

Chatters, Ford A., 229

Chavez, Richard, 229

Chiang, John, 229

Chicago's Pension Commission Board, 11, *11*

Chili Cook Offs, 225

China and CalPERS, 176-177

chronic disease care management, 196

CII (Council of Institutional Investors), 137, 139-145, *140*, *142*, *144-145*, 153, 160, 166, *166*, 168

cities joining SERS, 51-52, 52, 62, 63

CitiMortgage, 112

City of Thousand Oaks, 218, *218*

Civilian Conservation Corps (CCC), 39, *39*, 42

civil service reform, 2-3, 7, 9

Claremont Graduate School, 168

Clark, Thomas J., 160, *160*, 229

Cleantech, 191

Climate Risk Disclosure Initiative, 210

Clinton, Bill (President), 173

Coates, Barrett N., 11

Comcast Corporation, 171, 172, *172*

Commission on Pensions of State Employees (Pension Commission), 7, **9**, 9-16, *10-16*, 33

Committee on Economic Security, 42

commodities (natural resource), 193

Commons, John R., 39

common stock (equities), 56, **56**, 97, *97*, 110, *113-115*, 113-116, 129, 131, **131**, 139, **142**, 169-170, 174, 181

competitive model of negotiating health plans, 194

Connell, Kathleen, 229

consolidating California's retirement systems, 71, 73-74

Construction Industry Research Board, 171

consultants, 57-59, *58-59*, 61, 115-116, 131, 133, *133*

contract members, public agencies joining as, 35, 50-52, *50-52*, 53, 62, *63*, 76, 182-183, *182-183*

contributions
employees, 14, *15*, 15-16, 36, 48
gender-based rates, *15*, 15-16, 36, 48
gender-neutral rates, 128-129, *130*, 131
State, 14, 36, 48

Image Credits

Images not listed below appear courtesy of CalPERS.

Cover

Courtesy of the California History Room, California State Library, Sacramento, California

1: A Progressive Proposition

Intro: Courtesy of the California History Room, California State Library, Sacramento, California

Page 1: Courtesy of California State Employees Association

Page 2: Library of Congress, Prints & Photographs Division, National Child Labor Committee Collection, LC-DIG-nclc-04385

Page 3: Sacramento Archives & Museum Collection Center, Sacramento-El Dorado Medical Society Collection, 1998/12/24

Page 4: Sacramento Archives & Museum Collection Center, City of Sacramento Collection, 1999/X-04/58

Page 5: Library of Congress, Prints & Photographs Division, Panoramic Photographs Collection, PAN SUBJECT-Groups no. 267

Page 6: (*both*) The Bancroft Library, University of California, Berkeley

Page 8: Courtesy of the California History Room, California State Library, Sacramento, California

Page 10: Sacramento Archives & Museum Collection Center, Melvin Stover Collection, 1987/91/135

Page 11: DN-0079254, *Chicago Daily News* negatives collection, Chicago Historical Society

Page 13: Sacramento Archives & Museum Collection Center, City of Sacramento Collection, 1999/X-04/55

Page 14: Copyright, 1929, *Los Angeles Times*, Reprinted with permission

Page 15: Sacramento Archives & Museum Collection Center, Helen J. Astill Collection, 2001/56/63

Page 16: Sacramento Archives & Museum Collection Center, McCurry Collection, 1973/03/1474

Page 17: Library of Congress, Prints & Photographs Division, Panoramic Photographs Collection, PAN US GEOG-California no. 234

Page 18: Courtesy of the Oakland History Room, Oakland Public Library

Page 20: Whitaker-Baxter Collateral, California State Archives, Office of the Secretary of State, Sacramento

Page 21: Robert Lackenbach/*Time & Life* Pictures/Getty Images

Page 23: Library of Congress, Prints & Photographs Division, George Grantham Bain Collection, LC-DIG-ggbain-06374

Page 24: Courtesy of the San Francisco History Center, San Francisco Public Library

Page 25: (*left*) Sacramento Archives & Museum Collection Center, Norwood Silsbee Collection, 1969/206/55'B'

Page 27: (*right*) Courtesy of California State Employees Association

Page 29: Herald Examiner Photograph Collection, Los Angeles Public Library

Page 30: Courtesy of California State Employees Association

2: The Defining Years

Page 34: Sacramento Archives & Museum Collection Center, City of Sacramento Collection, 2004/X-01/004

Page 36: Copyright, 1931, *Los Angeles Times*, Reprinted with permission

Page 37: Sacramento Archives & Museum Collection Center, Melvin Stover Collection, 1987/091/132

Page 38: Courtesy of the California History Room, California State Library, Sacramento, California

Page 39: P-0687, Eastman's Originals Collection, D-51, Special Collections, University of California Library, Davis

Page 40: © Bettmann/Corbis

Page 41: Leonard McCombe/*Time & Life* Pictures/Getty Images

Page 42: Library of Congress, Prints & Photographs Division, FSA/OWI Collection, LC-USF34-018934-E

Page 43: Social Security Administration History Archives

Page 44: Courtesy of the California History Room, California State Library, Sacramento, California

Page 45: Library of Congress, Prints & Photographs Division, HABS CAL,49-SONO,5-1

Page 46: (*top*) Hank Walker/*Time & Life* Pictures/Getty Images
(*bottom*) Courtesy of the Coalinga District Library

Page 47: (*top*) Sacramento Archives & Museum Collection Center, *Sacramento Bee* Collection, 1983/01/SBPM1489
(*bottom*) Links Collection: F3254: 270, California State Archives, Office of the Secretary of State, Sacramento

Page 49: Sacramento Archives & Museum Collection Center, California Parks and Recreation Collection, 1989/01/272

Page 50: Courtesy of the Hayward Area Historical Society

Page 51: Courtesy of the Archives and Local History Collection, Redwood City Public Library

Page 114: Copyright, 1966, *Los Angeles Times*, Reprinted with permission

Page 115: Courtesy of the San Francisco History Center, San Francisco Public Library

Page 116: Courtesy of California State Employees Association

Page 117: Sacramento Archives & Museum Collection Center, *Sacramento Bee* Collection, 1983/01/SBPM2891

Page 118: Courtesy of the Frashers Fotos Collection

Page 120: Library of Congress, Prints & Photographs Division, LC-USZ62-122674

Page 121: Copyright © 1958 The *New York Times* Company

Page 122: AP Images

Page 123: David Hume Kennerly/*Time & Life* Pictures/Getty Images

Page 124: Copyright © 1976 The *New York Times* Company

Page 126: Employee Benefit Research Institute, www.ebri.org

Page 129: © Corbis

Page 130: Courtesy of the Palo Alto Historical Association Photograph Collection

Page 132: (*both*) Courtesy of the San Francisco History Center, San Francisco Public Library

Page 133: © Bettmann/Corbis

5: Influence & Integrity

Page 134: Courtesy of California State Employees Association

Page 136: Sacramento Archives & Museum Collection Center, McCurry's Collection, 1973/03/1076

Page 137: Copyright, 1984, *Los Angeles Times*, Reprinted with permission

Page 138: © Bettmann/Corbis

Page 139: Courtesy of Robert A.G. Monks, Portrait by G. Augusta

Page 140: A 1985 Herblock Cartoon, Copyright by the Herb Block Foundation

Page 141: Hugh Patrick Brown/*Time & Life* Pictures/Getty Images

Page 142: Shelly Katz/*Time & Life* Pictures/Getty Images

Page 143: Jim Britt/*Time & Life* Pictures/Getty Images

Page 144: Securities and Exchange Commission Historical Society—Virtual Museum and Archive of SEC and Securities History at www.sechistorical.org

Page 145: Jerome Magid/*Time & Life* Pictures/Getty Images

Page 146: Courtesy of the Big Bear Airport

Page 148: Sacramento Archives & Museum Collection Center, Dreyfus & Blackford Architects Collection, 2002/079/0705

Page 149: © Joseph Sohm/Visions of America/Corbis

Page 150: (*left*) Sacramento Archives & Museum Collection Center, Phyllis Alvedo Collection, 1985/39/04

Page 151: (*upper left*) © *Sacramento Bee*, 2006

Page 152: (*top*) F3757:55-58A, California State Archives, Office of the Secretary of State, Sacramento
(*bottom*) Sacramento Archives & Museum Collection Center, *Sacramento Bee* Portrait Collection, Charles Valdes

Page 153: Library of Congress, Prints & Photographs Division, HABS CAL, 34-SAC, 65-2

Page 154: (*top*) Alan Levenson/*Time & Life* Pictures/Getty Images

Page 156: (*all*) Reprinted with permission, *Pensions & Investments*. Copyright, Crain Communications, Inc.

Page 158: *Sacramento Union* Archives, D-350, Special Collections, University of California Library, Davis

Page 159: Courtesy of California State Employees Association

Page 160: (*top*) California State Archives, Office of the Secretary of State, Sacramento

Page 162: Courtesy of California State Employees Association

Page 163: Courtesy of California State Employees Association

Page 164: Courtesy of California State Employees Association

Page 165: Copyright © 1991 The *New York Times* Company

Page 166: Courtesy of the Council of Institutional Investors

Page 168: Copyright © 1990 The *New York Times* Company

Page 169: Copyright © 1992 The *New York Times* Company

Page 171: Courtesy of the Las Flores Community

Page 172: Tim Boyle/Getty Images News/Getty Images

Page 173: Dirck Halstead/*Time &Life* Pictures/Getty Images

Page 176: Trevor Samson/*Time & Life* Pictures/Getty Images

6: Building a Secure Tomorrow

Page 181: (*bottom*) Copyright © 1996 The *New York Times* Company

Page 182: (*left*) Courtesy of the CalPERS Unit of the Division of School Financial Services, Los Angeles County Office of Education
(*middle*) © Roger Ressmeyer/Corbis
(*right*) © Maggie Hallahan/Corbis

Page 183: (*upper left*) Courtesy of the Russian River Fire Protection District
(*upper right*) Courtesy of the Santa Cruz Consolidated Emergency Communications Center
(*lower left*) Courtesy of the Murrieta Valley Cemetery District
(*lower right*) Courtesy of the Nevada City Chamber of Commerce

Page 184: Rich Pedroncelli/AP Images

Page 185: Courtesy of California State Employees Association

Page 186: Reprinted with permission, *Pensions & Investments*. Copyright, Crain Communications, Inc.

Page 187: David McNew/Getty Images News/Getty Images

Page 190: Courtesy of Premier Pacific Vineyards

Page 191: Rich Pedroncelli/AP Images

Page 192: Katsumi Kasahara/AP Images

Page 193: © Copyright 2006 Tab, Reprinted with permission, Politicalcartoons.com

Page 194: Copyright © 2002 The *New York Times* Company

Page 195: © Copyright 2007 Pat Bagley, Reprinted with permission, Politicalcartoons.com

Page 196: Stewart Cairns/AP Images

Page 198: Reprinted with permission, *Pensions & Investments*. Copyright, Crain Communications, Inc.

Page 200: Mark Lennihan/AP Images

Page 201: © Greg Smith/Corbis

Page 202: © Reuters/Corbis

Page 203: (*top*) © Reuters/Corbis
(*bottom*) © Jeff Christensen/Reuters/Corbis

Page 204: Copyright © 2003 The *New York Times* Company

Page 205: © Lucy Nicholson/Corbis

Page 206: © Eric Miller/Reuters/Corbis

Page 207: Pat Crowe II/AP Images

Page 209: (*top*) Richard Drew/AP Images

Page 210: (*top*) Richard Drew/AP Images

Page 215: Courtesy of the Twin Cities Police Authority

Page 218: Courtesy of the City of Thousand Oaks